On the
Cutting
Edge

On the Cutting Edge

The Story
of a Surgeon and His Family
Who Served Country Folk
to Kings in Four Nations

by
E. ANNA NIXON
Missionary to India, 1940-1984

ON THE CUTTING EDGE

© 1987 by The Barclay Press

International Standard Book Number: 0-913342-61-0
Library of Congress Catalog Card Number: 87-72972

Other books by E. Anna Nixon:

MORE THAN SHADOW,
a story of village life in India

CHRISTIAN EDUCATION IN THE THIRD WORLD

"DELAYED, MANILA,"
autobiographical account of concentration camp experience
during World War II

DR. GRACE OF BUNDELKHAND,
biography of Bundelkhand's first woman doctor

A CENTURY OF PLANTING,
a history of the American Friends Mission in India

DeVol family photos illustrated on front and back covers
appear on pages xiv, 74, 91, 99, 116, and 186.
Cover design by Al Mendenhall
Interior design, composition, and lithography by
The Barclay Press, Newberg, Oregon, United States of America

Contents

How were a girl named Frances and a boy named Ezra, born
the same month half a world apart, destined to find one
another? She was from Austrian and British pioneer families
who helped to build the state of Michigan and homesteaded in
North Carolina. His forebears were Quakers from France who
settled in Ohio and sent missionaries to China.

What strange destiny orphaned Ezra at the age of ten and
brought Frances into the same devout Quaker community,
though they did not meet? What created in each of them such
deep hunger to know God?

Was divine providence back of the shaping of events that finally
brought Ezra and Frances together on a college campus? Did
mere human attraction and youthful idealism lead them to wade
through the depression to become medical missionaries? Or was
there something more?

Foreword

Being a career missionary means that one's sense of divine calling orders one's total life in mission for Christ. Numerous persons see a short term in missions as a service for Christ and the Church to be rendered as part of their life's work. But for Ezra and Frances DeVol, the calling of God meant missions as a lifestyle as well as a life service.

In this book, *On the Cutting Edge*, Anna Nixon, herself a veteran missionary, has shared with us a candid review of the very human and yet dedicated lives of several of God's choice servants. We are confronted with their vision, their faith, their struggles, their family, their achievements, their failures, their sorrows, their joys, and their fruit in very unusual years and settings of service. The story is a moving witness to the grace of God, to the centrality of Christ in calling and service, and to the forgiving and enabling work of the Spirit. The service of Ezra and Frances DeVol as a team of medical missionaries is a monumental expression of the contribution of many like persons who have, with their mission, also built good international relations and have strengthened the global network of faith, which we know to be the kingdom of God.

I first met Dr. DeVol at the Landour Missionary Conference, when Esther and I were invited by the Evangelical Fellowship of India to be their guest preacher in this period of renewal. At his urging, following Conference sessions in West Pakistan, I returned to India and then joined him in Kathmandu, Nepal, to minister to the hospital workers. During those days, I spent much time with Dr. DeVol as Frances had remained on vacation in India. It was an inspiration to observe his dedication and compassion for the people as he ministered to them. With pride and a deep sense of joy, he introduced me to the man operated on by his surgical colleague, Dr. Robert Berry. The patient had been the first to undergo heart surgery at the hospital. On another day he took me to the prison to visit a brother who was in jail for having converted and baptized a half-dozen persons. We talked and prayed with him, and as we left, Dr. DeVol shared his conviction that Christ's church would find the way to grow in Nepal, even though making converts to the Christian faith was against the laws of the land. And it has grown.

One of the strengths of this book is the realism with which the story is told. The author does not paint a picture of faultless people, but of conscientious, dedicated men and women who sought to serve Christ with integrity—at times with a constraint that later needed to be released by the freedom of grace. The story makes clear that the Christian life is a pilgrimage in which we continue to learn, to adjust, and to trust as we follow the Master.

We are given a history of missions without the book being designed as a missiology; however, in presenting a history that is built around families and their passages, there are missions principles presented and tested. The reader will be able to walk with the DeVols and their extended family, and in so doing will be able to sense and to test the convictions for mission that motivated these persons, and that will become a call to the reader.

As you read this book you will get the distinct impression that in the service of Christ we are always led to say with John the Baptist, "He must increase, and I must decrease."

—*Dr. Myron S. Augsburger*
Washington Community Fellowship
with the Mennonite Church
Washington, D.C. 20002

x

Acknowledgments

To Joyce Peele, a writer of drama for India's villages, goes credit for the concept that writing a book is something like having a baby. First the idea is conceived. This is followed by months of careful thought and research. Then comes the exciting labor of working night and day at the typewriter until the fuzzy, dog-eared manuscript lies complete on the desk. At last the writer leans back and exclaims to the world, "Look, there it is! Isn't it beautiful!"

Even if the baby looks like a squashed-up orange, Joyce said, the mother and everyone else agrees she's beautiful. However, from the day she is born, the parents and society begin working on that baby to bring her to perfection.

Just when does the baby—or book—reach perfection? A bumper sticker reminds us, "Be patient; God isn't through with me yet."

No less than thirty people have aided this biographer in writing the inspiring story of the lives of Ezra and Frances DeVol and their children. To the DeVol family members, friends, and co-workers who aided with interviews and editorial comments, I owe a debt of gratitude.

I wish to mention especially Mary Green of George Fox College, Newberg, Oregon, who put the whole manuscript onto a word processor. An author herself, she also contributed many helpful editorial suggestions. Ron Stansell of George Fox College, recently involved in studying and teaching missiology, and himself a missionary parent, read the script and made many valuable comments. S. Rickly Christian, Senior Book Editor for *Focus on the Family*, spoke of this book as innovative with its family emphasis. Cynthia Haynes, granddaughter of Dr. Ezra and Frances DeVol and a sophomore at Malone College, Canton, Ohio, skillfully pointed out needed updating of rules of grammar and phraseology. Her spiritual convictions had been tested on graduation from high school when in her salutatory address the right to mention her faith in Christ was challenged. Cynthia courteously and prayerfully stood her ground and won her point. She also won many points with me—and my admiration.

Finally, a word of thanks is due Ezra and Frances DeVol for sharing their lives, though at first reluctantly, yet so truthfully and completely. I have been enriched by this in the writing as I feel certain you will be in the reading.

—*E. Anna Nixon*

Dedicated
to Dr. W. Ezra and Frances DeVol,
whose hands and hearts were steadied
through faith and love
as they sought to bring wholeness
to everyone whose lives they touched.

A SURGEON AND HIS FAMILY
Dr. W. Ezra and Frances DeVol and their four children—
Philip DeVol, Priscilla Cox, Patricia Haynes, and Joseph DeVol
1986

1 Pursuing a Dream

Choose for yourselves this day whom you will serve.

Joshua 24:15

The Indian lawyer, Shiv Narain Khare, wiped away a tear as members of the Chhatarpur Municipal Council waited to hear what he was going to say. The buttons on his black, high-necked Nehru jacket threatened not to hold against his deep breathing as he lifted himself heavily out of his chair to stand and speak.

"They are leaving."

The judge at his bench leaned forward. "Dr. and Mrs. DeVol? The American surgeon and nurse? Oh, really? But maybe they'll come back to India again soon."

Lawyer Khare shook his head. He seemed unable to continue speaking. He was remembering how the doctor had cared for his little daughter on her deathbed. The court cases he had helped the doctor fight and win, the times of opening the Bible and finding a verse that gave them a promise to stand on when decisions threatened to go against them, the hours of fellowship when they talked of eternal matters—all these things suddenly crowded into his memory and choked off the sound of his voice.

Dr. Saxena, the civil surgeon, stood to speak as he peered knowingly over his glasses.

"I fear the DeVols won't be able to come back again, Sir. Dr. DeVol has had eight operations on his eyes. He has wasted his health here in India serving our people. Mrs. DeVol, who has assisted him in the operating theater, has had such severe heart attacks that the doctors have ordered her not to work any more.

1

They've given us the best twenty-five years of their lives, but now our climate has become too much for them. Besides, all their children and grandchildren are waiting for them in the United States."

"Ah!" sighed Dr. Dosajee. "What a treat it was to have their four children here in India with us! They lived just across the street from us. Their identical twin daughters—do you remember them? They left here almost twenty years ago! They were friends of my daughter, who is now a doctor. Their two sons were friends of my son. They've been gone now for eight to twelve years. All of them must be married now with several children."

"Well, what do you think, friends?" the chief municipal officer J. S. Chauhan asked. "Shouldn't we as a municipal council, in this city where they have saved so many lives, do something to show our appreciation for their service?"

"By all means!" spoke another official. "I have heard that Dr. DeVol is the best doctor in all of India and the fourth best in the world!"

"Where did you hear that?" another challenged. "Just try to name the three who are better! You will not be able to do it!"

Now, no one recorded the conversation that actually took place in the municipal council early in 1974 as these men planned the farewell they would give the DeVols. Their adulation exceeded all boundaries as they talked about how this couple had come to the remote Bundelkhandi area in India to witness to their Christian faith, strengthen the Church, build a general hospital, and train a staff who could carry on the work into the future. The words spoken would have been in Hindi, and in greater abundance, but the attitudes expressed by the people that day, as they made plans to honor the DeVols before they left India, would have been the same.

The sentiments of the people in Chhatarpur had not always been so favorable. When Dr. Ezra and Frances DeVol, soon to be forty, arrived in India in 1949, with their four children ranging in ages one to eleven, they met fear, ignorance, suspicion, and hostility. Many had no understanding of the dynamics that had brought this American family out of an established medical practice in the United States and into their midst. The truth was rumored through their ranks that the doctor's salary and also that of his wife was only $800 a year, a figure so fantastically low that no one could believe it. When the doctor enlarged the hospital and started asking for fees from those who could pay, in order that he would be able to more adequately treat the poor, he met with strong objection from wealthy members in the community who had grown up expecting mission medicine to be free. Battles ensued that took Dr. DeVol into courts, almost closed the hospital, and threatened to drive the DeVols from India.

Not being believed was the DeVols' constant disappointment in those early days. It was not the only one, however. Poverty worse than anything they had ever seen in country practice in the United States, or even in China, almost overcame them. Illness constantly took its toll of the whole family, as well as of the people around them. Lack of funds for development discouraged them. Corruption and downright opposition of people who opposed Christianity and anyone connected with it frustrated their efforts. Heartbreaking was the failure among Christian friends and colleagues who sometimes betrayed their trust and then, to defend themselves, turned against the DeVols and falsely maligned them.

Family separations, dogged with loneliness and the need to make tough decisions at a distance, made the balancing of responsibilities to children, as well as to patients who filled the hospital, an almost impossible feat. Failures often hurt and sometimes scarred. Others less dedicated might have given up, but the DeVols continued to stay and serve, day after day, month after month, and year after year, until they could no longer do so. The time had come to say goodbye.

Looking back over the past twenty-five years—like viewing a trail from Mt. Everest's summit—brought clearly into focus the journey that the DeVols had taken through "many dangers, toils, and snares." Memories flooded in of happy, rewarding times; of glittering celebrations; of fruitful periods of church renewal; of rich, shared experiences with the people of India in their struggles; of soul-expanding times, when out on treks through Indian jungles—sometimes with snowcapped peaks towering above them and roaring mountain streams paralleling their climbs—the father, mother, two daughters, and two sons had been knit together in the wonder and grandeur of nature, and the love and fellowship of family. No enjoyment excelled these all-too-few occasions together. Not only did the heavy demand on the time of the surgeon and the nurse in the hospital tend to pull the family apart, but so did the four hundred miles that separated their home in Chhatarpur from Woodstock School in Landour, Mussoorie, where all four children were in boarding nine months of the year.

The girls, Patricia Lee and Priscilla Ann, had joined the school in sixth grade and graduated in 1955. Joseph Edward and Philip Edmund had begun their formal education in Woodstock and had graduated from high school there, Joe in 1962, and Phil in 1966.

Eight years later, in 1974, the DeVols were returning to the United States and to their children—not just to four, but also to daughters-in-law and sons-in-law, to granddaughters and grandsons—a total of nineteen in all.

What had impelled this gifted and well-trained surgeon and nurse team to take their four children halfway around the world to the "uttermost part of the earth," to give the best years of their lives on a pittance of a salary in the face of such opposition? What formed their dreams? How had they prepared themselves to fulfil them? What did it cost them? What did it cost their children? Was it worth it? Chapter by chapter, this book will unfold the answers to these questions.

2 Richly Rooted

Surely I have a delightful inheritance.

Psalm 16:6 NIV

A Girl Born in Brighton

"Brighton, the corner where you are!" The punctuation and spelling in the Sunday school song is different, but the truth is that Brighton, Michigan, was the corner where Frances Hyne Hodgin was born on September 22, 1909. She brightened Brighton that day. No one would have dared to prophesy then how she would live to brighten the life of a surgeon and lives of people around the world.

This first daughter born in the home of Daniel and Elsie Hyne Hodgin would live quite a while before she would understand the significance of her name. The whole community in Brighton, however, understood it immediately and valued it from the moment the announcement came.

Elsie Frederica Hodgin, the mother (known as Frieda), had grown up in Brighton and had already lost all but one of her six brothers and sisters, most of them in their infancy or childhood. The last one, a sister named Frances, had lived to be nineteen. Sister Frances was known for her grace, her sweet and cheerful disposition, and for being—in the words of people in the neighborhood—"an ideal Christian young lady." But at seventeen she became ill with Addison's disease and slipped away the year before the baby girl named after her was born.

Grandfather Frederick and Grandmother Sarah and a host of other Hyne relatives came to see the baby. Grandmother Hyne,

5

holding little Frances in her arms, blinked back hot tears of recent grief but smiled in excited anticipation as she said, "If only this little Frances Hyne can live to be like her aunt!" Maternal Grandfather Hyne, standing erect and tall in dignified alertness, could not help being just a little proud that the Hodgins had chosen his last name as her middle one.

Grandfather Frederick Hyne knew who he was in Brighton. His father and a brother had come there from Prussia. After settling on tracts of land in that area, Charles T. Hyne, his father, had married Marie Hannah Westphal of Brighton. Her parents also had come from Prussia. Their fiftieth wedding anniversary was attended by all eight of their children and their families, and by Frederick's uncle, who also had eight children. By that time Frederick's father, Charles, was known as one of the wealthiest men in the area. Frederick was the son who joined his father in business and inherited the large grain elevator built by his father in 1871. On becoming the proprietor, Frederick prospered and added a lumber and coal business. He then erected a splendid home into which he welcomed his bride.

By the time Frances Hodgin was born, her Uncle Erwin was in business with her grandfather, Frederick Hyne, and the Hyne influence had grown through the generations. In time they also ran the bank and Hyne Brothers Brighton Mills. They were called upon not only to serve in the Wesleyan Methodist Church, where they were active members, but also to sit on councils and give advice on the development of the city of Brighton. Grandfather Frederick Hyne's Christian character and integrity were unquestioned. His life testified to his acceptance of his father's business motto: "Honesty in Business and Courtesy Towards All." His wife, Sarah Hicks Hyne, had a keen mind, and her undergirding and quiet support of her husband and two living children was a real delight to them all. She was one of the first two trained teachers in Brighton, and she also was a devoted Christian and worker in the church. "Together they have earned the love and respect of the community," was a public tribute to Frederick and Sarah Hyne.

Frances Hyne Hodgin carried a name that reflected great expectations and deep roots in Brighton. She already had a brother one-and-a-half years old named Jonathan Theodore. By the time she was old enough to crawl across the floor, Jonathan was piloting her around and teaching her to talk. A closeness developed between them that would last through life. Two years later, twin boys, Mendel and Melvin, doubled the number of the Hodgin children, but Melvin lived only a day. The mingled joy and grief tearing at the emotions of a family with a newly born son in a crib and another in a casket must have been deeply felt even by the nearly two-year-old Frances who all her life exhibited unusual depths of empathy.

When Frances was three years old, another brother, Daniel Garfield Hodgin, Jr., joined the family in Brighton. For six years Frances held the distinction of being the only girl in the family until on December 22, 1915, Elsie Frederica, the last of Daniel and Frieda Hodgin's children, was born in Mt. Pleasant, Ohio.

Daniel Hodgin, Frances' father, was a farmer's son from Pleasant Garden, North Carolina. He was converted in a Quaker Church. He took theological training in Guilford College in North Carolina and in God's Bible College in Cincinnati, Ohio. He was a forceful, earnest, and energetic evangelist in demand for revival meetings in Wesleyan Methodist, Friends, and other churches. From the age of twenty he traveled in a number of states, part of the time in a team with Rev. Fred DeWeerd and Clarence Cosand. While this team was in Brighton for revival services at the Wesleyan Methodist Church, Daniel Hodgin met Frieda Hyne, and they fell in love. She was a talented and avid church worker, and their common concern and love for Christ and His Church drew them together. After they were married June 5, 1907, they took a pastorate for a year in Wabash, Indiana. Frieda planned to travel with her husband in evangelistic meetings, but early pregnancy cut short those dreams. Before Frances was born, Daniel Hodgin moved back to Brighton. He had to go by himself on evangelistic tours, leaving his wife at home with the children, near her parents and relatives.

Daniel Hodgin loved taking his wife, three sons and daughter down to the beautiful Pleasant Garden, North Carolina, homestead where he grew up. The children would run among the tall trees surrounding the spacious farmhouse as their laughter and bouncing energy delighted Grandfather Jonathan and

Grandmother Virginia Neeley Hodgin, three aunts, and an uncle. The Hodgins shared the same faith as Daniel, and others of his relatives were also in Christian service. One cousin, Arnold Hodgin, would minister worldwide and also one day become the president of a Bible school. Another cousin, Tom Hodgin, was also in the ministry.

Frances felt rich in aunts, uncles, and cousins on both sides of her family. Because of them, she did not greatly miss her father who was absent most of the time. Daniel Hodgin, however, found it increasingly difficult to be away from his family. Each time there was an opportunity to go home between meetings, he felt more and more a stranger in his own household. Sensitivity to the needs of people made him a good evangelist, but constant evangelizing drained his nervous energy and made his spirit heavy.

"Be quiet, children. Daddy needs rest," Mother Hodgin would caution. "Why don't you get your wraps on and go outside? Or why not go into the bedroom and draw a picture?"

Daniel Hodgin was grateful for his wife's understanding, but he sensed he was not meeting the needs of his wife and growing children. He was not home when Frances at the age of five nearly died. While playing at Cousin Josephine Hyne's house, she suddenly began to feel very ill.

"I want to go home," she said.

"Shall I go with you?" Josephine asked.

"No," answered Frances as she started out the door. She lost consciousness then and never regained it until sometime later when she became aware, as she opened her eyes, that Grandfather Hyne was sitting by her bed scraping an apple with a knife. Frances had the feeling she had been on a very long and distant trip. She had been floating as if in a stream of water. It was soft and very pleasant, and everything was light. Very happy people were around her, and the whole scene was lovely and beautiful. Frances felt peaceful, loved, content, and joyful. Then she heard her name.

"Frances," Grandfather said.

Frances opened her eyes and saw him sitting there. Jaundiced and uncomfortable, she was ill for several days, but she would remember that experience the rest of her life as her first taste of heaven. It created in her a great desire to get ready to go there.

When Frances was five years old, her father became pastor of the Mt. Pleasant Friends Church in Ohio. Monthly income for a pastor was less than that of an evangelist, but the Hodgins' life was not focused on economic security. Their desire was to fulfill the will of God and guide their children in the same path. Therefore, they felt at this time that they should combine ministry with the care of their growing family. This pastorate, though far from the Hyne relatives, was closer to the Hodgins in North Carolina. The opportunities for Christian ministry and nurture of the children seemed adequate. A staunch Christian community in a peaceful country setting among tall trees and rolling hills and a good school in walking distance for the children appealed to them.

At first, the Hodgins made their home with Elisabeth Jenkins, an elderly and stately Quaker, who lived in a spacious, comfortable home on a large estate. She told Frances and Johnny fascinating stories of how as a child she had helped her mother free the slaves. She showed them rooms in which the runaway slaves had been hidden as they escaped from the South and sought refuge in the North. She also took the children to hear a missionary speak about China. Frances was fascinated by the Chinese dolls and pictures of Luho and Nanking. The missionary, Myrtle Williams, held the children spellbound with stories of how Drs. George and Isabella DeVol had built a hospital in China.

Frances started to school that fall of 1915 in Mt. Pleasant. Just three days before Christmas that year, she received a most wonderful surprise. Elsie, her baby sister, was born.

A Boy Born in Kuling

In 1915 on Christmas night in Mt. Pleasant, Ohio, as Frances Hyne Hodgin was allowed to hold her three-day-old sister Elsie before going to bed, it was already time for breakfast the next day in Luho, China. It could have been at the same time that Ezra, the six-year-old son of Dr. George DeVol, was leaning forward to see all the details of his father's matchstick illustration. Dr. George Fox DeVol, always the teacher, grasped such moments as these when he and his wife, Dr. Isabella DeVol, and their three children were together around the table. Charles, twelve, and Catherine, nine, were home from school. They all crowded around their father's end of the table, and Mother leaned forward with keen, calm, and supportive interest as if she, too, were a learner.

"You see, Ezra," Father explained as the others knowingly looked on, having heard it before, "your body is always carrying on a war. Inside you, right now, are white corpuscles ready to attack any invading microbes that would like to make you sick or kill you."

Ezra pressed a little closer as his father broke off a tip of a toothpick and put it in a dish. Then he surrounded the little bit of wood with a drop of water. "See how that water engulfs the little piece of wood? That's how your white blood corpuscles attack and destroy the microbes and carry them out of your body before they can do you any harm."

Ezra's attention never wavered. It could be said that his medical training began on September 7, 1909, the day he was born. Even before he learned how to read or write, he already knew not only the beatitudes but also the names of the bones in the human body. He had carefully watched Charles in preparation for mounting a bird make an incision down its abdomen. More exciting than that, many times already he had sat in the corner of the operating theater at Peace Hospital in Luho and observed his parents perform surgery. His eyes and ears seemed always open to medical happenings, and the wonder of healing had gripped him before he had any experience of a blackboard, textbook, or classroom.

Ezra had been born in Kuling, 350 miles up the Yangtze River. That summer resort was located in the mountains 3,600 feet above sea level where as many as two thousand missionaries lived for six weeks to three months of the year during the summer. The Friends Mission owned two houses there on the mountainside. There many children of missionaries went to boarding school and enjoyed the woods, mountain streams, birds, and flowers. During summers, missionary families shared the houses, and when Ezra was born, Charles and Catherine were introduced to their baby brother lying in a suitcase that opened up to make a little bassinet. Dr. Isabella DeVol's smiles did not completely detract their attention from a few tears in her eyes. They understood, for though they had never seen their sister Mary, they had visited her tiny grave in Kuling cemetery with its marker clearly stating, "Born January, 1902; died August, 1902."

Less than a month after Ezra was born, Mother Isabella returned with him to Luho. Walter and Myrtle Williams and their nine-month-old son Walter, Jr., arrived in China and came to Luho. There were no other American children in the Mission except the DeVols and the Williamses; thus Walter, Jr., and Ezra were destined to develop a relationship that would last through their lives. Every summer in Kuling for the next few years, Ezra's *amah* (nursemaid), Liu Da Ma, would carry him up and down the eighty-one steps between the houses where the DeVols and Williamses lived. As he and Walter, Jr., grew they would hike over Hankow Gorge, view Poyang Lake, and wade in the mountain stream that ran between the mission property and the community church. Parents would take them swimming at the Emerald Pool. They would go with Charles through wooded areas around Kuling in search of lilies and ferns, and with Catherine through Pine Ridge Mountain Pass above their mission house. They would get to know boys and girls of many countries, languages, and cultures in Kuling. However, they had growing to do before that could take place.

Luho was a walled city of less than a square mile with a population of 26,000. Most of the homes consisted of one-story buildings, each joined to another along narrow streets. The DeVol home was a bit nicer, but an open drain flowed in front of it. In the streets, humanity jostled with sedan chairs carried by coolies; herds of donkeys; hunched men, pushing wheelbarrows loaded with oil, cloth, and rice; salesmen with cotton candy. As Ezra grew a little older, he began to remember with distaste the donkey rides when he got blisters, the smell of the drain in front of his home, and the feasts in Chinese homes followed by doses of castor oil when he got home.

Neither Walter, Jr., nor Ezra were old enough to remember the turmoil that brought upheaval to China through their early years, but in 1911 when Nationalist China toppled the Manchurian conquerers, Ezra's nervous system recorded the rushed boat trip up the Yangtze River with his very ill mother on a stretcher. He felt the frustration of missionary families huddled together in a room in Shanghai waiting for the war to end. He heard stories later of how his and Walter, Jr.'s, fathers both offered their services to the Red Cross and returned to Nanking and Luho to minister to the mass of Chinese suffering and wounded. He also heard how the Nationalist China Government prohibited the practice of binding the feet of baby girls and ordered men to cut off their long black braids (queues).

Dr. Isabella DeVol was allowed to go back home with her children to Luho in February 1912. She carried with her a new determination to "speak more gently than the year before; pray a little oftener; love a little more." That image of his mother imprinted on Ezra's mind would go with him through life.

Home for Ezra during his early years would sometimes be Kuling, sometimes Luho, and sometimes Nanking. In 1912 when the Nanking missionary doctor died of typhus fever, Dr. George DeVol had to carry on in Luho and allow his wife, Dr. Isabella DeVol, to take Ezra and go to Nanking to keep the hospital open there.

Twenty-five miles from Luho, Nanking was a prestigious, large, walled city where emperors had once ruled. Purple Mountain guarded it. Just inside overlooking a river was Lion Hill. Nanking bulged with many non-Chinese Westerners. The University of Nanking overshadowed the mission school, and the University Hospital overshadowed the mission hospital, but to the Friends missionaries in China, the heart of the city was the Quakerage, a home for missionaries built in 1890, reached from Old Drum Tower by a road through one of its three arches.

Not until he had passed his third birthday and spoke both Chinese and English fluently did Ezra realize there was any country different from China or that he had American relatives. But while the German Hynes were pioneering in Michigan and the Hodgins in North Carolina, William Ezra DeVol's paternal great grandfather, a Quaker coming from England, but of French descent, had settled on a farm near Glen Falls, New York. Ezra's maternal great grandfather was a direct descendant of Thomas French, who had come to New Jersey with William Penn. He eventually settled near Salem, Ohio. In those days Quaker men wore broad-brimmed hats and homespun coats, the women wore Quaker bonnets and untrimmed gowns of grey, and everyone in the Quaker community addressed each other as "thee" and "thou."

Ezra never knew any of his grandparents. His father had been orphaned at the age of seventeen. Dr. Isabella's father, Ezra French, had died ten years before his namesake was born. Grandmother Mary French died in 1910 without seeing either Catherine or Ezra. Therefore, aside from his siblings and parents, Ezra had a limited concept of family. But in his early years, he never got tired hearing stories about his parents' early lives.

Mother Isabella DeVol's story hour about their early life probably went something like this:

"When Daddy was seventeen, his parents died and he became an orphan."

"What's an orphan?"

"A boy or girl whose mother and daddy have died and who have no one to care for them. However, your daddy knew God cared for him. So he prayed."

"Did Daddy pray even when he was little?"

"Of course, Ezra Boy! And when he got big like your brother Charles, he still prayed. Did you know your daddy also has a big brother named Charles? He is your uncle."

"What's an uncle?"

"You'll see when we go on furlough. In America you have uncles, aunts, and cousins. They'll help you celebrate your fourth birthday this year."

Dr. Isabella DeVol adored her husband and delighted in telling her children about how he worked as a farmhand, not shunning the hard labor of milking cows, currying horses, feeding sheep, gathering eggs, following a plow, and flailing out rye.

The principal of the school, however, wanted George DeVol to continue his education and arranged for him to enroll and pay later. This he did.

Another man paid for George DeVol's first year to Earlham College. The open door for medical training came through a tragedy. A man's son in premedical courses suddenly died and the man turned to George DeVol to take the place of his son. "God works in mysterious ways, his wonders to perform." Many others helped, and finally in 1897, George DeVol graduated from the medical college of New York University. He soon set up practice in the city of Staten Island.

It was impossible for Ezra to grasp all of this even in simplified form, but he liked his mother's nearness and the sound of her voice.

"When we reach California, we'll get on a train and go to Damascus, Ohio," Mother continued. "There is where I grew up and went to school. We will meet the people there at Yearly Meeting who send us the parcels."

By this time Mother Isabella would have felt the loosening of her son's handclasp. There would be another time to tell him of her side of the family and how God had called her to China as a medical missionary when she was a young woman in Earlham College. The uncle who paid her way through college said, "Thee must go, my dear," and wouldn't let her pay him back. But there was no money for medical school, and while she waited to know what to do next, she taught in the academy in Damascus. By the end of that year, the Women's Missionary Society of the Friends Church let her know they had accepted her application for a scholarship for three years to the Wooster Medical College in Cleveland (now called the School of Medicine of Case Western Reserve). She graduated in 1897 and went that summer to New York for some graduate studies. There she met Dr. George DeVol at New York Yearly Meeting. Their love for each other was mutual and their calls identical. They acknowledged with joy that their lives should be joined together in medical service in China.

Dr. Isabella French left for China on her twenty-eighth birthday, November 18, 1897; Dr. George DeVol planned to follow her just as soon as he had cleared his medical college debts. Five days after his arrival in China, they were married in Nanking at the Quakerage, on January 17, 1900.

The Boxer uprising, illness, missionary work in Nanking and Luho, straightening bound feet, delivering patients from the opium habit, and caring for a host of illnesses ate away the doctors' time. More than that, there were evangelistic services, conferences, building the churches, and praying for the lost. There was the birth of a son, Charles Edward, October 2, 1903. Then came their first furlough.

When the DeVols returned in 1905, they brought money enough to build Peace Hospital in Luho near their home at West Gate. Catherine was born January 30, 1906, the hospital was finished in 1907, and Ezra arrived September 7, 1909. Six weeks later, the Walter Williams family joined them, and until they could build their house across town at Little North Gate, they lived with Margaret Holme near the church. They opened a boys' school and constructed Friends Academy and their home nearby. This greatly strengthened the educational work in Luho.

The second furlough the DeVol family looked forward to finally began in June 1913. When they reached America, Ezra felt the half had not been told him. He was overcome with wonder at the unbelievable sights of motor cars on paved roads; open spaces without mobs of people; grassy, rolling hills around Sunnyslope farm; and wonderful feasts not followed by castor oil. The screeching sirens, thundering horses, and ringing bells of a speeding red fire truck, belching smoke and flinging traffic this way and that off the road, captured his attention to the point of deflecting him temporarily from his purpose to become a doctor. A fire chief in helmet and boots dashing to the fire suddenly seemed far more important.

Furlough quickly came to an end, and the DeVol family started back to China on the SS *Tenyo Maru* in late 1914 at the beginning of World War I. Out in the middle of the Pacific Ocean, the ship was suddenly plunged into darkness. A blackout order had been given and the ship veered sharply in its course and began to pick up speed. Apprehension mounted, and Ezra shook with fear as his father brought the whole family together into their cabin.

"A German cruise ship [the Emden] is after us," he said, "but we do not need to be afraid. The Bible tells us to trust and not be afraid. We can ask God to protect us. Let's get on our knees and pray."

His parents and then Charles and Catherine prayed. "It's your turn, Ezra Boy," said Father. So five-year old Ezra prayed, too, and as he did, his fears melted away and a new sense of the reality of God's living presence was awakened in him. The danger was soon over, and in due time they arrived unharmed in China.

Drs. George and Isabella DeVol left Charles and Catherine in the Shanghai American School and proceeded to Luho to open Peace Hospital again. That summer Ezra attended kindergarten in Kuling. He was of a mind, however, not to let his mother out of his sight. She finally gave in and sat with him the entire morning. When she left at noon, Ezra felt abandoned and stirred up something of a storm. He soon settled into the school routine, but as summer ended, his mother took him back with her to Luho, where he again sat in the corner of the operating theater observing the surgery when not with his friend, Walter, Jr.

Walter, Jr., had been waiting for Ezra, for he had been lonely during their furlough. Also during the DeVols' furlough, Walter, Jr.'s, baby sister Grace, just a year-and-a-half, had died. The two boys started going back and forth to see each other. That fifteen minutes' walk from the school to the hospital through the crowded streets was considered too much for even a six-year-old, so a gateman accompanied Walter, Jr., to the DeVol home.

The boys enjoyed being in the yard together. Dr. George DeVol's bicycle was a mystery to them. They could not figure out how a person might achieve balance on only two wheels. They explored the trees and plants and delighted in the birds. Once a beautiful heron accidentally flew into the ancient pagoda near Peace Hospital and injured a wing. It fell into the DeVol yard. Walter, Jr., and Ezra ran to pick it up but realized they were too late. It seemed tragic that anything so beautiful could be dead.

Before Charles and Catherine went to school, they insisted on being in complete charge of the Edison phonograph. Ezra was not allowed to touch it, but he was determined not to be left out. So regardless of what the music was, band or stately hymn, he entertained the guests with amazing acrobatic stunts. However, with his older brother and sister away at school and Walter, Jr., looking on, Ezra delighted in secretly slipping on a record. Then they would watch the startled Chinese visitors as their eyes darted here and there trying to locate the invisible speaker.

When Ezra went to the Friends Academy area to visit Walter, Jr., he loved rollicking with Walter, Jr.'s, dog Dick, and then under the hallway stairs finding his mechano set and teddy bear. Chinese friends helped them fly kites and also made for the boys a little wagon from a wooden Carnation milk box.

When Charles and Catherine came home and the four children played together, there were situations that sometimes got out of hand. "Who shall we blame?" Walter, Jr., son of the school principal, would call out in an authoritative voice. One thing was certain, Ezra knew that he, the youngest, would not be able to defend himself against the mighty. One day he finally rebelled, and such a quarrel ensued that not even Brother Charles was able to mitigate the tension. They appealed to a higher tribunal, and as Mother Isabella DeVol sat in judgment, she listened with calm and intent silence. When they had finished presenting their points of view, she had much to say to each of them.

"Ezra Boy, you must apologize," she ordered. Apologies were duly made, and all might have ended there if Ezra's eyes had not at that moment fallen on a bed caster. Disregarding all consequences, he grabbed it and gave Walter, Jr., such a blow on the head that, had he been stronger, Walter, Jr., might not have lived to develop his brilliant educational career in later years. Mother, with a hair brush, evened the score and demanded another apology on the spot. Both boys, hurting a lot in different places, soon forgot what the quarrel was about, and Walter, Jr., remained Ezra's loyal friend. It was about that time, however, that everyone quit saying "Ezra Boy."

Dr. Isabella DeVol was a discerning mother as well as a skillful doctor. Therefore, she did not send Ezra off with Charles and Catherine to boarding school when he was six, but kept him at home. She tried to guide him in his studies through the mornings. He was lonely with Walter, Jr., gone on furlough, but he spent more time with his mother on hospital rounds. All things medical interested him, like the story of the microbes. The parents had no doubt that one day he would become a doctor. They only hoped that he would be a doctor to China.

FOUR HYNE GENERATIONS OF BRIGHTON, MICHIGAN
Grandfather Frederick Hyne, Mother Frederica Hyne Hodgin, Great Grandmother Hannah Westphal Hyne, Jonathan and Frances Hyne Hodgin

Frances' Grandfather Frederick and Grandmother Sarah Hicks Hyne, Uncle Erwin Hyne, front, Mother Frieda Hyne, and Aunt Frances Hyne for whom she was named, back

The Hodgin Children, Brighton, Michigan—Frances, 5; Jonathan, 6; Mendel, 3; and Daniel, 1

Evangelist Daniel G. and Frieda Hyne Hodgin

The Hodgin-Hyne Home (bottom) in Brighton, Michigan

China Missionaries—Left: Myrtle, Walter, Jr., Walter, Sr., and Grace Williams; center back: Margaret Holme; right: Catherine, Dr. Isabella, Dr. George, Charles, and Ezra DeVol on mother's lap

Walter, Jr., pulls Ezra in a Carnation carton wagon made by Chinese friends

The 1916 DeVol Home
in Luho, China

Peace Hospital built in 1907 by
the DeVols at Luho

Peace Hospital Chapel, front row
center, left to right, Dr. George,
Charles, Catherine, Ezra, and Dr.
Isabella DeVol, 1913

Drs. George and Isabella DeVol in
China with their youngest son,
Ezra—a doctor in the making

Catherine
Charles
Ezra
(all born in China)

3 Agonies and Aspirations of Growing Up

May the Lord make you increase, both you and your children. May you be blessed by the Lord, the maker of heaven and earth.   *Psalm 115:14, 15*

Torn from China through Tragedy

Frances, the evangelist and pastor's daughter in Mt. Pleasant, and Ezra, the missionaries' son in Nanking, had no way of knowing the tragic events in their early lives that would gradually lead them together. The series of upsets began in 1916 just after the DeVols had moved into their new $1600 home near Peace Hospital in Luho. For a short while, work progressed rapidly as they enlarged the hospital and laid plans for evangelization, health care, and development for 300,000 people in Luho District.

Dr. George DeVol, not only a physician and a surgeon, but also a preacher and a soul-winner, envisioned great wholeness for all. He and his wife worked side by side in the operating room and in the clinic. Along with the demonstration of their skills, they trained paramedical workers, doctors, and a surgeon, sharing their medical knowledge with China's sons and daughters in the hope that many more hospitals would eventually dot the district. That, however, was only half the story.

Beyond the medical, the Doctors DeVol envisioned spiritual healing, and every one of the workers in training was exposed to their high hope of wholeness through the Lord Jesus Christ. Dr. George DeVol preached in all the churches and also in the hospital waiting room before opening the clinic each morning. Every patient, as he left the hospital, took away tracts in his hands and

23

the knowledge of Christian hope in his heart. Dr. George DeVol kept the patient's picture on file with a brief description of what had happened to him not only medically, but also spiritually: Had he been converted? Was he interested? Did he show no interest at all?

With these cards in hand, the evangelists went into the villages, and the people warmly welcomed them into their homes and listened to their message. Out from these homes the evangelists witnessed throughout the country. As confidence grew, the census in the hospital went up and the membership in the church increased.

Another welcome change at this time was the opening of Hillcrest School in Nanking. Charles and Catherine were both enrolled there, just 25 miles from home instead of 350. They could come home for some weekends and for special days, and Ezra also could soon be enrolled there. Ezra welcomed the opening of Hillcrest School, for he realized that soon he would have to leave home for study.

"Not this year," Dr. Isabella said.

Gratefully on his seventh birthday, Ezra stood on the porch of their summer home in Kuling and watched the sun disappear while his mother prepared for the trip back to Luho. Suddenly a very sober thought popped into his mind: I am seven, and I have reached the age of accountability!

He felt awed by the fact that he had an eternal destiny, and that he had a choice in the matter. Had his mother known of this mature insight, she might have reconsidered and sent him into boarding at the Quakerage in Nanking, but Ezra kept his thoughts to himself.

Shortly after the family returned to Luho and Charles and Catherine went to Nanking, the reverses began. Esther Butler, the superintendent of the Mission, became ill. As in 1912, Dr. Isabella DeVol again had to move to Nanking to keep the work going. Once more her husband was left alone in Luho with the entire burden of the enlarged hospital and growing evangelistic demands.

Early in December 1917, Dr. Isabella received an urgent message from her husband in Luho: "I am ill and need you here."

Leaving the Nanking hospital without a doctor, she rushed to Luho and found her husband critically ill with a carbuncle on the back of his neck. Charles and Catherine were called home from school in Nanking. Catherine helped look after Ezra, and Charles stood by to assist as Dr. Macklin of Nanking operated. Dr. Isabella gave the anesthetic.

On Christmas Day, Dr. George had to go through a second surgery. There were no antibiotics, penicillin, or wonder drugs. There was persistence, patience, and prayer—and peace—even though the family could not understand why five days later Dr. George DeVol had to die. Charles, 14, became a man overnight. Catherine, nearly 12, mothered 8-year-old Ezra, and together they joined the procession to the graveyard with the 3,000 people who attended the funeral. The Gospel had truly reached every corner of Luho County.

Not well herself, Dr. Isabella DeVol had to return to Luho to care for Peace Hospital. By summer, she was so ill she had to take the family to the cooler climate of Kuling, where she was hospitalized and diagnosed as having sprue. In spite of rest, she made no improvement, but returned to Nanking with the children. Charles was enrolled in high school, Catherine in seventh grade, and Ezra in third. It soon became evident that her health was deteriorating rapidly and that early furlough was necessary. Charles helped with the arrangements for sailing.

"I always feel safe when Charles is around," Ezra said as he followed his brother from place to place.

Leaving China at the end of November 1919, they found themselves transported to the U.S.A. for Christmas, leaving behind their enlarged hospital, their brand-new home in Luho, their father's and sister's graves, and their childhood friends of China.

In Santa Rosa, California, famous as the home of Luther Burbank, Dr. George's brother Charles took them in. His three children, Arthur, Ethel, and George, nearly matched ages with their China cousins. Uncle Charles put the children into school with his children, and Ezra continued in the third grade.

As spring came on, Dr. Isabella proceeded on to Ohio and took up residence with Elbert and Martha Benedict on Sunny-slope farm. This was really home to Ezra, since at the age of four he had spent his first year in the United States there. Now at the age of ten, he loved more than ever the rolling hills, the new green grass, the freshly plowed fields, the wind in the trees, and the horses, cows, and chickens in the barnyard. He took full advantage of the wide-open spaces with no end of places to run and hide while he watched the birds and rabbits. Charles and Catherine went to school in Ashley, and Ezra was immediately enrolled in the third grade in a nearby one-room school called Alum Creek Special District Academy.

That summer the family all went to New York to visit relatives, who provided for them to stay on and study in a private academy in Glen Falls. Ezra was again placed in the third grade, a humiliating experience, even though they taught new subjects such as art, French, music, and dancing. He was determined to master everything and eventually escape from the third grade.

That winter, blizzards exceeded anything the old timers in New York could remember. The children went to school through a tunnel of snow as temperatures bottomed. Dr. Isabella's health deteriorated again in the excessive cold, and it became obvious she must return to Sunnyslope Farm in Ohio.

Ezra returned to Alum Creek Special District Academy—and was again enrolled in the third grade!

"Oh, please, please don't put me in the third grade again!" he pleaded.

And even though there were only ten days left in the term, Myrta Windsor, his teacher, listened to him and enrolled him in the fourth grade. Ezra was so grateful and worked so hard those ten days that when the term ended he was transferred from fourth grade directly into fifth!

Learning at this country school became a fascinating pursuit. Ezra loved his teachers, and particularly J. B. Henry, who had lived at Sunnyslope and rented the farm while all the DeVols were there. J. B. Henry also loved this peppery young student, son of doctors, on whom he could depend for emergencies. In his desk Ezra kept a little first-aid kit and treated all the students' scratches and cuts.

Other attractions were skating on Alum Creek in the winter, fishing in the spring, and playing ball and "anti-over" at noon and recess. Life at Sunnyslope seemed wonderfully bright, except for the fact that even a ten-year-old boy could see his mother was fading away.

Father had died at Christmas time. Why did Mother also have to die at Christmas time? Others were singing their hearts out, wrapping gifts, and filling the air with laughter; at Sunnyslope, hope was gone.

There was talk of who would take the children. People softly tiptoed back and forth into Dr. Isabella's room. Ezra did not hear everything, but word got through that Dan Wilbur, a cousin in New York, wanted Charles. Amy Marvel, another cousin, who was married to a surgeon in Richmond, Indiana, wanted Catherine.

In all the muted conversation, however, Ezra did not hear his name mentioned. He lived with the horrible thought of having nowhere to turn when his mother died. He neither knew that Aunt Louisa Sweet had offered to take him, nor that his mother was saying "No" to all these requests in order that the three children could stay together at Sunnyslope in the care of the Benedicts, who had offered to be their guardians. Nor did he know that the mission board had agreed to educate them.

On prayer meeting night, December 22, 1920, the Benedicts and DeVols were missed. They were gathered about Dr. Isabella's bed. Dr. Isabella was at peace about God's care for her children, and her final thoughts were of the needs of China.

Her last words were: "Who will go?"

Charles and Catherine pressed close. Ezra remained in the background. He loved his mother intensely, but China not at all. He remembered the times he had shivered with malaria, the bumpy rides on donkeys, the offensive smells, and the castor oil after feasts. In America there were apples in the cellar and fresh pies cooling in the kitchen. Classy cars sped down the highways. He could run through the meadows where birds flew and sang. While Charles and Catherine were saying, "I will go," eleven-year-old Ezra kept his distance, steeling his will in the resolve neither to lie nor to commit himself.

The next morning as funeral arrangements were being made, Uncle Elbert and Aunt Martha gathered Charles, Catherine, and Ezra for morning prayer as was their custom.

"Your name will still be DeVol but you will live with us," Uncle Elbert told them. "We are your Aunt Martha and Uncle Elbert. This is your home from now on."

Gratitude deeper than he had ever known flooded Ezra's grieving heart. The kindness of Uncle Elbert and Aunt Martha shown to them in giving them a home would stay with him for the rest of his life.

Moved Nearer by Illness

Frances Hodgin in Mt. Pleasant, Ohio, was delighted with Elsie, her little sister. She also enjoyed all she was learning in school. As she came home from the Christmas program and looked up at the stars, she skipped along feeling God was very close. She ran races with her older brother Johnny and she enjoyed reading her first grade books to Mendel and Dan.

Frances did not understand what was happening to her mother. Frieda Hodgin spent more and more time in bed, and eventually she was unable to care for all her children. Johnny and Frances had to move over to the big home of Elizabeth Jenkins for a second time, where they stayed for six weeks. That was a long time for a little girl not yet seven, and she counted the days until they could all be home together again as a family.

That time arrived in the spring of 1916 when Grandfather Frederick and Grandmother Sarah Hyne came by Mt. Pleasant on their way back to Brighton from their winter vacation in Florida. Alarmed at their daughter's condition, they persuaded Daniel Hodgin to let them take her back to Brighton. Though the trip by train was long and arduous, Frieda was able to make it, and the others came by car. Then followed a tremendous battle to save her life. Daniel Hodgin resigned his pastorate in Mt. Pleasant and moved again to Brighton. He and the children prayed earnestly for Frieda's survival as she went through the valley of shadow, suffering tetanus following a goiter operation.

Two years passed before Frieda regained her health, and Daniel stayed on in Brighton with the family, assisting his father-in-law in business and taking evangelistic services as time and opportunity afforded.

The insecurity felt by the children at this time was partly overcome by the return to their relatives and former friends in Brighton. For the next four years, Frances attended school and enjoyed having children around her. People up and down the street called her "little mother." She "taught school," reading the children stories from her school books.

With wild accounts about the six o'clock freight train, Frances frightened her cousin, Josephine Hyne, who lived across the street. Tramps and hoboes sometimes appeared on the streets after the train went through, and Frances' description of how they would sometimes catch children and run off with them left a vivid impression on Josephine. Every time she was outside when the six o'clock freight whistle blew, she would run for home as fast as her legs could carry her.

Frances loved the changing scenes in Brighton. She enjoyed raking the leaves and the lovely smell of fall. When the snow came, she took delight in playing fox and geese on the big lawn. One night when she was about nine, the Northern Lights flashed with such brilliance across Brighton's sky that people came out of their homes saying, "This must be the Lord's coming!"

She went to bed that night, filled with awe and wonder. As she looked out her small window at the pine branches against the flashing sky, she thought of the unknown course of life and cried out in her aloneness, "O God, You seem so far away!"

There was nothing Daniel Hodgin wanted more for his children than that they would recognize God was near to help them in all of their problems. Away so often preaching this message to others, he felt the time had come again to take a pastorate, this time in the Highland Avenue Friends Church (Westgate) in Columbus, Ohio.

World War I was over. Frances was eleven years old. She and her brothers and younger sister all made new friendships quickly in the new location. She plunged into junior high studies and music. Matilda Stewart, a former missionary to China, taught piano to both Frances and Johnny. They began to play so well they often gave recitals together.

Both in the church and from Matilda Stewart, Frances heard a great deal about missions. So when Dr. Isabella DeVol died, Frances was aware of the tragedy that left three orphaned children. Her father was one of ten Quaker ministers who attended the funeral in Damascus, Ohio, where Dr. Isabella was buried. Though he had only recently moved to Ohio, he was a highly respected evangelist and was asked to take part in the service. He led in prayer.

Another minister spoke of Dr. Isabella DeVol as a "quiet, poised, devoted, merciful, reverent, and sincere" woman.

Another quoted her as having said, "I am most impressed with the blessing that there is in sorrow."

Ezra heard it all probably with a more profound sense of loss than anyone, as he had never before been separated for long from his mother.

Struggling toward Spiritual Reality

Frances heard about Dr. Isabella DeVol's funeral at family prayers and felt sorrow for the children without parents. She prayed for China, too. New experiences, however, soon captured her attention as she formed new friendships and became interested in her music lessons, in which she excelled.

Frances enjoyed the church services and the Sunday school. Her father was a dynamic preacher and her mother a prayer warrior. She reveled in going with them to Quarterly Meeting, often held in the Alum Creek Friends Church. The Hodgins invariably stayed in a home just across the creek from Sunnyslope, and Frances thought it was a lovely farm. There is no doubt that often Frances and Ezra were in the same meetings, but being eleven-year-olds, they did not notice one another.

In the services Charles and Catherine DeVol sometimes gave testimonies and led in prayer. Frances yearned to know God as they seemed to, but she was too proud or too shy to go to the altar, and in her failure to surrender completely, she began trying in her own strength to live right. This led to her becoming critical of others, especially her brothers, who did not try as hard. They resented her attitude, and the result was sibling disharmony, which made Frances feel very insecure.

During the winter of Dr. Isabella DeVol's illness and death, Ezra knelt at the altar at Goshen. He did not want to go to China, but he did not want to go to hell. How to avoid both and still fulfill the will of God was an issue with which he yet had to deal. Charles had made his peace with God at the age of six, the year Ezra was born. He would always remain to his little brother the model of true Christian commitment, an ideal Ezra admired but was still not quite ready to follow completely.

After three years in Columbus, Daniel Hodgin and his family again returned to Brighton, and he resumed evangelistic work. Frances was ready for high school. The pastor of the Brighton Wesleyan Methodist Church, a gifted musician, quickly enrolled Johnny and Frances in a young people's orchestra and choir. This group was in demand for revival meetings, and they met many people as they traveled.

Frances was gentle, vivacious, friendly, and attractive, but terrified of dates. She preferred meeting friends in groups. Her willingness to enter into the services caused the leaders in the Wesleyan Methodist Church to invite her to become a member. Not yet fifteen, Frances felt confused. She wanted to be a Christian, but she knew there were unsurrendered areas in her life. How could she explain? The adults attributed her hesitance to shyness and urged her to join. She finally went forward to the altar along with others and agreed to become a member of the church, wistfully hoping to feel different. Afterward, however, she felt no change and was deeply disappointed.

Frances had no illusions about her state of grace, especially when her father came home from his long trips in evangelistic work and took over the ordering of the household. Because resentment was hard to hide, she stayed out of his way as much as possible, feeling more guilty on every occasion. She was well aware that church member or not, she had an attitude that was anything but Christian. Even so, classmates at her senior graduation seemed not to have sensed her feelings. They foretold in the class prophecy that she would become a nurse in a foreign land.

To Frances, it seemed she would never become anything. After graduation there was no money for college, and she could not get a job. John and Mendel moved away from home to work. Daniel and Frieda Hodgin moved with Frances, Dan, and Elsie to Coldwater, Michigan. There Daniel Hodgin began his fourth pastorate, and Frances got work in the library and sought to improve her skills in typing and other subjects by enrolling for a postgraduate course in the Coldwater High School. The resentment she felt against her father now began to torment her, and in spite of good friends in church, she avoided going and began slipping away to movies, not approved by her parents.

The climax came one evening as she started out of the house and her father called her back.

"Frances, Elsie needs your help in algebra," he said.

"I don't want to help her," Frances answered and turned toward the door.

"Frances!" her father commanded. "After you have helped Elsie, you may go, and not before."

Frances returned and took up the algebra book. She was torn with resentment and remorse, and felt more confused and unworthy than ever before. Frances would not have known that the model Charles was to Ezra, she was to her little sister Elsie, who often followed her to the library and sought to be helpful. Once Frances allowed her to take the library coin box to the office. On her way, she dropped it and felt sure she had fallen from grace in the eyes of her sister, Frances. Instead, Frances, observing the calamity, smiled and stooped to help Elsie pick up the money. Frances' graciousness left an indelible mark in Elsie's memory.

Frances' torment ended in 1928 on Mothers' Day at the Coldwater Wesleyan Methodist Church. The well-known evangelist from Columbus, Charles Stalker, was in her father's pulpit that day, and after the message, the altar was lined with seekers. Frances stumbled forward and knelt at a chair on the front row to ask God for forgiveness of her sins.

The congregation was singing:

"The cleansing stream, I see, I see!
I plunge, and Oh, it cleanseth me!"

God met her that day and flooded her life with His joy, love, and peace. She did not notice that in the pew behind her a twelve-year-old girl was also kneeling and sobbing out her commitment as she prayed for Frances. She was Frances' little sister, Elsie.

Back in Ohio on Sunnyslope farm, Ezra was going through similar spiritual battles. Even though the elders came and offered to take him in as a birthright member of the Friends Church at the age of eleven, he refused. At the age of twelve, however, he became a member in his own right and immediately accepted appointment to the kindling committee. All this, however, even the trip to the altar in Goshen, had left him no angel. Grateful as he was for the home given him by Uncle Elbert and Aunt Martha, he did not appreciate the long hours of daily chores, especially when there was a conflict with school sports. As a matter of principle, Uncle Elbert felt the upbringing of the DeVol children should be strict. Since Charles was already grown and Catherine nearly so, it was Ezra who most often broke the rules and suffered the rebukes.

A serious error in caring for the car was a case in point. To save the cost of antifreeze, the rule was to drain the radiator of the car when coming home, and fill it again just before leaving. Ezra remembered to fill it before taking off to Cardington, but he forgot to drain it when he got home. As a result, it froze and broke, and he paid the full penalty for his failure. However, the next night, Uncle Elbert made a similar mistake. He forgot to drain the tractor. To his utter dismay, it froze and broke both the radiator and the block! Ezra did not weep!

In 1924 after eighth-grade graduation from the academy at Alum Creek, Ezra moved on to Ashley High School, riding the horse, Midget, which was a slight improvement over donkeys in China. Football became his chief love, and in Ezra's eyes Uncle Elbert became a tyrant in his refusal to let him play. Uncle Elbert seemed to have one eye on the kind of company Ezra was beginning to keep, and the other on the vast amount of chores to be done at Sunnyslope.

Ezra's rebellion was mounting, however, and in desperation Uncle Elbert decided for the sake of Ezra's soul to give up his help on the farm and send him to Marion, Indiana. Charles was already a senior in Marion College as Ezra joined him as a room-mate and enrolled in the Marion College Academy for his sophomore year.

Catherine was also a student there, and during his junior year in high school, Ezra roomed with her fiance, Everett Cattell. They became fast friends, especially after the day Everett saved his life.

A group of young men had gone swimming in Deer Creek, and Ezra, who had not yet learned how to swim, jumped in beyond his depth. He came straight up out of the water and went down again. He came up the second time and fought for his life, but there was nothing on which he could lay hold. As he went down the third time, all the sins of his life came before him with great clarity.

"I never had any idea that one's mind could be so electrified at a given moment," Ezra said later.

He was so terrified that when Everett Cattell reached him, Ezra pulled him under. Then another friend came to the rescue. Clarence Moore (who later went to Quito, Ecuador, in HCJB Radio work) jumped in and helped Everett bring Ezra to shore.

Charles married Leora Van Matre on July 28, 1926, and they went to China. Catherine married Everett Cattell August 31, 1927, and they moved to a pastorate in Columbus, Ohio.

For his senior year in high school, Ezra moved back to Sunnyslope to help Uncle Elbert. He completed all his remaining credits by midterm in Cardington and was able to show his gratitude to Uncle Elbert and Aunt Martha by helping them full time on the farm until Marion College opened in the fall of 1928.

In spite of membership, regular church attendance, daily devotions, and family prayers, Ezra did not experience the peace he had seen in his mother's face. He wanted it, but even more, he wanted to choose his own course. He enrolled in Marion College with the determination to get "A's" in all his courses so that he would not be barred from medical school later. To guarantee the attaining of high marks, he vowed not to have any dates his first year. All went well for the first two weeks until he saw, crossing the street, a student who had just arrived. She was wearing a light blue hat, and as he noted her beauty and poise and sensed the spirit within her, Ezra gasped and stood transfixed. He bit his lip, regretting his vow. She was Frances Hodgin.

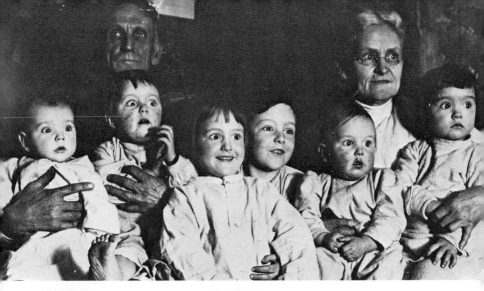

"I like what I see," Frances (center) says, surrounded by brothers, sister, cousins, and Hyne grandparents.

Ezra with his mother

"Charles, Catherine, and Ezra," Uncle Elbert and Aunt Martha Benedict said, "your name is still DeVol."

4 College Romance and a Sense of Direction

So do not fear, for I am with you; do not be dismayed, for I am your God. I will strengthen you and help you; I will uphold you with my righteous right hand.

Isaiah 41:9, 10 NIV

College Days of Pain and Pleasure

Frances Hodgin's plans to enroll in Asbury College were hindered by the development of a leg infection. She despaired of ever getting to college, but her father and mother encouraged her to enroll in the Wesleyan Methodist college in Marion, Indiana, even though classes had begun before she recovered. She enrolled in the same class as Ezra, and they soon became acquainted.

Stern and purposeful, Ezra doggedly pursued his studies and kept his vow while another young man stepped ahead to woo and win the girl of his dreams. With Frances in mind but temporarily out of reach, Ezra was not distracted in his effort to attain high grades.

Financial difficulties for both Ezra and Frances, exaggerated by the Great Depression, sent them off in different directions for jobs to cover tuition, books, and pocket money. Ezra carried out ashes from potbellied stoves, waxed floors, and planted strawberries. If possible, he worked Saturdays at Blumenthals, a department store, for they paid $4.50 a day. Otherwise, he sold men's shoes at Tom McAnn's, where the wages were only $2.50. By his third year in college, he got a comparatively lucrative job at $12.00 a week as chauffeur for a wealthy lady in town.

In 1927, because of war in China, Charles and Leora DeVol had to come home. Charles was immediately put on the

37

Marion College staff, and he and Leora provided Ezra with free room and board. That summer, while Charles was working at Indiana University in Bloomington on his master's degree in botany and Leora was at Sunnyslope, Ezra lived on oatmeal for a dollar a week and saved the rest of his earnings for college expenses.

To earn her way, Frances worked in the college kitchen, did housework for a lady in town, and clerked on Saturdays in a Sears department store. Her musical ability was appreciated, and she was paid to sing in a mixed quartet at a Presbyterian Church each Sunday.

One of the young men in the quartet hoped to capture Frances' undivided attention, but he was frustrated as she began to notice surprising sides in the temperament and character of that serious-minded, disciplined, premedical student, Ezra DeVol. He became a freshman class hero over the incident of the "senior log." The seniors brought this heavy log onto the campus to use as a bench, and the next day a haughty senior stood up in assembly and announced:

"This is a *senior* log. We don't mind a junior sitting on it, if he sits by the side of a senior. If a sophomore is invited by a senior to sit on it, then, and only then, may he do so. But a freshman? NEVER!"

Frances observed who picked up the gauntlet. Ezra, accompanied by his cousin, Edward Benedict, and a friend, Clark Shreve, called on John Williams, the treasurer of Marion College. John Williams was a practical man who believed one should not separate his religion from his public service.

"Could we borrow your crosscut saw? We'll bring it back in the morning, " Ezra promised.

John Williams's eyes sparkled a little more than usual. He had been around the college for a number of years and no doubt anticipated what was going to happen. He had no hesitation in loaning the saw.

While Clark Shreve stood guard at midnight, Ezra and Edward sawed the log into two-foot lengths and distributed it all over the campus.

On talent night during Ezra's sophomore year, he and a friend did an Amos 'n Andy type of skit. Some students thought their jokes corny, and Ezra felt it fell flat, but his sense of humor delighted Frances, who laughed heartily.

"Do you see any change in me?" Ezra, as "Amos" asked "Andy."

"No," answered "Andy."

"Well, you should. I just swallowed a dime!" ·

Ezra enjoyed jokes, but he did not have a happy-go-lucky attitude. Most of the time he impressed people as a person dead in earnest. Nowhere was this more evident than in spiritual matters, a facet of character increasingly appreciated by Frances.

The Beginning of College Romance

As they entered their junior year in the fall of 1930, both Ezra and Frances were active in college affairs. They were members of the Gospel League, a national organization for spreading scriptural holiness. Ezra was president of his class and president of Amphictyon, the literary society, and Frances served as its secretary. Ezra played basketball and belonged to the Latin and German Clubs. Frances belonged to the Spanish and French Clubs. Both were on the yearbook staff, and Ezra was the editor. Frances had quit dating her former friend, and Charles DeVol's astute wife, Leora, guessing the reason, invited Frances to Thanksgiving dinner. Margaret, their two-month old baby, delighted them with her gurgles. The turkey, dressing, and pumpkin pie were served with such genuine gratitude that Frances felt immediately at home. Through the cozy, rich afternoon, a romance began. Ezra and Frances both knew they were falling in love. They began their dating by attending a Rachmaninoff concert and were thrilled with the music and also with each other's company.

Spiritual Commitment and a Call

Ezra knew he was moving toward becoming a doctor, but he had so blocked out the thought of being a missionary that he dreaded to hear Frances even speak of the mission field. She showed great interest in missions, however, and there was some talk going around the college that Frances felt she should be a single missionary. Having no distinct idea as to what direction her life should take, she felt drawn to teaching, and by taking a few more subjects, she learned she could not only qualify for a B.A. but also a B.S. degree in education.

This new relationship with Frances was no doubt one major factor in Ezra's growing conviction that he was missing God's best in his life. Another occurrence also shook him to the depths. Driving down South Washington Street, he was dazzled by the oncoming lights and did not see a man stepping off the curb to get onto a streetcar. A sudden thud sent the man across the tracks, where he fell in a heap. Ezra slammed on the brakes, ran to the man, picked him up, and carried him to the car. An angry crowd gathered as he sped down the street to a doctor's office. As the man was being treated, Ezra reported the incident to the police. The man proved not to be seriously injured, and nothing came of the case except to leave a devastatingly nervous chauffeur, Ezra, amazed at the seemingly miraculous deliverance.

This incident awakened Ezra to his dependence on the Lord. To show his gratitude, he went to a students' prayer meeting on December 18, 1930, and as an invitation to come forward was given, deep conviction gripped him and he sat trembling in his pew.

Fearing an emotional response, he prayed: "Lord, if You really want me to go to the altar, send my friend, Bill Emerson, to speak to me."

Suddenly, he felt a hand on his shoulder, and there stood Bill Emerson.

"Ezra, don't you want to go forward?" he asked.

Ezra surrendered to the Lord that night and was gloriously forgiven and renewed. At last he was at peace with God.

Before Frances went home for Christmas, she and Ezra shared some thoughts about their future plans. She was not yet at peace. She was a prolific reader and had been influenced by many books about single women who had served God unencumbered. Ezra did not want to hinder God's full will for her. He had not yet heard any missionary call. Frances' parents approved of Ezra and were doing nothing to discourage her in that relationship.

As Frances reached home, she discovered Charles Stalker, a prominent evangelist, was holding meetings in the church. His wife, Catherine, was with him. She had a listening ear and an understanding heart, and Frances found it easy to share her secrets with this discerning lady.

"My dear," said Catherine Stalker after hearing her through and praying with her, "in my humble opinion you are not the kind of young woman God would call to be a single missionary. Many of us find our greater service in God's will by standing by and supporting another."

These words seemed right and beautiful to Frances as her indecision evaporated and rays of assurance beamed comfort into her conscience. Returning to Marion College, she found no difficulty through smiles and glances to let Ezra know, for nearly every time she looked at him, she found him looking at her. On Valentine's Day he brought her roses, and for the first time spoke the words that were drawing them together.

"Frances, every rose means I love you."

On February 27, 1931, they became engaged.

Nine days later, Marion College held its annual missionary convention. Responding warmly in their newly found love for their Lord and for one another, both Ezra and Frances listened to the challenging messages with open hearts— until the last day.

Suddenly, Ezra began to feel very uncomfortable. Having previously settled in his mind never to be a missionary, the thought seemed not to have occurred to him that his commitment might also include that.

I'm getting pulled in by my emotions, he thought. *I won't go to the meeting tonight, and this feeling will pass.*

So he stayed in his room, read magazines, and listened to the radio. As the evening wore on, peace fled from his heart, and the fear of losing his soul gripped him. Finally just as the meeting was being drawn to a conclusion, he walked in, went forward, and knelt at the altar.

Am I just being emotional? Does God really want me to be a missionary? These thoughts kept going through his mind.

"Oh, God," he prayed, "You allowed Gideon to put out a fleece. Let me put out one. You know there are already over seven hundred applicants for the seventy-eight places in the [Case] Western Reserve University School of Medicine, and that so far no one has ever been accepted from Marion College.

If You *really* want me to be a missionary, help me get into medical school in the next three months."

The very next day, the way opened for Ezra to go to Western Reserve for an interview. He ran to tell Frances, and she put aside the book she was reading on the life of Hudson Taylor to exult in this beginning of God's clear leading in their lives. He stayed to talk about what she was reading and sensed her intensified longing to be with him in God's service.

"It's all coming together so beautifully," she said.

The next morning as he left for Cleveland, she watched out the window for him to go by and said, half to herself and half in prayer, "My prayers will follow you, Ezra, all the way."

In three weeks—not three months— Ezra was accepted in medical school.

"Oh, God," Ezra prayed again, "You let Gideon put out the fleece the second time. You know I haven't a penny to my name. Show me where I can go for financial help. If that comes, then I will know beyond doubt that You have truly called me."

He thought of his mother's cousin, John Johnson. When Isabella DeVol had needed money for Western Reserve medical training in the 1890s, John Johnson's father, who was Isabella's uncle, had loaned it to her. Thinking of John Johnson as a possible source of financial help, therefore, surely was no miracle, but the directness of his answer seemed to be, as on May 30, 1931, Ezra stood before him in Richmond, Indiana.

"How much do you need?" John Johnson asked.

"About $600 a year," answered Ezra.

"Well, I'll loan you the money for two years."

Becoming Acquainted with the Hynes

That fall, two weeks before entering Western Reserve, Ezra was invited to Brighton. Frances, her parents, brothers Jonathan, Mendel, and Dan, and sister Elsie were all waiting to meet him. The next day, he was introduced to the grandparents.

Grandfather Frederick and Grandmother Sarah Hyne dominated Brighton. Head of the bank, the lumber business, the mill, the coal industry, and active in the church, Grandfather Hyne stood tall, slender, and straight as a ramrod. There was no doubt who was in charge, but his grey eyes were kindly and his bearing quiet, poised, and dignified. Frederick Hyne was German and Sarah English. Grandmother Hyne, with her crown of white hair, was a short five-foot-two with sparkling blue eyes. Words between her and her husband were scarce, but understanding was deep. This showed up even in the way she poured him a cup of tea. A slight jiggle of the cup showed her he had enough. They were love birds, smiling across the table.

"I felt like a moth in a butterfly box," Ezra later explained. "But he accepted me. I loved to watch him play with children. Mendel, Frances' brother, bought two balloons, and Grandpa filled them with gas. We all stood with the children and watched them go out of sight. Suddenly Grandpa shouted, 'Look, I see four up there!' and we all laughed as he poked fun at his double vision from cataracts."

Frances remembered a time in her girlhood riding with Grandfather through a forest. The going got rough and Frances got nervous, but Grandfather Hyne held the wheel tightly and never took his foot off the accelerator. "They are alike in some ways," Frances thought as she observed how Ezra and her grandfather liked each other from the start.

Struggles in Medical School and College

Two weeks later, Ezra entered medical school and moved into a scholastic enrrironment different from any he had previously encountered. Brought up in a home of Quaker doctors, nurtured in a Quaker community, educated in a Quaker school and a Wesleyan Methodist college, he thoroughly believed the Bible, not just because of what he had been taught, but because of his own dealings with God. God spoke to him through the Bible. It guided him as he sat under teachers who professed to be agnostics, and as he rubbed shoulders with students whose ethical philosophy differed from his.

He decided early not to join a fraternity. Ezra stated his reasons clearly, realizing social ostracism might be the price, but, to his surprise, the leaders with whom he had spoken seemed to understand him and respect his convictions. Snickers in class also died quickly when Ezra presented logical reasons for his disagreement with interpretations of life in terms of atheistic evolution.

There were dark days, but he found an anchor in Dr. T. Wingate Todd, a Scotch Presbyterian professor of anatomy, whose faith was based on the inspired Word.

Another anchor was his mother, Dr. Isabella French DeVol, whose picture was among the Western Reserve graduates of the class of 1897. Knowing that she had gone through classes at this same medical college and had made it all the way brought courage. One such day was November 3, 1931, as Ezra and a staunch Quaker, John Pennington, stood together in the halls of Western Reserve looking at Dr. Isabella DeVol's picture.

"When I have doubts," Ezra said, "I remember that what my mother had was no 'make-believe.' Her spiritual life was a reality. She demonstrated it. My doubts vanish when I remember her quiet, radiant spirit and her love for the Lord."

Struggles with faith were almost secondary to the financial plight, and it seemed providential that just before Thanksgiving, Ezra was able to earn $50 by giving his first blood transfusion. That same year, Everett and Catherine Cattell, Ezra's brother-in-law and sister, moved to Cleveland and took up the pastorate at First Friends Church. They provided his room and board all through medical school.

Dr. Byron Osborne, a father of four children and a teacher at Cleveland Bible Institute, had observed that Ezra always wore the same threadbare trousers to church services and prayer meetings. Though money was hard to come by, Dr. Osborne suddenly received a small inheritance, and his first thought was to use it to help Ezra. Investing some in order to be able to give further donations to Ezra from the interest, Dr. Osborne took the rest and bought a brown suit, hat, and matching overcoat. Ezra had them for his college graduation.

Another test was academic. Dr. Frederick Waite, the cytology teacher, had been around a long time. He remembered Ezra's mother. He was gruff at times, and on the first day of classes he let his students know where he stood.

"Western Reserve didn't send for any of you, and I personally don't care how long any of you stay. It's up to you to decide who'll remain and who'll be flunked out."

Dr. Todd was a terrifying figure at the quarterly orals in anatomy. Six doctors examined each student individually for thirty minutes, firing questions intended not only to ascertain the student's knowledge of the subject but also to test his emotional stability. He was supposed to learn that equanimity was one of the watchwords of medicine, as Marcus Aurelius said: "Thou must be like a promontory of the sea against which, though the waves beat continually, yet both itself stands and about it those swelling waves are stilled and quieted."

Frances Hodgin, his fiancee, encouraged Ezra through all these tests, sending regular letters and spending every holiday season with him. She was a senior, and on June 6, 1932, by transfer of certain credits from Western Reserve, Ezra and Frances graduated from Marion College, he with a B.S. and she with a B.S. and a B.A. degree.

The last year in college was a significant one for Frances. She had her first taste of the agonies of separation from the one she loved. She learned more about the real meaning of the missionary call—to China, of course—for Ezra's sake.

Music meant a lot to her, but a change in the music department caused a drop in her interest. At meetings in Columbus, Clarence Moore of HCJB, Equador—the man who helped Everett Cattell rescue Ezra from drowning—was scouting for talent. He heard Frances sing, "God Is Working Out His Purpose," and he awarded her a music scholarship for her complete senior year in Marion. Frances, regretfully, neglected to take advantage of it. Her full attention was on Ezra and missions.

Before graduation, Frances felt the stinging financial pinch of the times. Library work and clerking in a store downtown on Saturdays was not enough to clear her tuition debt, which had to be paid before registering for the spring term. That day arrived, and there was still no money. She went for a walk, praying that somehow she could finish school. As she came back, she found a special delivery letter from her brother Mendel, who had been working in the state of Washington. She opened his letter and found it contained his first apple-picking paycheck for $208. The tuition was $200!

"The Lord does provide on time, abundantly!" Frances gratefully acknowledged, with very tender thoughts of the sacrifice of her brother.

Financial tests did not end for Frances on graduation day. Her hardest trial came the next year back in Michigan when, with her B.S. degree in education, she found no teaching position. She had to settle for housework at $3.00 a week.

Daniel Hodgin appreciated his daughter's assistance at the piano and in leading music for evangelistic meetings. Therefore as time and opportunity afforded, she traveled with him, enriched by his sermons and blessed by his concern for the people who lined the altars. She developed a greater sense of the spiritual battles every individual must fight to enter the Kingdom. She entered into their struggles and felt the time was not ill-spent. Still no schools opened their doors. Discouragement came from being so far from Ezra with no remunerative work through which she coud help either him or herself.

At the same time, Ezra was in trouble at medical school. Shortly after enrolling for his sophomore year, the sponsor of his class, Dr. Wiggers, broke the news to him as gently as he could. The bottom line of what he said was:

"You don't have what it takes to be a doctor. You could employ a tutor to help you, but he would charge about $10 an hour."

Both Dr. Wiggers and Ezra knew that hiring a tutor was completely out of sight financially. For the next ten days, Ezra was in the deepest depression and darkness he had ever experienced. He knew where to turn, however, and as he read 2 Chronicles 14:11, he found comfort:

"Lord, it is nothing to thee to help, whether with many, or with them that have no power."

He had no power, but he did trust in God. In prayer on the tenth day, he began to hear a still, small voice:

"Do you serve Me because I am getting you through medical school or because you love Me?"

"You know everything, Lord, You know I love You," Ezra confirmed.

"Then go back home and be a failure for Me."

Ezra shuddered! What? *Go home?* It was the last place he wanted to be seen! *Be a fellow who couldn't make the grade? Oh, God!*

The still, small voice came again. "Go to Sunday School, church, and Christian Endeavor, and be a witness for Me. Walk with Me in humility, and keep sweet about it."

Before rising from his knees, Ezra said "Yes" to the most difficult order he had ever received. In prayer meeting that night, his testimony had a ring of certainty that blessed other people, and Ezra felt the joy of spiritual victory.

Less than twenty-four hours later as he stood by the Western Reserve bulletin board looking at announcements, Dr. Wiggers came by, put his hand on Ezra's shoulder, and said: "It's all right, DeVol. You're getting along OK. Forget what I told you the other day."

Dr. Wiggers taught physiology, and in it Ezra not only did "OK"; he proved his excellence in an assigned paper on "The Coronory Flow During Systole and Dystole." By extra research he came across and included in his paper a theory that reversed the accepted theories of the day.

"This has revolutionized my physiological concept," exclaimed Dr. Wiggers, the teacher, as he handed back the paper. That day Dr. Wiggers became a humble learner at the feet of his student. He and Ezra became fast friends.

Lest Ezra become too secure, histopathology rose up to give him another blow. Dr. Howard Karsner, the teacher, required a quiz every week with nearly perfect scores. Students sat four at a table with their microscopes to diagnose tissue. It was not a single kind of tissue, like a piece of lung, heart, or muscle; it was lung, heart, muscle, and nerve, ground together like hamburger. The students had to look through a microscope and then draw a map identifying the various tissues.

"This is so tough, we'll never make it unless we help one another," the other three students agreed.

"I can't do that," Ezra said. "I have to do my own work or I can't expect the Lord's help."

The other three students, dumbfounded, finally shrugged their shoulders, turned to one another, and walled him out. They passed the first three tests and Ezra failed—one, two, three. He was distressed. Catherine Cattell, his sister, heard him groaning in his room.

"It takes more than prayer, Ezra," the still, small voice whispered.

Ezra got the message. Not a miracle, but an accumulation of knowledge was the requirement. He must study longer hours and concentrate more intensely on histopathology with the help of a microscope. Ezra responded with all the discipline he could muster, and God gave him a verse from the Bible, Isaiah 50:7, on which he could stand.

"The LORD God will help me; therefore shall I not be confounded: therefore have I set my face like a flint, and I know that I shall not be ashamed."

On the rest of the quizzes until the end of the course his scores were nearly always ten for ten.

Changing the Course in Turbulent Waters

As Frances received letters from Ezra telling of God's gracious victories, she felt more of a failure than ever and even suggested to Ezra that they break their engagement. Of all the tests Ezra had gone through, this one was no doubt the most difficult. There was no money for a trip to Brighton. In fact, Ezra had just received $1000 of his loan from John Johnson. The day after he had deposited it, the bank failed, and he lost all but $50!

Though he was stunned by this loss, it seemed infinitesimal compared with the possibility of losing Frances. Ezra longed for her to be near him. He wrote, "Why don't you consider coming to the Frances Payne Bolton School of Nursing here at Western Reserve?"

On reading Ezra's letter, Frances recalled her school prophecy, that she would be a nurse in a foreign land, and smiled. She had no desire to be a nurse, but if that was what Ezra wanted, and if the Lord opened the way, she was willing to consider it.

So on July 14, 1933, Frances and a friend from Ann Arbor went to Western Reserve, took their aptitude tests, and were accepted. Since there was no money available to pay the fees, a wise family sat in council and finally decided that in any case, Frances should go to Cleveland, get a job in a home, attend Cleveland Bible Institute part-time for the intellectual and spiritual challenge, and be near Ezra.

Shortly after Frances arrived at the Cattell's home in Cleveland where Ezra was staying, two nurses from the Frances Payne Bolton School of Nursing came to visit Catherine Cattell, met Frances, and learned of her problem.

"I didn't have any money, either," one of them said, "but I applied for a scholarship and got it."

"I didn't know there were scholarships," answered Frances, "but anyway, it's too late now. The term has already begun."

The next day as Everett Cattell took Frances to Cleveland Bible Institute to register and apply for work, she told him what the nurse had said. They were just at that time passing Western Reserve University. Everett quickly turned off the road and into the parking lot of the school of nursing.

"Go in, Frances, and find out what the possibilities are," Everett urged.

Timidly she ascended the stairs, knocked on the dean's door and received a gracious welcome. As soon as she gave her name, the dean said:

"Frances Hodgin? Where have you been? We've been waiting for you!"

In no time at all, Frances told her story and filled the forms for scholarship.

"There's no question about the scholarship," the dean said. "Now get your books and go right to classes. It will take only a little time to complete the formalities."

Four days later, September 22, 1933, the three-year scholarship came through, and Frances moved into the dormitory to begin her new career. She was happy, grateful, and terribly busy. She was able to go to prayer meeting and church with Ezra and sometimes spend a holiday with him.

However, contemplating a career change at the age of twenty-four with three more years of study ahead before marriage was not all easy. There were times when Frances felt she could not go through with it. For three months she rode the roller-coaster of indecision and depression, which affected her physically, spiritually, and emotionally. Ezra suffered with her. Before they found themselves again one in heart and sure of God's purpose, both had to be willing to give each other up.

With assurance renewed, Frances found her attitude toward nursing turned around, and she wrote in her diary:

"I want to be a good nurse. With God's help, I believe I can."

Ezra wrote in his: "Frances witnesses to victory. I am so very happy."

On May 21, 1934, when Frances was capped in a beautiful service, Ezra's heart swelled with love and gratitude.

"A milestone along the way," he wrote. "God loves to interweave the golden threads of His love along the warp and woof of our everyday experiences."

A Renewed Sense of Direction

From then on with vision clear, Ezra and Frances pulled together. Financial problems dogged their every step, but they were touched by the gifts of children in Sunday schools and the way people at church would press fifty cents or a dollar into their hands.

Unique financial answers came in 1934. For the summer Ezra was offered a job at Harkness Camp on Lake Erie, a camp for two hundred young people. Just before going, he developed whooping cough for the second time in his life. Doctors gave him medicine which suppressed it, and then they cleared him to go. On arrival, he started coughing again. He got into the car, knowing he could not possibly stay at the camp with such a cough. He told the Lord that the camp needed a doctor and he needed the money. He sat there, expecting to cough again, but soon realized he was well. Marveling at God's ability to heal—a fact he would experience often in his life and practice—he got out of the car and went to work.

In April 1934, money came so that Ezra was able to go with Frances to Brighton when her Grandmother Hyne died, and again in September when Grandfather Hyne died. In November Ezra's Aunt Martha was in her last illness, and since he did not have a cent, Ezra prayed for money to go to see her.

"I can loan you my car," Everett Cattell offered, "but I don't have any money for gas."

The only day in the week Ezra could get away from his medical studies was Wednesday. He watched the mail on Monday, hoping for one of those miracles of God's rich supply. Nothing came. Tuesday, nothing came. Wednesday's mail would be too late.

Tuesday evening a five-dollar telegraphed money order arrived with no signature. With it Ezra bought gas to fill Everett's car and went to see his Aunt Martha for the last time. She died December 16, 1934. (Roy Skipper in Columbus had sent the money. "I felt impressed to send it on Sunday," he said later, "but I forgot to put it in the mail; so when I did think of it, I just felt I should send it by telegram.")

Some gifts were not in dollars and cents. Ezra needed a car to answer the call on home-delivery obstetric cases. Western Reserve demanded that each doctor in training answer twenty-one such calls successfully, accurately estimating the time of birth in order to call the resident and have him present to observe the delivery. A friend, Fred Gallagher, loaned Ezra a car. Calls kept him jumping, but getting the resident there on time was something else! After being called, the resident had to travel through city traffic ten or twenty miles, and if he was a minute late, the case did not count. After Ezra failed the first three times, he began to pray earnestly, for time was running out.

In his morning devotions, reading Isaiah 41:9, 10, he felt an unusual sense of the presence of God.

"I have chosen thee and not cast thee away," and "Fear not, I am with thee!"

These words stood out as if in letters of gold. Ezra claimed these promises. His next obstetrical case came November 8, 1934, and Delwin Davidson, born at West 104th Street, cooperated perfectly without wasting the resident's time by a minute or frustrating Ezra. In due time Ezra had the required twenty-one deliveries to his credit in obstetrics; he then returned the car to his friend with thanks.

From Hudson Taylor, Ezra and Frances had learned this principle: *Move man through God by prayer alone.* In his last year, Ezra estimated he would need an extra $400 beyond his loans in order to graduate. The money did not come in great sums, but in many small ones. At the end of his medical course, he counted the total of what had been received, and it was $403! All bills were paid and a sum of three dollars was left over!

Then came the climax. Three eight-hour days of state board examinations, one of practicals and two of writtens. Ezra knew as he left the building that he had passed. That evening he went home to Sunnyslope and woke up the next morning with the most glorious feeling he had ever experienced. The sun was shining, and the trees were clapping their hands. He walked out and spotted wrens, orioles, cardinals, and thrushes, and felt like joining them in song.

A few days later, June 12, 1935, was graduation. Everett, Catherine, and David Cattell, Uncle Elbert Benedict, and Daniel, Frieda, and Elsie Hodgin all joined Frances to watch the ceremonies. Talk about Elsie's recent engagement and about the airplane Mendel had built and flown seventy hours up to 2,500 feet came to a hush as the ceremonies began. The music rose to a crescendo, and the [Case] Western Reserve University School of Medicine graduates marched in. Speeches were soon over and the great moment finally arrived. Frances, breathless and intent, her hands tightly clasped, her face radiant, and her eyes shining like stars, watched Ezra step forward. Praise to God rose in her heart. The degree was conferred, and as he stepped back to his place, she could hardly contain the joy she shared with him at that moment of his completion of a lifetime goal. He was now Dr. William Ezra DeVol.

Marion College "Senior Log" *No Freshmen Allowed!* Marion College Graduation, Ezra and Frances, 1932. W. Ezra DeVol, M.D. (below). Frances, the nurse (lower right), in Frances Payne Bolton School of Nursing, Cleveland, 1933-1936. Ezra with Frances the day he graduated from [Case] Western Reserve University School of Medicine, Cleveland, 1935.

5 Meeting God at the Corners

My God in His love will meet me at every corner.
Psalm 59:10 as paraphrased by Amy Carmichael

A Long Year of Waiting

Following graduation from medical school, Dr. DeVol advanced to meet the future. He was clearly led to Cleveland City Hospital for his internship, beginning on July 1, 1935. The work there was strenuous and of great variety. He liked that, as he wanted all the experience possible before undertaking a missionary career. Two weeks later, he called Frances and told her that he had done twelve deliveries that day. The next day he applied to the mission board. Before the end of the month he had his license to practice, and before the end of August it was probated.

"Oh, I hope this year goes fast," Frances said. "Our whole thought and aim is to get to the field." She also sent her application to the mission board. She had one more year in training, and the challenges for her were equally as great as for Ezra in his internship.

"My heart is in the work, and I enjoy it so much," she wrote.

The greatest trial of this last year was that Ezra and Frances now lived ten miles apart and their heavy schedules and no transportation made it impossible for them to see each other often.

That winter Ezra was put into quarantine with scarlet fever. Everett and Catherine Cattell drove Frances over to Cleveland

City Hospital where she talked to him through the isolation ward window.

A few days later, Catherine was admitted into the obstetric ward where Frances was working, and on December 10, 1935, Barbara Ann was born.

As Frances, the nurse, took Barbara in her arms, she said, "I love nursing, and obstetrics more than any other part of it." The ten days she was able to nurse Catherine in the hospital was a time of special joy.

The year surely was speeding by, and to her delight, Frances' training in psychotherapy and physiotherapy took her to Cleveland City Hospital from January to April, 1936. Ezra was well again and doing a lot of surgery. They saw each other more often and attended prayer meeting and church together as heavy schedules allowed.

Wedding plans began to dominate their conversation, and a tentative date was set for late fall when Frances would be finished with all her requirements. Graduation day was June 10, 1936, but illness had delayed the completion of her required hours of nursing, and Frances Payne Bolton School of Nursing had a rule that no student could get married until those hours were completed.

Though their engagement exceeded five years, they had every intention of abiding by the rule, until Everett and Catherine Cattell announced their plans to go to India as missionaries in September. With Charles in China and Catherine's departure for India, Ezra felt keen disappointment that not one of his family would be present at his wedding. He explained the extenuating circumstances to Dean Howell, who gave special permission for the rule to be set aside for Frances. They moved the wedding date forward to August 15, 1936, while the Cattells were still in America.

"Only seven weeks away!" exclaimed Frances when the news came. "I didn't know anyone could be so happy!"

Those seven weeks evaporated. Dr. Ezra had been accepted as assistant resident in Fairview Park Hospital and moved into his new job at the end of June. He was delighted that, as in City Hospital, Fairview Park also offered a wide variety of medical procedures and numerous opportunities to perform surgery.

Fumbling attempts to witness for Christ, however, sometimes brought embarrassment. When Ezra failed to let his light shine, conviction tormented him. He wanted to be a good doctor; he was also learning to be a Christian doctor. Feeling constrained to speak to a badly burned woman who was going to die, he put it off. She died before he could get back to her, and his conscience tortured him. Another time, he felt he just had to speak to a woman with terminal cancer. He approached her gently and asked:

"Has your minister been to see you?"

She began to weep uncontrollably. "Oh, you think I am going to die!"

Shocked by the reaction, Dr. DeVol withdrew from the room. His conscience now struck him on the other side. What technique was there that would help him match faith with practice? Later he dreaded facing the woman during rounds, but to his surprise, she opened the conversation and ended up committing her life to Christ. These experiences convinced him of the need to listen perceptively to God's still small voice and to follow His leading.

At the same time, Frances was thinking very practically about their wedding arrangements. Her grandparents had businesses and property, but in those days of depression they had very little cash. Evangelist Daniel Hodgin and his wife had always lived frugally, but somehow they managed to send Frances $50. On her first day off, she went shopping and found a wedding dress for $10.

Frances sat up late at night addressing wedding invitations. On her day off, she cleaned the apartment on Rosedale she and Ezra had chosen for their first home. But as the days flew by, there was very little time to do anything but assist in surgery, take examinations, and work overtime. Just before the wedding, she worked a twelve-hour shift in the surgical suite, where that day fifty-nine operations were performed.

The Wedding

The day before the wedding, two friends from the church, Willard and Florence Farren, met Ezra and Frances at work and took them to Brighton. They arrived an hour after midnight.

On August 15, 1936, at two p.m., Frances came down the aisle of Brighton Wesleyan Methodist Church. Ezra, waiting at the altar for her, was awed by her beauty in the white satin, princess fashion gown with its high neckline, softly draped sleeves, long train, and the three-tiered tulle veil fashioned to a crown of orange blossoms. She wore silver sandals and carried a bouquet of pure white roses, delphinium, and maiden hair fern, tied with wide, white satin ribbon. Wearing a full-length pink organza dress, carrying pink roses, Elsie's heart pounded with pride as she stood at her sister's side as the maid of honor and only attendant.

For his best man, Ezra had chosen Edward Benedict, a cousin and college friend. Elsie's fiance, Kenneth Eyler, and Frances' brothers served as ushers. Mendel's girlfriend, Kathryn Swartz, was there for her first meeting with some of the Hodgins, including the bride. Rev. Daniel Hodgin, father of the bride, assisted by Rev. Everett Cattell, performed the ceremony. Sixty guests attended the reception, where the four-tier silver and white wedding cake was served.

Rice throwing and a honeymoon were omitted. Arrangements were made for the six-o'clock Flint-Detroit train to make a whistle stop at Brighton, where the bride and groom boarded. From Detroit they took a night steamer across Lake Erie and were back in Cleveland by morning and soon at work—he at Fairview Park Hospital, and she in Lakeside, completing her required hours.

Beginning Life Together—Apart

Frances got home to their Rosedale apartment from Lakeside Hospital only on some weekends. Not until October did Frances complete her course work and really move into her own home. In December she took her state board examinations in Columbus. Unlike Ezra, who walked away from his state boards with assurance that he had passed everything, Frances left in a state of depression, with the feeling that she had failed. The cloud did not lift until results came to prove otherwise.

Opening and Closing Doors to China

That fall, the DeVols moved to the house of some friends who were wintering in Florida. Their new home was quite some distance from the hospital where Frances worked, but it saved rent, and that was very important. There were debts to pay.

In December, Fairview Park Hospital Chief Resident, Dr. Palomake, called Dr. DeVol into his office.

"We have been satisfied with your work," he said. "There are going to be some changes. As you know, we have a tremendous amount of surgery. You are being requested to accept the position as chief resident. Here are the application forms. What is you reaction to that?"

Dr. DeVol was dumbfounded. At such a time, was this not God's wonderful provision? This offer seemed all he longed for as he waited for China's doors to open. Here was the opportunity to improve his skill as a surgeon and at the same time earn money to pay his debts. Gratefully, he took the application to his office and while singing praises to God, filled it out meticulously.

Thinking of all he would say to Frances as soon as he got home that evening, Ezra bounded down the stairs to turn the application in at the desk. Arriving there, he found it impossible to let go of that application. He stood there, turning it over and over again in his hand. Was he on the right course? Was God really leading him in this direction? Why this sudden feeling of indecision? He turned and went back upstairs to his office and sat down to pray.

This is foolish, he thought. *Of course I should hand this in. It has to be God's provision at this time.*

Rising from his chair, Ezra deliberately walked down the stairs to the desk and stood there again. Conviction gripped him that such a commitment might stand in their way of going to China. Therefore, instead of the application, he submitted his apologies and resigned as of July 1, 1937.

About a week later, the mission board notified the DeVols of their acceptance as missionary candidates for China. This confirmed to Ezra that he had been guided on the right path. The medical debt still had to be cleared before they could proceed, and they had no idea of what was going on behind the scenes in answer to their prayers about that.

Dr. Walter R. Williams, Jr., Dr. DeVol's boyhood friend, had applied to go to China as a missionary in 1931, but financial difficulty made it impossible for the mission board to send him.

He and his wife, Helen, were deeply disappointed. He turned to a career in education, and in 1936 had just signed a three-year contract with Oberlin Public Schools in Ohio when a letter arrived from the board requesting him and his wife to go to China in the fall. He felt that he could not break his contract. After a visit with Ezra and Frances, he became aware of their eagerness to go as soon as their debts were paid. Walter, Jr., and Helen Williams put down the first $500 to erase the debts, and with permission of the mission board, they solicited gifts from other friends.

January 1937 ushered in a very significant year for the new bride and groom. The debts were cleared, their courses were finished, and they were now uncommitted and ready to accept the call. But another development brought further changes. On January 4, Ezra made a special trip home from Fairview Park Hospital to break some special news to Frances.

"Yes," he said, "the Ashheim Zondek test is positive!"

Marriage! Parenthood! The mission field! Frances could hardly take it all in. She did not handle pregnancy very well, and by March she had to resign her job and go to Brighton. Her physician husband had some second thoughts about her condition and asked her to return to Cleveland for a test in July. His eyes twinkled as he told her what he found, but Frances was both alarmed and happy in undulating waves. She went to Myrtle Williams to share the news.

"We're going to have twins!"

"Twins? What? But you're going to China this fall!"

Practical, realistic Myrtle Williams gained her balance as soon as she read the mercurial emotions in Frances' face. Myrtle Williams's big brown eyes began to sparkle as she reached out motherly arms. Then both of them burst into laughter.

A few days later, without jobs, Ezra and Frances closed their apartment and went to Brighton. While waiting for the birth of the twins due in three weeks, they began to prepare for China. Even before the twins arrived, news came that the Sino-Japanese War, which started July 7, was making missionary work in China impossible, and they would not be able to go. They were dumbfounded! Degrees in hand, but the door to China closed in their faces? No jobs! No home! The impending responsibility of double parenthood! What was the meaning of all this?

A One-Hundred Percent Increase in the Family

On August 3, 1937, Dr. DeVol rushed his wife to the hospital at Howell, Michigan. On August 4, two little red-headed girls made their appearance and doubled the family. Patricia Lee arrived at 2:34 a.m., Priscilla Ann at 3:04. As mirror twins, left-handed Patricia and right-handed Priscilla had to be identified with arm bands and would often confuse even their parents.

"They're both here and they're fine!" the nurse jubilantly announced.

The twins thrived, bringing joy and also wakeful nights when both had colic. What a cushion of warmth and love they found in Brighton with parents who knew how to love and pray! The DeVols were not alone as they sought to know what corner they would need to turn next. At the end of the month when Frances was ready to travel with the twins, the family went to Sunnyslope. Uncle Elbert Benedict, alone and lonely, welcomed them. The peace and quiet of the farm comforted them as they waited and prayed for new direction.

A City Practice

The DeVols did not have long to wait to hear the words, "This is the way, walk ye in it." (Isaiah 30:21)

LeRoy Skipper's physician, Dr. G. T. Mathews on West Broad Street in Columbus, Ohio, needed an assistant. In October, the DeVols found an apartment near Highland Avenue Friends Church [Westgate], and Dr. DeVol started to work for $50 per week. Even in those days this salary was not adequate for a family of four, but in a sense they were still going through preparation for their life work.

Five significant benefits came from those three years in Columbus. First, they decided to tithe their income whether they could afford it or not. The first year and a half they could not afford it, but a few gifts from friends and relatives helped them keep going.

Second, Dr. DeVol learned that answering home calls helped to establish a reputation as a doctor who really cared for people. He answered as many as four calls a night.

Dr. DeVol did care about people. They were never mere "cases." They had names and needs—more than the physical.

What he lacked in office personnel, he took on himself. For example, Esther Garner (later Mrs. W. Robert Hess), age 11, came to his office and had her tonsils removed. Afterward, the doctor himself carried her down to his car, took her home, and carried her upstairs to her bed. Mrs. Garner, Esther's mother, though deeply grateful, was alarmed, for Dr. DeVol, just two weeks earlier, had himself undergone appendectomy surgery with complications that nearly cost him his life. Her confidence in him, however, was firmly established, and she took her second daughter, Martha, to him for the same operation.

The third significant benefit of these years in Columbus was the lifelong relationship developed with the people at Highland Avenue Friends Church [Westgate], such as the Langdons, Skippers, Stahlys, Hannes, Foxes, Wheelocks, and many others. In that fellowship, spiritual life was deepened and commitments were made. Galatians 2:20 became very real:

"I am crucified with Christ: nevertheless I live; yet not I, but Christ liveth in me: and the life which I now live in the flesh I live by the faith of the Son of God, who loved me, and gave himself for me."

Paul and Marjorie Langdon just naturally turned to Dr. DeVol for the delivery of their son. Dr. DeVol even named him, calling him Larry.

Paul Langdon appreciated Dr. DeVol's spiritual depth, good medicine, and sense of humor. He instigated a practical joke on Ezra one day with the help of Perry Hayden, the miller from Tecumseh, Michigan, who developed "Dynamic Kernels."

Ezra did not know that Perry was in town. Paul and friends thoroughly bandaged Perry, using bottles of catsup to create the illusion of serious injury, and took him into Dr. DeVol's office. The doctor leaped to attention, got the man on the operating table at once, removed the bandages, and looked into Perry's smiling face. Only then did he smell the catsup.

One evening a patient came to church and stood up to give testimony to his healing of a cough. To their embarrassment, Dr. DeVol heard the man thanking him over and over without much mention of the Lord. Others also were becoming a bit weary of it when suddenly the man started to cough, and cough, and cough! Dr. DeVol never lived that down.

Not only in Columbus were relations cemented, but being near Sunnyslope, the DeVols often took time off to visit Uncle Elbert, who now lived alone. Ezra and he went hunting together and talked over old times. This brought much happiness to Uncle Elbert and relaxation to a weary physician.

By April 1939 Dr. DeVol felt he had gained sufficient experience to survive in practice alone, and he opened his own office on West Broad in Columbus. The very first week he made more than twice as much money as he had before, and the practice grew. His experience broadened, and this was the fourth benefit he appreciated during those years. E. L. Skipper helped him again, loaning him money for basic office furniture. He paid $65 for a two-door used Chevrolet, at a considerable reduction in price because the doors opened backwards.

A fifth benefit was the opportunity to practice the lessons he had learned in witnessing in Fairview Park Hospital. He remained sensitive to the still small voice. One house call took him to the home of a huge man named Jewel Dobson, a warehouse worker. He had had a heart attack and was in terrible pain. His blasphemy made the air blue as Dr. DeVol tried to give him an injection of morphine. When the pastor came, the man's language became even worse. He was near death, but there was no clear way to reach him spiritually.

One day when Dr. DeVol went to check on him, he felt the nudge in his conscience: "Talk to Jewel about his soul."

Cautious, Dr. DeVol waited for another nudge, and then another. Finally he got up his courage and said, "Dad, are you a Christian?"

"Nope."

"Do you want to be?"

"Yep." The tears started rolling down Jewel's cheeks.

With his wife kneeling on one side of the bed and the doctor on the other, Jewel made his peace with God. They did not know then that at the same time, down in his wife's church, the pastor and his congregation were also praying for Jewel. He made a wonderful recovery and lived two years more in spiritual victory. This was only one of many such opportunities Dr. DeVol seized to combine physical and spiritual healing.

Charles DeVol's daughter Margaret often stayed with her Uncle Ezra and Aunt Frances, and delighted in baby-sitting the twins. Often, however, Frances was alone and found the care of Pat and Pris more than a handful. One day they got the gate open at the top of the stairs and tumbled down. Frances caught them at the landing. Whenever they got outside, they invariably chose to run in opposite directions, forcing Frances to call for help. They stimulated each other and generated excitement for the family and for the neighborhood.

Margaret Curran, sister of Mrs. LeRoy Skipper, made a point of dropping in at appropriate times. She came in one day and found Frances beside herself, with food on the stove and both girls crying.

"Take them both!" Frances exclaimed.

Margaret Curran did just that, and sent Frances out for a walk.

Amazingly, Frances and the twins were regularly by Dr. DeVol's side in church, prayer meeting, and Sunday school, though sitting through an entire service was rarely possible. Frances encouraged her husband in his practice and often longed to be with him. This, however, would have to wait until later years. For the time being, she was an efficient wife, mother, and homemaker, and was drinking in spiritual truths offered them through their rich relationships in the Friends Church.

To China at Last

By 1940 the way cleared for the DeVols to go to China. Dr. DeVol sold his practice to a trusted friend, Dr. Jack Miles. Collecting bills, he was told, would be impossible if his patients knew he was leaving. Nevertheless, he felt people should know not only that he was going, but why. The fact that he collected 98 percent of all outstanding bills testified to God's faithfulness and to the confidence that existed between the doctor and his patients.

On August 20, 1940, Ezra and Frances DeVol, with three-year-old Pat and Pris, took a train to San Francisco and boarded the *SS Asama Maru* for China. The ship had to stop for repair in Yokohama, where they ran into the Black Dragon Society of Japan. These people openly urged war with the United States. The DeVols realized trouble lay ahead. On arriving in Shanghai October 1, they were almost washed ashore by the very severe storm (typhoon) that whipped through the city leaving the streets flooded.

Before they had cleared customs, political winds threatened to drive them right back to America. The American Embassy in Peking warned American citizens, particularly women and children, to leave.

A Corner with a U-Turn

How could Ezra and Frances DeVol follow God all the way to China only to turn back? Surely, they felt, this was not right for them. After consultation with the missionaries who had come to Shanghai to meet them, they decided to proceed on to Nanking and then to Luho to the home of Charles DeVol, who had returned to China with his family in 1939. Ezra's home town of Luho welcomed him and his family with a 32-course dinner. Cousins Margaret and her little sister Esther entertained the twins who, in turn, entertained them by bouncing back and forth on the davenport.

After their delightful visit in Luho, where they expected to live eventually, the DeVols returned to Nanking and took up language study. Six weeks later the officials of the American

Embassy not only warned all women, children, and "unessential men" to leave, they sent in the *SS Washington* of the President Lines to take them out. Though classified as surgical resident in University Hospital in Nanking, Dr. DeVol had as yet no permanent assignment and was considered "unessential." Not only the missionaries, but Dr. H. Daniels of the University Hospital advised him to return home with his family, and they decided to follow that course. Each reluctant step in that direction became slower and slower. Neither felt right about what they were doing. Finally they came to a dead stop and sat down, alternately staring at the wall and their half-filled suitcases.

Suddenly they noticed the words of a faded motto on the wall:

"TRUST IN THE LORD AND DO GOOD" Psalm 37:3

This was exactly what they wanted to do. Ezra reached for his *Amplified Bible* to find the verse in context, and he read:

"Trust . . . in the Lord, and do good . . . *dwell in the land* and feed surely on His faithfulness."

The verse struck him like lightning—and light. He was convinced he had heard from God and should stay.

"I knew this last week," Frances confessed. "I couldn't sleep, and the Lord made it plain to me that I was to go home, but you were not to go home with us. I thought I could not bear it, but now I am ready."

"Unless God helps me, I cannot bear it either," said Ezra. "Who knows for how long? Yet we must go on trusting Him."

The next day Ezra read *Streams in the Desert* in morning devotions, and this verse underlined their convictions:

"What? Could you not watch with me one hour?" (Matthew 26:40) On their knees the matter was settled.

That morning after prayers, Ezra and Frances went together to the University Hospital for a scheduled operation. On arrival, they found all the doctors and nurses in the hospital on strike except the operating nurse, who had things ready with the patient on the table. But there was no surgical team to assist in the operation. Dr. DeVol persuaded a young Chinese doctor to assist, and the operation was finally over. The experience so unnerved Dr. Ezra that he questioned why he was staying after all. Back at the Quakerage, however, he began removing his things from the suitcases and "set his face like a flint."

Just then Charles DeVol appeared at the door and called Frances into the hall. "Frances, are you really sure that you should go?"

It was Frances' turn to feel unnerved, for she trusted Charles' judgment and wisdom; but, this time she found herself answering calmly, "Yes, Charles, I am as sure it is God's will for me to go as I am that Ezra should stay."

At the ship in Shanghai, Ezra could hardly bear to say goodbye. Boarding the boat that would take them to the SS *Washington*, Frances held Pat's left hand and Pris's right. She swallowed hard as tears that would not stop coursed down her cheeks. The girls were crying and calling out, "Daddy!"

As distance between them grew greater, Ezra and Frances were thinking, *Oh, Lord, how long? Will we ever see each other again? What lies ahead— prison, torture, death? Oh, God, watch over us as we are separated. Keep us loving You and one another. Keep us true even unto death.*

A Long and Distant Separation

The SS *Washington* sailed out, and soon Frances could not see even a speck on the vast horizon. *We are really leaving him behind. It is not a bad dream. I will not wake up and find him here beside me. Oh, God, how I need You!* Holding tightly to the hands of her three-year-olds, she turned and went down to her cabin. Darkness enveloped them, and before long winds arose, tossing the ship mercilessly on huge, restless waves. They were all seasick. The storm outside, however, was but a shadow of the turmoil inside as Frances increasingly became aware of her aloneness and inadequacy. What would she have done without the assurance that God was in charge and leading even through the darkness of the storm!

In spite of rough seas, the ship continued plowing through the waters and finally steamed into port. Before Christmas, Frances, Pat, and Pris were back once again in Brighton, Michigan, in the shelter of the big house of their loved ones, Daniel and Frieda Hodgin. What a wonderful Christmas the Hodgins and all the Hyne relatives gave them!

Early in January the girls got admission to a preschool operated by the Henry Ford Foundation and Frances found work in a hospital in Tecumseh, Michigan. An English family, Edward and Ella Escolme and their twelve-year-old daughter Beppy, took them in and made them feel at home. The Escolmes were a longtime pastoral family in Tecumseh Friends Church. Edward Escolme had been converted under the ministry of Daniel Hodgin, Frances' father. Solid and reliable as the custom of afternoon tea, the Escolmes, who had come many decades ago from England to the United States, still communicated the sturdiness of the British Empire.

On December 7, 1941, the hospital radio blared out the news of Pearl Harbor. Frances wept all the way home. The radio at Escolmes' was turned on to a program entitled, "Life Can Be Beautiful." Frances threw herself into the rocking chair where she would often sit and knit in the evenings to keep hands busy and mind at peace. Unaware of little listening ears just around the corner in the next room, with tears in her voice, she blurted out:

"Who says life can be beautiful?"

Peering over the top of his glasses, Edward Escolme turned and said in a gentle, reproving voice, "Oh, yes, Frances. Life can be beautiful, if—"

Before he had time to quote a text to substantiate his claim, Frances put her head in her hands and cried, "I can't stand it!"

Ella Escolme rose and put her hand on Frances' shoulder. "Yes, you can stand it, Frances. You have to!" Her voice sounded like the Rock of Gibraltar.

Frances did stand it; she stood much more than that. At the hospital her good training made her a valuable nurse, and rich experience enhanced her ability. The staff depended on her more each day and drew encouragement from her strength and faithfulness. She set aside her evenings for time with Pat and Pris. She told them stories and played exercise games with them at bedtime. Life for all of them in the Escolme home began to be very pleasant. Beppy was a friend to the twins and also a built-in baby-sitter.

"Let's play the Quaker game," she would say. "We'll see who can get to sleep first." It was a game that worked every time.

The girls loved hearing Aunt Ella say in her English accent, "Now finish your porridge, girls, or Uncle will be vexed." The words fascinated them, though they never saw Uncle vexed.

With the Escolmes' help, Frances had movies made periodically to later share the girls' stages of growth with their father. In 1941 she made a phonograph record for him and sent it to China. Just as she finished it, the twins called out:

"Come home sometime, Daddy!"

The record reached him, and the last groove stuck and repeated over and over, "Come, come, come, come!" That was hard on Daddy when there was no way to come, or even to send a letter.

One day in June 1942, a very important letter from the U.S.A. State Department brought word that Dr. Ezra DeVol was on his way home and would arrive in New York late in August. Frances went to New York and was present as the huge Swedish diplomatic exchange ship, the *SS Gripsholm*, pulled into the harbor with its 1,600 passengers. These repatriates all came from interior China in exchange for 1,600 Japanese sent home from the United States. Wartime secrecy kept the news out of the papers, and precautions against air raids and espionage kept Frances waiting in the dark for many hours not knowing how she would ever make contact with her husband. Amidst all the pandemonium, she could not find him. The next morning she went down early. The place was almost deserted. Suddenly she heard a voice behind her:

"Frances!"

She turned and saw him coming toward her.

"Ezra!"

Understanding God's Purpose and Direction

Yearly Meeting in Damascus was already in session, and Ezra and Frances went directly by train to Salem, Ohio, where they were met by the Escolmes with Pat and Pris and other friends and relatives. They went on to Damascus, where with Frances by his side and a little five-year-old red-head clinging tightly to each leg, Ezra managed piece by piece to share the experiences of serving God in China during World War II. This is the way he told it:

The hardest experience of my life to date was standing on the shores and watching my family sail away from me into stormy seas. Returning on the train to Nanking alone, I suddenly sensed a Presence in the empty seat beside me, and the Lord reassured me: "I am going back to Nanking with you." I was filled with joy and I knew I wasn't alone.

Fortunately, on return, I was so busy with surgery in the University Hospital of Nanking that I had no time for introspection. Chinese wounded filled our wards. I didn't forget I was a missionary, and I sought to witness for Christ at every opportunity. I witnessed to dying soldiers and some were converted. When I did not witness and they died, I felt remorse. An eight-year-old Chinese boy named Wang Shu Pang brought joy to my heart. He had pneumonia and empyema. I had to remove a piece of his rib and drain pus from the pleural cavity behind it. As he recovered, he read tracts eagerly. He learned to know Christ and accepted Him as Savior.

As the Japanese took control of Nanking, it became increasingly clear that no one could work under their occupation. My brother Charles and I decided it was time to follow our wives to the U.S.A. Charles went to Shanghai and secured two options. We could sail either on December 4th or 11th, 1941. However, my exit visa had lapsed, and it was impossible to get it renewed. Charles, therefore, secured two tickets for the 11th, and finally I got a pass to leave Nanking on the 8th. That morning my devotional reading included 1 Corinthians 17:8,9:

"But I will tarry, for a great door and effectual is opened unto me, and there are many adversaries."

I had hardly closed the book when the news came:

THE JAPANESE HAVE BOMBED PEARL HARBOR!

World War II was on. Neither Charles in Shanghai nor I in Nanking were going anywhere. The American Embassy in Nanking was immediately inaccessible, surrounded by Japanese guards. Charles and Elsie Matti and I were isolated in the Nanking Quakerage in blackout, our suitcases packed, expecting any moment to be taken to a concentration camp. Eight days later the Japanese came in an ambulance and ordered me back to work.

Dr. H. Daniels had gone on the ship leaving December 4th and was interned in Santo Tomas Internment Camp, Manila. Dr. C. S. Trimer of the Methodist Mission and I were the only American doctors left in Nanking. He took over as superintendent and I was put in charge of surgical service.

The verse that held me in China, "... dwell in the land...." also had a phrase in it, "Feed on His faithfulness." Our meals were cut down to two a day as all U.S.A. funds were frozen. But other ways opened up for us.

A Chinese banker, Mr. Hsia, appreciated our pneumothorax treatment for his daughter who had tuberculosis. Every two weeks as he brought her for treatment, he delivered to us twelve dozen eggs. Sometimes he also gave us cookies, cakes, and Japanese yen. He helped us feed the whole community.

The only legal way of getting money was to write a check for only $5.00 and send it to be cashed to a Shanghai bank, but it was illegal for anyone to take the check to Shanghai. James Ging, a young Christian studying in Shanghai, went to see Charles DeVol who was not allowed to leave the city. Charles, knowing the difficulties of people in the interior, asked James to go to Nanking and bring signed checks for as large amounts as possible from the Mattis and me.

On his return with the checks in his pocket, he watched Japanese soldiers board the train and start a search of every passenger, stripping them and turning their socks inside out. James began to pray. Confiscating money and beating passengers, the soldiers proceeded down the aisle until they came to James. He handed them his ticket, his cholera inoculation certificate, and his pass. The checks were in his pocket. They proceeded on down the aisle without searching him. The checks reached Charles who got the money and sent it to us by the French consul, Pierre Salat, who gladly brought it because I had operated on his wife.

We froze during those days because we couldn't afford fuel. At mealtime even the water in our glasses froze. Only layers of clothing kept us alive.

More trying than lack of food or money or fuel was the harassment in the hospital work. The occupying forces turned off the lights at the hospital and the home in which we were staying and demanded an excessive bribe of four hundred yen to turn them on again.

"That's fine," Dr. Trimer said graciously. "We'll just get along with kerosene and candles."

Japanese patience gave out before Dr. Trimer's. Finally they came down to twenty-five yen, and to let them save face, Dr. Trimer gave in.

The Japanese took charge of every department in the hospital. They demanded that English names of medicines be obliterated and substituted with Chinese. This brought chaos in the pharmacy since there were no substitute Chinese names for tetanus antitoxin, sulfonilamide, morphine, or even aspirin or castor oil. Inspections went on continuously by at least four groups: the Navy, the Army, the Military Intelligence, and the Japanese Civilian Authorities. They became alarmed on discovering a discarded X-ray machine. They felt certain it was being used in some way to transmit messages to the Allies.

One day, a Chinese gateman saved my life. I heard loud voices out at the gate house and sent a servant to see what was going on. He returned some time later and told me this story:

"I found a samurai sword being held against the neck of the gateman by a drunken Japanese officer who demanded to be taken to you. The gateman adroitly took the officer over to the outpatient department and sat him down in the waiting room. Then the gateman went from door to door, pounding and shouting your name. We Chinese understand these things, Doctor. When the depressive effect of alcohol took over and the officer began to cry, the gateman tenderly escorted him outside the door and bolted it."

After the Japanese occupation, our church services were stopped, but we continued to have prayer meeting at the hospital. Chinese Christians sometimes brought food to our house and stayed to pray. It was dangerous, but they came anyway. Stories reached us of the many Christians who were demonstrating courage and faith in spite of opposition, and we knew that God was meeting the deepest needs of their lives.

One day in June my Chinese colleague Dr. T. Y. Chen called me into his room and, after closing the door, said very quietly, "Do you know that you are going home?" I couldn't believe it. The Japanese had repeatedly said to me: "Maybe some of these old white-haired missionaries will go, but you, never! You are military age and you're going to stay here for the duration."

But, you see, I am here in the U.S.A.! I thank God for my American heritage! I thank Him for my Christian heritage, and for your prayers. God has kept His promises, and He has led us all the way. Great has been His faithfulness!

On the next trip of the *SS Gripsholm* in 1943, Charles DeVol came home from Shanghai. He was able to explain more fully what Dr. Ezra DeVol's presence had meant in Nanking from 1940 to 1942. In his answering calls to the British, American, Italian, and French embassies, Dr. DeVol had spread the love of Christ. In turn, they spread it. There was the French consul who was so appreciative that he said over and over again to Dr. Ezra DeVol, "What can I do for you?"

Finally, Dr. Ezra said, "Well, maybe sometime you can help my brother Charles. He's being held in Shanghai."

Pierre Salat, the French Consul, not only helped James Ging and Charles get money to the missionaries, but he also loaned Charles $2,000 for the Luho/Nanking Christians. This gift kept the work going during the war years.

Proceeds from the sale of Dr. Ezra DeVol's medical books as he left China went to Charles and helped him buy back from a pawn shop a watch Dr. Ezra had given him earlier, which had been stolen from his pocket on a crowded bus.

These and many other wonderful experiences in answer to prayer increased and solidified faith in the lives of Dr. Ezra and Frances DeVol as once again they turned a corner and sensed God in His love meeting them there.

Ezra and Frances on their wedding day with Best Man Edward Benedict and Maid of Honor Elsie Hodgin, August 15, 1936, Brighton

Proud parents of identical twins,
Patricia Lee and Priscilla Ann,
born August 4, 1937

Ella and Edward Escolme (above) provided a home for Frances when she had to bring the twins home from China in 1940 and find work in Tecumseh, Michigan. They arrived from China in time to spend Christmas with Grandpa and Grandma Hodgin (above right).

The University Hospital, Nanking, China, 1940. Back, left to right, Drs. T. Y. Chen, Chao, Daniels, Trimmer, E. Kraus, DeVol, A. Kraus, Li, Tien, Shen; seated, Drs. Hsu, Sze, Chen, Chang, Djlang.

James Ging (right), a student in Shanghai, risked his life to get money to Ezra and his colleagues (above), Charles, Leora, Margaret and Esther DeVol, Frieda Gersberger, and Elsie and Charles Matti.

Dr. DeVol operated on Wang Shu Pang in 1941, and he gained health and also became a Christian

The DeVol family reunited, August 1942

6 A Country Practice Interlude

*By faith Abraham, when called to go . . . obeyed and went,
even though he did not know where he was going.*
Hebrews 11:8

Opening a Practice in Marengo

After Yearly Meeting in Damascus, Ohio, and a visit to Frances'
parents, Daniel and Frieda Hodgin in Brighton, Michigan, the
DeVols went to Sunnyslope near Marengo, Ohio, to visit Uncle
Elbert Benedict and his new wife, Mary. There in the beauty
and quiet of the country home, they relaxed, prayed, and
sought to get their bearings before returning to Columbus to
open a new practice. Three weeks slipped by without any indication of which direction to go until one day in Marengo when
Dr. DeVol went shopping. At the grocery store, a merchant,
Mr. Wheeler, casually asked where he was going to practice.

"Probably in Columbus," the doctor answered.

"Why not set up a practice here in Marengo?" Mr. Wheeler
suggested. "Our former doctor left. The house is still empty."

Dr. DeVol listened courteously, thinking to himself, *It's not
surprising the doctor left. The population of this town must be less than
three hundred.* Picking up his groceries, he walked across the
street to get a haircut.

Delmar Dye, the barber, said, "Doctor, why don't you come
here and settle down?"

His next stop was the hardware. "We're short of doctors in
Morrow County," one of the owners, Clyde Rogers, said.
"There's a vacant building in town you could probably rent."

79

At home that night as Ezra shared this news with Frances and wondered what to make of the three consecutive invitations, the phone rang. A man from the other side of Sparta needed a doctor for his wife.

"I'm sorry," Dr. DeVol answered, "but I'm not in practice yet."

"I don't care whether you're in practice or not!" the man insisted. "Come on over and see my wife."

Dr. DeVol did not have the heart to refuse him, so finding the medical bag he had left behind in 1940, he started out to locate the place according to the man's directions. Country roads, he discovered, were not well marked, and in no time he was hopelessly lost. At last about two a.m. he spotted a house with a light. The man was still waiting, and his wife was in agony with pain in her back. The doctor had a spinal needle and some novocaine and was able to bring almost instant relief to the suffering woman.

Convinced that God was leading through these simultaneous happenings, the DeVols opened a practice in Marengo. They rented a house for an office, and Dr. DeVol went to Columbus to Wendt-Bristol for equipment, medicines, and supplies. He put up his shingle and posted his prices:

Office Call	$ 1.50
House Call	3.00
Appendectomy	100.00
Hysterectomy or more difficult operation	150.00

Word soon spread that there was a doctor in Marengo who did surgery, general practice, and deliveries, and also made house calls. In no time at all, Dr. DeVol was driving his brown secondhand four-door V-8 Ford an average of one hundred miles a day, and taking surgical cases to Jane Case Hospital in Delaware, Ohio. Later he changed to Mercy Hospital in Mt. Vernon because they had more ample facilities.

From the beginning Dr. DeVol felt the need of a hospital in Mt. Gilead. He began even then talking with his medical colleagues in the area about such a possibility. The idea germinated, and a committee was appointed. It took many years for the dream to materialize, but in 1952 such a hospital was built.

To keep himself alive, Dr. DeVol realized the necessity for rules governing the use of his time. House calls and hospital visits were posted for morning, and office hours for afternoons and evenings. Thursday afternoon and Sunday, his office was closed. Rules had to be flexible, of course, but no rules at all led to chaos.

It was not long until the practice had outgrown the little rented office, and Dr. DeVol borrowed $4,000 to buy a house on Walnut and Main. He was able to pay off the debt within one year.

Inner Healing at Sunnyslope

Uncle Elbert was delighted to have the DeVols stay in Marengo and live at Sunnyslope. He seemed to have forgotten the discipline Ezra had required during boyhood, and the gratitude Ezra had always felt toward the Benedicts for giving him a home in Sunnyslope as a child grew into full flower at this time. Dr. Ezra skillfully cared for his Uncle Elbert in his last illness. Aunt Mary, Uncle Elbert's second wife, bustled about doing the housecleaning, churning the butter, and cooking the meals. She always baked two pies on Sunday morning, and always apologized for doing it on Sunday. She moved to Delaware after Uncle Elbert died on June 13, 1943.

Dr. George and Isabella DeVol's children inherited the farm, and Dr. Ezra secured the help of Zell Wire, an elderly man from across the road, to do the farming. Until this time, Frances had been able to carve out time to help her husband in his medical practice—something she dearly loved to do. They had fixed up a little room above the office where the girls, on coming home from school, could rest and play, and where the DeVols, with hot plate and toaster, would sometimes prepare a light supper before going home at night after the patients had all been attended. Now with complete charge of Sunnyslope's six-bedroom house, which was nearly always overflowing with guests, Frances had to turn her full attention to being a hostess. As she had earlier accepted the challenge of nursing, now she made a career of homemaking. How the children loved it! Pat and Pris often found treats laid out for them when they came home from school. They especially enjoyed the custard in little brown cups. Though mother was very active in church programs and missionary meetings, her daughters' memory of her was of her charm, control, and fresh appearance. They wanted to be like her.

The family enjoyed Thursdays, Sundays, and mealtimes, when they could all be together. Taking Pat and Pris by the hand, Ezra would run with the wind under the maple trees across the yard. The girls loved riding in the wagon behind the tractor.

One day their daddy went to gather stones to build a fireplace out back where they grilled hamburgers and had picnics. They also built bird feeders, one outside the kitchen where chickadees and cardinals often came. They put suet out for "Donny," the downey woodpecker, who sounded like an electric drill digging a hole in the trees. Out in the middle of the yard on a stump, the blue jays and doves alighted for food. A nuthatch perched on the edge of the feeding tray by the window for hours (nuthatch time) listening to the "Hallelujah Chorus" on a record. Ezra loved finches. One day when he was discouraged, Frances prayed:

"Lord, send us a finch."

When Ezra came home for lunch, there outside the window was a finch.

Pat and Pris protected the birds from the big, black-and-gray-striped cat. In the fall, they rolled in the fallen leaves. In the winter as the wind howled and snow blanketed the hills and trees, they felt cozy and warm in the farmhouse with its furnace and the fireplace, where the logs snapped and sent up sparks as they gathered around the piano to sing or sat close to Mom as she read stories while waiting for Daddy to come home from house calls. In the spring, they made flower gardens and planted trees for each child. Summer was a great time to pick raspberries and strawberries.

The foundation of their home life, however, was laid in their regular morning family devotions.

"We were never too busy each morning after breakfast to kneel in a circle in the living room," Pat recalled in later years. "I can remember Dad. He always knelt on one knee. I always felt he had that stern quality of doing something because it was right whether it was tough or not. He would pray for college students. They were the hope of the world in his eyes. He would ask God to *keep them in the hollow of His hand*. That is a phrase I have not forgotten. It's so safe to grow up where God is handling the universe!"

"Dad always read the Bible," Pris recalled. "Then he prayed, Mom prayed, and we prayed in the order in which we were born. It wasn't that we discussed anything necessarily; we prayed to God. If there were concerns for us children, they were spoken to God and they weren't gone over in detail first. In those prayers, we got a lot of insight for living. It wasn't 'I want you to do this or that,' but it was a prayer to God about that issue."

The first DeVol son, Joseph Edward, was born at Jane Case Hospital in Delaware, Ohio, on February 24, 1944. That year Ezra bought his first new car. His practice now kept him away from home up to sixteen hours a day except on days off, and he cherished more and more the time he could have with his family.

During their first year in school, Pat and Pris and three other girls in their school contracted tuberculosis. Pat came down first, then Pris. To facilitate their care, their parents transferred them to the large downstairs bedroom, where there was a pot-bellied stove into which they surreptitiously threw the food they did not want to eat. Dr. Drake, whom Dr. DeVol called in for consultation, laughingly said to the girls later:

"Blessed are the Marengoites,
For they have Dr. DeVol!"

The girls heard echoes of this from many places, and they were proud of their father.

Ezra and Frances' second son, Philip Edmund, was born July 16, 1947, at Mt. Vernon, Ohio. Joseph was old enough to remember this occasion. He missed his mother very much while she was in the hospital. When she was ready to come home, his father took him to the hospital and asked him to pick out the baby he wanted. When he saw Philip, he said, "That one!"

When Phil was born, Pat and Pris were in Michigan visiting Grandpa and Grandma Hodgin, whom they adored. Daniel Hodgin was the most wonderful grandpa possible in their eyes. They went out for a boat ride, and, while they were sailing, he took his gold watch out of his vest pocket and looking at it thoughtfully, he said to them, "You probably have a surprise waiting for you at home."

When the twins returned to Marengo, sure enough, there was their new brother, Phil, born at the very hour Grandpa Hodgin had looked at his watch.

The DeVol family was now complete. There was no place like Sunnyslope, they felt, to bring up a family and guide them toward God.

Ezra bought his second new car, a Pontiac, black with red and chrome trim, large enough to accommodate the whole family and his growing practice.

Spiritual Outreach

Barring emergencies, the DeVol family were all together in Alum Creek Friends Church on Sunday mornings, evenings, and Wednesday night prayer meetings. Pastors Leon Roby and Hiram Bridenstine preached good sermons. The Robys were a musical family and enhanced their worship services with piano and violin. Frances often sang solos in the services, sometimes accompanied by her niece, Margaret DeVol, who spent her summers with them. The DeVols' presence encouraged others in regular attendance, and as the members worked together, the church grew.

Former "kindling committee chairman" of 1920, Ezra inspired a wood-cutting bee on Sunnyslope farm. Frances and the women of the community prepared the dinner, and Ezra and the men sawed the logs and distributed the wood to church members needing fuel. When the church was remodeled, they all pitched in again, digging and building, as well as molding a group of believers into a living church.

Dr. DeVol was prospering in his practice, and other members were doing well in their businesses and on their farms. It came as a shock, therefore, to realize that they were still paying their pastor only $25 a week. Dr. DeVol led a campaign to raise the pastor's salary. While in Columbus, he and Frances had started the practice of tithing. Now they were far exceeding the tithe. Needs, like the pastor's salary, drew additional offerings from their pockets, and so did appeals for the college and for missions. Their treasure went where their hearts were.

Revival services were planned for the church, but Dr. DeVol feared he would not be able to attend. The practice was too heavy. At family prayers he mentioned this and suggested they might pray for fewer patients during the meetings. Pat and Pris took this very seriously. As the meetings began, Dr. DeVol found that, for the first time, his office was nearly empty and the telephone almost silent. It remained that way for two weeks, and he began to wonder how he would be able to pay his pledges if things did not pick up. He attended the special meetings, but as they closed, he asked the family again to pray for his work. So Pat and Pris prayed for sick people to come so that his work would increase, and it did!

Sunnyslope itself became a beehive of spiritual activity. The barn floor was opened to the community for showing Christian and cultural films—and sometimes Donald Duck, just for the fun of it.

Dr. DeVol, however, was not a man who could let activity substitute for genuine spiritual life. At Yearly Meeting in 1944, he felt dead and dry, and he prayed for the Lord to revive him. He felt the power of the Holy Spirit rekindle his love, and when he spoke at the elders and overseers meeting on Saturday afternoon, there was a great movement of revival. This did not go without testing. On reaching home, Dr. DeVol became angry about a doctor's treatment of one of his patients. He had no peace until he went back and apologized to the doctor. Later a nurse's aide failed in her duty, and he lost his temper. He had to ask her forgiveness before he felt at peace with himself again.

Two verses from the Bible helped him. Proverbs 14:17: "He that is soon angry dealeth foolishly." And, 1 John 1:7: "If we walk in the light as He is in the light, we have fellowship with one another, and the blood of Jesus, His Son, purifies us from all sin." He came to realize that "walking in the light" meant dealing drastically with his problem of temper and being willing every time he failed to make amends. This made him seek to be sensitive to the leading of the Holy Spirit in his life in every situation.

After getting more deeply into the life of his community, Dr. DeVol became concerned for Marengo's youth. He observed in his office the increase in venereal disease and teenage pregnancies. Something needed to be done on a broad scale to remedy this. He asked his family to pray about this, and Frances joined her husband at a meeting of Youth for Christ leaders in Medicine Lake, Minnesota, in 1946. There they took advice from Dawson Trotman, Billy Graham, Beverly Shea, and others.

Back home, Dr. DeVol talked first with Dale Riggs, pastor of the Methodist Church. Together they visited the Marengo High School superintendent, John Florence, and the result was that every other Saturday night in the high school gymnasium there were meetings for young people. Many pastors in Morrow county cooperated. College choirs and orchestras by the bus load came to sing in these meetings and stayed as guests at Sunnyslope. Pat and Pris helped their mother, making hors d'oeuvres, putting out the guest towels, and setting the tables. They loved the excitement, and they learned many choruses they never forgot. Through the spiritual impact of these meetings, many young people came to know the Lord Jesus Christ.

The effort to win youth inspired the pastors and leaders to plan cooperative prayer meetings and other activities. The most inspiring service of this kind was at Easter, year after year, as they met at sunrise at such places as Mt. Gilead or Alum Creek cemeteries, in one of the churches, or at the State Lakes Park. These cooperative meetings continued many years to promote united effort in key ministries and evangelism.

Hospitality was always extended at Sunnyslope as friends and relatives came and went. Rosy Hatten, a high school girl, lived with them and was a great help to Frances. Margaret DeVol made Sunnyslope her summer home while her parents and sister Esther were in China. When they came home, they also came to live at Sunnyslope.

In 1945, the Cattells came from India and made their headquarters there. At Christmas that year, all six bedrooms in Sunnyslope were filled. The last time Charles, Catherine, and Ezra had been together was in 1931; this time, fourteen years later, their families came with them. The cousins became acquainted, and the farm was filled with the laughter and singing of the fifteen relatives, a Chinese guest, and the hired girl.

A Country Doctor among Country Folk

Medical practice in Marengo was far different from the practice Dr. Ezra and Frances had anticipated being engaged in at the Peace Hospital established by his parents in Luho, China. Nevertheless, Ezra enthusiastically devoted himself to this country practice and before long had mastered the roads and their twists, turns, and treacherous spots. With the expanding work, he secured the help of Lois Patterson and Garnell Lloyd to assist in the office and do the accounts. Doctors in Mt. Gilead and Cardington were near for consultation and came to give anesthesia for tonsillectomies. He served the people from three counties, and he tried never to fail in an emergency, even if the snow was deep, the wind strong, and his body weary with having already been up most of the night.

On one such occasion, Dr. DeVol, having worked all night, stopped just at sunrise to make a final call at the house of a family he had never met. He was so weary that he literally staggered up the walk.

"He's drunk!" the woman said to her husband as she opened the door. Warily, she invited him in, offered him a chair, and asked, "Would you like a cup of coffee?"

"I surely would!"

The sound of his voice caused her to revise her first conclusion.

"And how about some breakfast?"

"That would be great!" Dr. DeVol answered, trying not to sound too enthusiastic.

"Please be seated a few moments," the housewife said as she pulled out the pans and tied on her apron. "I'll have toast, ham, and eggs ready in no time."

When the meal was ready, the housewife woke up the weary doctor for the most adequate breakfast he had ever remembered. Having eaten, rested, and treated the patient, the "drunk doc" and this family parted, friends for life, laughing heartily at the first impression he had made.

Most country people were gracious and friendly. One day on a call in winter, an untimely thaw had ruined the roads. Pushing the car, bogged down in mud up to the axles, Dr. DeVol heard a friendly farmer's voice.

"Could you use a little help, Doc?"

"Sure could! A baby's on the way, and I'm afraid I'm late for the party!"

The farmer flew into high gear, raced home, and brought his horses. He had "Doc"—mud-splattered and thankful—on his way in no time.

All country people, however, were not always as thoughtful as this. A call came from near Chesterville one blizzardy night in the dead of winter. Frances, for once, felt the wind was so strong and the roads so treacherous that she should not let him go. A call was a call, however, so they prayed and committed themselves to whatever might happen. The wind had drifted the snow so high in the lane from the highway to the house of the patient that Ezra had to get his shovel from the back of the car to clear his way down the drive. In spite of the sub-zero wind chill, he had worked himself into a perfect lather of sweat by the time he reached the house.

Opening the door a small crack, the housewife peered out.

"Oh, Doc, it's you! I have good news! My child is better and we don't need you after all." To keep out the cold, she closed the door in his face. The wind had already made a new snowdrift over the lane, and "Doc" had to shovel his way out to the highway again!

One day a call came from fifteen miles away as Dr. DeVol was in his office with a waiting room full of patients.

"Come quickly, Doc, you know my babies are born fast!"

The doctor flew into action.

"Excuse me, it's an emergency," he explained to his patients. "Wait, please. I'll be back as soon as possible."

Ezra dashed out of his office, jumped into his car, and sped past a chicken farm where white leghorns lined both sides of the road. *I don't dare stop*, he thought, and seemingly not too well acquainted with the ways of chickens, he honked his horn. This excited the chickens, and those on the right side crossed to the left and those on the left to the right. Many failed to make it as feathers flew like a snowstorm before the onrushing vehicle. Covering the fifteen miles in record time, he rushed into the house only to find that the labor had stopped. Doing the needful, Dr. DeVol waited for some time. The patients in his office also waited the rest of the day. When he returned, he had so much to do that he forgot all about the chickens. Years later, in the "stilly watches of the night" when sleep was slow in coming, he suddenly remembered he had not gone back to the farmer as he should have done to make amends for the chickens that did not make it to the other side of the road.

Patients would not always cooperate with the doctor. One little fellow came in to have his tooth pulled. He eyed with hostility the needle and syringe with the novocaine. As Dr. DeVol put his left finger in the boy's mouth and barely inserted the needle, the boy bit down in all his fury. The doctor dropped his needle and gave the boy a sound slap on the left cheek. The boy's mouth flew open, and before feeling returned to the doctor's finger, the boy was off the table and out the door, never to return.

Some patients who needed better care than could be given in the doctor's office or in the home flatly refused to go to the hospital. Instead of just walking out the door, Dr. DeVol tried old home remedies, like the 2-4-6 enema for intestinal obstepation. Two ounces of epsom salts, four ounces of glycerine, and six ounces of water worked like a charm in many cases.

Some country medicine, however, the doctor had no more faith in than the stories he had heard when he was in China. Sometimes he told such stories about odd medical practices in the Orient. For example, the surgeons were called "outside doctors" and "inside doctors." If a man was shot with an arrow, the "outside doctor" would cut off the arrow at the surface of the skin. The "inside doctor" had to get the rest of the arrow out.

He quit telling such stories after the following conversation in his office.

"What's this thing tied around your child's neck?" he asked.

"That's the eye tooth of a hog," the mother answered.

"What's it for?"

"To keep the kid from having fits."

"Does it work?"

"Why, sure! He's never had any fits."

In all the busy rush, the country doctor did not forget he was a Christian. The sensitivity to God's voice he had developed in his early years stayed with him through the days of his many-faceted country practice. Some, therefore, were led into faith in the office and during his calls in the homes.

One very stormy night a call came from a home up on Highway 229. Dr. DeVol found a very deaf, elderly man named Mont shivering in his rocking chair by a pot-bellied stove with the coals burnt to ashes. He was so ill with pneumonia and congestive heart failure that Dr. DeVol offered to take him immediately to the hospital. He refused to go, even though he was entirely alone and not on speaking terms with his relatives. There seemed to be no way to help him. Dr. DeVol, however, did not walk away to leave the stubborn old man to die alone. He gave him a penicillin injection and various kinds of pills, built up a good fire in the stove, and left extra coal nearby. He advised Mont to get into bed. He refused.

"Who will stoke the fire?" Mont asked.

That made sense. So the doctor put water, his pills, and some food on a table within his reach, found an extra quilt and a few pillows, and made him as comfortable as possible. It was time for the doctor to walk out the door, but something held him. Pulling up a chair, he sat down, sensing a concern to witness for Christ to this deaf old man.

How can I do it? he questioned, for his throat already ached from shouting into the man's deaf ears the necessary questions and instructions in relation to the illness. Nevertheless, he rose from his chair, knelt down on the dirty, cold, linoleum floor, put his mouth to Mont's ear, and shouted:

"Mont, don't you want to be saved?"

The sentences were short and simple, and repeated many times, but they led Mont to a direct encounter with God, who forgave his sins and made him His child. Not only was he saved, but he recovered his health, was reconciled to his family, and became another trophy of the redeeming, transforming love of the Lord Jesus Christ.

The Country Doctor's Honor

Among the pieces of mail received one day on the rural route serving Sunnyslope was a letter from the American College of Surgeons. It was a request for Dr. DeVol to submit his application to become a member. He had not considered himself qualified, as he knew three years residency in surgery was required. He had completed one year in Fairview Park Hospital and done surgery two years in University Hospital in Nanking. However, those two years in China had not been under supervision, as the rule required, because the supervisor had left Nanking just as the war began. This had left Dr. DeVol in full charge. He wrote explaining all this.

The American College of Surgeons pursued the matter, requesting descriptions of all the operations he had performed within the last twelve months. After complying, Dr. DeVol received another letter requesting descriptions of fifty operations performed during his practice. He submitted these with detail and pictures.

When the honor was awarded in New York, September 12, 1947, Frances went with her husband, representing not only herself but also the country folk around Marengo, who were bursting with pride that *their* doctor was now a Fellow of the American College of Surgeons.

Recalled to Missionary Service

The draft board had declared Dr. DeVol essential to Morrow County during the war, but as peace opened doors to travel, the DeVols remembered their call to China. Early in 1948, they began taking steps to find a doctor to replace them in Marengo. A longtime friend, Dr. Al Shreve, doing his residency in Timken-Mercy Hospital in Canton, Ohio, mentioned the possibility to Dr. William S. Deffinger, who was interning at Aultman Hospital in the same city. As the two doctors came to know one another, both felt this was an answer to prayer.

"Why do you want to come to this farming community?" Dr. DeVol asked.

"I feel as much called to come to Marengo as you feel called to go to China," Dr. Deffinger answered.

The DeVols planned to turn over the practice in March and leave for China in early summer. Dr. Deffinger agreed to commute until he could move to Marengo July 1. Lawrence and Flossie Westbrook moved into Sunnyslope as the DeVols moved to temporary quarters in the rooms above the office.

"Caring for the farm is something we can do while you DeVols serve the Lord overseas," Lawrence said as he moved his family in to stay for several years.

Then came a terrible disappointment. The DeVols' visas were refused. Hostilities in China closed the door. With suitcases packed, the Westbrooks in their home, and Dr. Deffinger taking over their practice, they had to revise plans quickly. Dr. Deffinger was happy for them to continue with the practice until July; so they continued, living in the rooms above the office in Marengo. Margaret Curran, who had helped with the twins in Columbus, now came to give a hand with the four children as Frances stepped in as receptionist-nurse.

During these weeks the girls became much more aware of their father's medical practice and their mother's professional skill as through the registers in the ceiling they sometimes heard what was going on. They still remember a man laughing while his wife was coughing and sputtering as their father was trying to locate the fishbone caught in her throat. They often heard expressions of gratitude for treatment received. They roller-skated to school, got ice cream across the street, and enjoyed their closeness as a family in the little town of Marengo and in the smaller quarters. They entered into the prayers for China's doors to open and felt they, too, had a real part in the mission for which their parents were willing to give their lives.

The DeVols planned to take time off in June, first of all to attend Margaret DeVol's graduation from Marion High School. While they lived in Sunnyslope, they had practically adopted Margaret during the time her parents and sister Esther were in China. Margaret could hardly bear the thought of Uncle Ezra and Aunt Frances going, too.

After a visit to meet the mission board in Cleveland, the DeVols planned a trip to visit relatives and to store in their memories some of the beautiful sights of the eastern United States. They sent word to Margaret to meet them. They left eleven-month-old Philip in Brighton with his Hodgin grandparents, and Margaret sat in the back seat spinning stories for the fascinated twins seated on either side of her. Joe sat in front between his parents. They visited relatives in New York, and went from there on up through the mountains to Vermont. From one peak they could see five states at once. They stayed with families who had signs out, "Rooms for Tourists." For two weeks they had a wonderful family time, returning refreshed and full of hope.

Dr. Deffinger moved to Marengo July 1, and plans for China began to take shape again. Pat and Pris had their first and only day in Ashley school in the sixth grade. The next day, September 7, 1948, on their father's 39th birthday, one-year-old Phil, four-year-old Joe, the eleven-year-old twins, Ezra, and Frances all said goodbye to the host of friends of the Columbus and Marengo areas, who saw them off on their way to Los Angeles.

"We are going out with joy and being led forth with peace" (Isaiah 55:12), Frances wrote as they traveled. "Let me encourage you, our friends at home, to pray.... We are en route... not knowing what is ahead. Another promise coming to us is Isaiah 42:16: 'And I will bring the blind by a way that they knew not; I will lead them in paths that they have not known: I will make darkness light before them, and crooked things straight. These things will I do unto them, and not forsake them.'"

Frances would not have considered herself a prophetess, but in the next six months in their faith and obedience, step by step, the DeVol family would learn with amazement how God would lead them around many devious and treacherous corners, through "blind alleys," and finally into the light of such certainty that any questions about the process would be forgotten.

Just before leaving Marengo, the DeVols had heard of a longshoremen's strike, which might further hinder them, but they hoped the strike would be over by the time they reached Los Angeles. Though that did not happen, Elizabeth Jenkins opened her doors to the family. Years before she had taken Frances into her home in Mt. Pleasant. She was now retired, living with a nephew in Hollywood. The nephew and his wife were gone on vacation, and Elizabeth Jenkins was alone and in a wheelchair, being cared for by a nurse. The DeVols walked to nearby restaurants for meals, carrying Phil and pushing Joe along in a stroller.

For six weeks they followed this routine as they waited. During this time, Ezra became ill with a cold, and Joe came down with rheumatic fever. Phil was fussy and could not sleep at night. Frances had a hard time knowing where to dry the diapers.

Pat and Pris were enrolled in a Christian school to which they commuted from Hollywood on two buses, going through Los Angeles and Pasadena. They took this in stride, but both felt a trip to Disneyland and Knotts Berry Farm was more important than a day in school. Their parents did not think so. Later they felt even worse when they saw the pictures of their parents with Joe and Phil enjoying that trip.

"This was one of my few disappointments," Pris recalled later.

Pat and Pris wondered how they would fit into missionary life. Both of them had come to terms with the Lord of their lives, and while in California, they received word that Alum Creek had taken them in as members of the church. Still, they had questions.

"I think missionaries should be brave," Pat said, "but I don't feel very brave."

Joe, pathetically thin after his fever, was feeling very homesick. One day Frances went into the bathroom and found him sitting crossways on the toilet seat.

"I'm turned toward the farm, aren't I?" he asked. Yes, he was facing east!

Regular family prayers still held the family together. When they sought for sailing on a military ship, they were refused. Specific prayers for the shipping strike to end seemed unheard. The day they had planned to arrive in Shanghai, the DeVols began a study of Norman Grubb's book, *The Law of Faith*. They sought to follow that law.

Letters coming from China were not bright, but at the end of October the DeVols went to Oakland, California, to the Home of Peace, a missionary home where fifty-four other missionaries in similar circumstances lived. Meals were provided daily, and life was easier. The girls enrolled in their third school in three months, and Joe went into kindergarten. Phil kept falling out of bed until they found a crib for him. He was full of ginger, running everywhere and darting out open doors. He required a watchful eye.

By mid-November, cables brought word that Friends missionaries were leaving interior China and that John and Geraldine Williams, the newest missionaries there, were waiting in Shanghai for a ship to Japan.

"Because we have felt a drawing to Japan, our spirits lifted at the word that the Williamses were on their way there," Frances wrote. Hopes in that direction, however, were short-lived as a letter came almost immediately saying that the mission board was not considering opening a work in Japan. Instead, on November 12, 1948, they wrote asking the DeVols to consider India.

Anywhere but India, was the first thought of both Ezra and Frances. Other doors were open, such as a possible practice in Damascus, Ohio.

"I think we should go to India," both Pat and Pris agreed as the matter was discussed during family prayers.

By the end of November the longshoreman's strike was settled, but their sailing to China had already been cancelled, and the China missionaries were on their way home. That week the DeVols also heard a message they felt was just for them:

"Delays don't just happen.
They are planned of God."

Ezra and Frances each went into a separate room to pray for God's direction about India, and the same message came to both of them from Isaiah 30:18-21: ". . . This is the way, walk ye in it."

Applications went immediately for visas, known to take a long time. Frances started buying thin cloth and making cotton dresses. They repacked, leaving behind the heavy warm clothes required in China. They sold the electric refrigerator and washing machine and bought an operating table, an X-ray unit, a generator, a truck, a trailer, and various other items of medical equipment. They met the China missionaries coming home and took care of the Williamses' children, who had the measles.

Visas came January 6, 1949. They bought tickets on the *M. V. Borneo* freighter of the Java-Pacific Lines, which brought a retiring missionary, Carrie Wood, home from India. On February 12, 1949, five months and five days after leaving Marengo, the DeVol family, with great joy and a sense of freedom, sailed to India.

Sunnyslope farm near Marengo, Ohio, became the possession of Drs. George and Isabella DeVol's children in 1943 and the home of Ezra, Frances, and family

Everett and Catherine DeVol Cattell, Ezra and Frances DeVol, Charles and Leora DeVol

Pat and Joe have their turns at closeness

Sunnyslope provided Pat, Phil, Pris, and Joe
with solid comfort

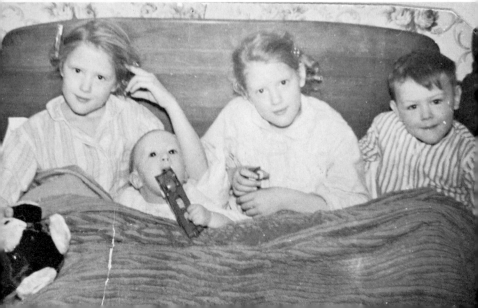

Youth for Christ had the cooperation of Morrow County pastors, like Rev. Dale Riggs.

Frances in Oakland at the Home of Peace

On the way to China the DeVols were delayed five months on the West Coast. When Ezra and Frances were thirty-nine, they took Joe, 4, Priscilla and Patricia, 11, and Phil, 1, to India, on the *M. V. Borneo* February 12, 1949.

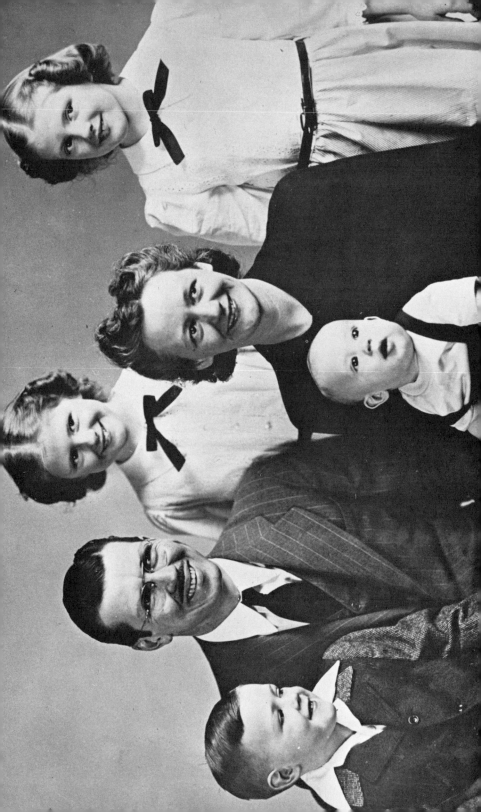

7 The Challenge of Changing India

The Trip

On the move at last through the mighty waters of the Pacific, the DeVol family proved to be good sailors. Passengers on the freighter numbered fifteen children and twenty-one adults. They all helped Joe celebrate his fifth birthday in a way he would never forget. The ship's captain blew the whistle. Home of Peace in Oakland sent a cable, "Happy birthday, Joe, we miss you horribly." While Joe's father helped him put together a little boat house with his new carpenter set, eighteen-month-old Phil kept Frances and his sisters on the run to prevent him from falling overboard.

Phil, practicing his new walking skill all over the ship, made wide acquaintance quickly. Josephene Hwang, a Chinese lady, begged for the privilege of keeping him when the ship docked in ports. Frances appreciated this gracious offer because it freed her to go ashore with the rest of the family to visit missions and do sightseeing in the many ports in which they stopped. These included the islands of the Pacific, Borneo, Java, Sumatra, the Philippines, Singapore, Rangoon, Malay, and Penang.

Near Saipan they saw mushroom clouds rise and spread into the heavens. These were not atomic explosions as they first believed, but mere navy maneuvers. They saw active volcanoes just off Negros in the Philippines. They learned of fierce

101

battles fought in the very waters through which they traveled peacefully.

Pat and Pris regularly gathered the prekindergarten children in the morning for games and stories, something they enjoyed and the parents appreciated immensely.

The weather got warmer and warmer, and Joe kept asking, "When will we get to the hot place?"

Arriving in India

On April 6, 1949, they got to the hottest place they had ever been: INDIA, 105° F! Land of the Taj Mahal, the high Himalayas, the mighty Ganges! Massive jungles, where elephants, tigers, and the great *nilgay* (blue bull) share haunts with cobras, monkeys, and panthers! Languages—fourteen spoken by millions, hundreds more spoken by thousands! Religions—ancient, fanatical, fatalistic, divisive—Hindu, Moslem, Christian, Sikh, Jain, Buddhist! The country had been torn apart by Hindu-Moslem animosity. Mahatma Gandhi, leader to freedom from British rule, was dead and enshrined in Delhi. Politically, the country was still in turmoil. Even as the surgeon and his wife arrived to serve the people, each with an annual salary of $800, the Maharajah of Chhatarpur State, stripped of political powers, was left with an annual pension of $26,000. India, land of contrasts!

Ezra's brother-in-law and sister, Everett and Catherine Cattell, welcomed the DeVol family as they arrived in Bombay. After customs, Everett drove the loaded truck and trailer back to Chhatarpur, the small city of 26,000 people that would eventually be the DeVols' home. Catherine and the family boarded the train for the seventeen-hour trip from Bombay to Jhansi. It was the hot season, and burning winds blew dust and soot into the open windows as they sped through dry, rocky wastes past barren fields.

Bumping and swaying through changing and unfamiliar scenes, Ezra realized with sudden finality that he was in India—not China, his boyhood home. The rest of the family had gone into a forward compartment to have lunch while he remained behind to watch the luggage. Alone, he thought of the millions of people bound in caste and poverty, all so different from the Chinese. His sense of inadequacy mounted. Overwhelmed with thoughts of the future, as the train moved along, he knelt to pray. He turned naturally to God's promises, and his eyes came to rest on Exodus 33:14: "My presence shall go with thee and I will give thee rest." What more could he ask? As he claimed that promise, his fears evaporated.

Just then Pat and Pris bounced into the compartment.

"It's our turn to watch the luggage now while you have a sandwich," they said. "We left plenty of tea in the thermos for you!"

The DeVol family arrived in Jhansi at noon the next day and received a warm welcome from Canadian Presbyterian missionaries before boarding another train for sixty more miles to Harpalpur. Milton Coleman met them there and took them by jeep the remaining nineteen miles to Nowgong. Anna Nixon, with Indian school children waving palm branches, welcomed them into the large mission compound where they would live the first year while studying the language.

"We have arrived!" Dr. DeVol wrote home to the mission board. "All the delays, the days of indecision, and the problems of the past few months have faded into insignificance because we are conscious of being in the place of God's choosing."

Later they went to Chhatarpur, fourteen miles on up the road, and were greeted by Alena Calkins, Norma Freer, Rebecca Coleman, Clifton and Betty Robinson, and Victor Mangalwadi, the pastor of the Friends Church. He presented them with a wooden cross on which he had carved the words, "Sir, we want to see Jesus!"

To Landour for Woodstock School and Language Study

A few days later, Pat and Pris and other missionaries' children were taken by the Robinsons to Woodstock School in Landour. They took the train back through Jhansi, then 256 miles to Delhi and overnight from there to Dehra Dun at the base of India's Himalaya Mountains. There they boarded a bus that took them the twenty-six miles up hairpin curves to Mussoorie. From the bus stop they were taken for a jolting, hair-raising ride in a ricksha pulled by men who ran along Tehri Road, a mountain trail with a sheer drop into deep valleys to the right. The men finally stopped, panting, at the gates of Woodstock School. Pat and Pris entered their fourth school that year. They were late, and the standard of education was higher than in any school they had previously attended. They knew they would have to study hard during their school days in India.

Ezra, Frances, and the boys stayed a bit longer in Bundelkhand. They visited the twenty-five-bed women's hospital in Chhatarpur, and became acquainted with Dr. Grace Jones Singh, who was in charge, and with Alena Calkins, a missionary nurse who assisted her. Dr. Grace, the first woman of the area to be trained as a doctor, had served there for twenty-five years and, for the past ten years, had often been the only doctor. Frances was shocked to see many of the paitents in such anemic conditions. Their hemoglobin tests went far below the normal of 80 to 95. Many were recorded as having only 25 or 30, and one was as low as 15.

Out in the villages of mud houses with sun-dried tile roofs, the DeVols greeted children who were wearing nothing, men in unbleached muslin "dhotis" bound around their hips, and women with dark red "saris" draped over their bodies, including their faces. *How different from China*, thought Ezra as he listened to the unintelligible Hindi while thinking in Chinese.

A few days later the rest of the DeVols took the same route Pat and Pris had taken to Landour. Riding through the bazaar in rickshas, they met the girls coming to meet them. They all went together to Pinepoint, a Friends Mission house just beyond Woodstock School, where they had lunch with the Robinsons. Then they climbed to an altitude of 7,500 feet to their first hill home, called Rosebank.

The view from Rosebank, high on a cliff, captivated them. The cool mountain air was brisk and refreshing, and the snow-capped peaks of the Himalayas rose high above them.

"We see mountain after mountain from our house, all in the 20,000-foot class," Frances wrote. "When we look away to the hills in the distance to the eternal snows, all our problems dissolve!"

Some of the problems were the lack of curtain rods at the windows, the inconvenience of having to go to the kitchen through the girls' bedroom, the dark butterscotch color of the walls, and the general disrepair of the house. Woodstock School was a one-thousand-foot drop below. The girls walked back and forth. Joe walked down, but a coolie with a *khandi*—a little basket tied to his back—carried Joe up at noon each day.

Landour Language School was not far away, and as Ezra and Frances joined Hindi classes with one hundred other missionaries, Frances had to hire a man to do the cooking and a woman to look after Phil, who seemed bent on finding all the cliffs from which he could fall. He also found the flowers, and once came in smiling with a handful of dahlias, hyacinths, and orchids, mixed with ferns.

"Come see the mosquitoes and the larvae in the water!" Phil said. His vocabulary amazed his parents, and his activities kept them on their toes.

Not until the rains began did the family notice the condition of the tin roof, but almost immediately the bathroom was flooded. Pans and buckets were shifted from here to there to catch the drips, and neither the typewriter nor the beds were spared as the wind shifted. Raincoats and boots were inadequate when the monsoon really set in. By turns sandflies, fleas, mosquitoes, and scorpions had to be reckoned with. All the children suffered, but Pat seemed most vulnerable and itched for months.

In addition, the moldy odors of the rains and the garlic smell of Indian food, as well as the high singing of cicadas and the roar of continual rain "like a hundred kegs of nails being dumped on the tin roof" got to Pat. She hated the spiders, leeches, and gnats. She even disliked the moss and ferns that softened the hillside trees. Sleep fled. She developed pleurisy, so painful it became unbearable to cry.

For Pat and Pris's twelfth birthday, their parents saved the rationed kerosene, flour, and sugar to bake a cake. They borrowed a slide projector, invited in other missionaries, and showed pictures of Sunnyslope. All of them got terribly homesick. Joe asked: "How long will it be before we can go back to the farm? I just loved the barn!"

As Pat went to school the next morning after another sleepless night, she felt she could bear the weight of India no longer. Sensing her struggle, Frances stayed home from language school to pray. Without knowing why, Pat came home from school at noon that day, and found her mother there to listen. That evening the family prayed together, especially for Pat, aware that only the power of God could help them be the missionaries they had come to India to be. Gradually Pat and Pris, as well as Joe and Phil, adjusted to India.

"I hated the ferns at first because the monsoons brought them," Pat said. "Later I loved the monsoons because they brought the ferns." There had, however, been a price to pay, and they paid it, supported in a family committed to the will of God.

Ezra soon became very active in the Landour community, which grew to about a thousand as missionaries flocked to the hills from April through September for a month or so of respite from the heat on the plains. Frances longed to join the choir but gave it up because of family needs and the demanding language school schedule. The witnessing Ezra had learned to do in his medical practice was not neglected here, and through personal contact and in prayer groups he led other missionaries into new experiences of personal faith. Others, filled with doubt, were revived. A Hindu Brahmin language school teacher, Mr. B. L. Tripathi, became a Christian.

The Landour Community Hospital was short of doctors, and the DeVols were barely settled before calls for surgery began to eat into the doctor's time for language study. His first operation was on Chandra Prakash, a 37-year-old shopkeeper, considered hopeless with intestinal obstruction for eight days. Dr. DeVol dreaded the thought of losing his first patient, so as he prayed, he noticed a motto on the wall: "I will not fail thee." Claiming that promise, he operated. For the next twenty years each summer, as he went through the bazaar, he stopped to greet Chandra Prakash in his shop.

Dr. DeVol's next operation was on a princess with a dislocated shoulder; the next, a hairlip of a six-year-old temple girl; and the next, a spiral fractured femur of another doctor's daughter.

Medical attention to missionary colleagues and their families received priority. Alena Calkins developed illness for which she had to be sent home the next year. Max Banker, Everett Cattell, and Clifton Robinson all had malaria. Hepatitis took its toll. Everyone, at some time or other, suffered from dysentery. Everett had chronic phlebitis. Frances had to undergo major surgery just before her first language examination. Phil seemed accident and illness prone. If not in bandages, sling, or splints, he often had an earache, tonsillitis, or dysentery. Once with no other surgeon around, his own father had to "screw [his] courage to the sticking point" and perform an emergency hernia operation on him. Ezra was encouraged by the bravery and trust of his son. Meeting such needs always took priority over language study.

A different kind of interruption, and one Ezra occasionally welcomed, was a good hunt with some of his friends. Back in the mountains there were panthers, bears, and deer. A night in the hilly jungle sometimes ended with venison steak, and always with tales of adventure.

Going into Boarding

In September, the DeVols prepared to return to Nowgong, continuing language study on the plains with Pastor G. M. Roberts as their Hindi language tutor, and Pat and Pris went into boarding at Woodstock Long Dorm. Double sets of clothes, for the twins enjoyed dressing alike, had to be made ready. Sewing name tags on each piece, Frances was overwhelmed by the clothing requirements for each girl: 14 cotton dresses, 7 long-sleeved dresses, 7 cotton slips, a good supply of underwear and stockings, 4 pair of brown oxfords, 1 pair of white strap shoes, and 1 pair of other type shoes. This seemed twice too much, but the laundry system required it. The *dhobi* (laundry man with his donkey) brought the clean clothes only once a week and gathered up the next week's laundry. He took it to the river, beat it clean (?) on the rocks, and then spread it out on the river bank in the sun to dry.

Before leaving, Frances gave each twin a "Toni" home permanent. As time was running out, Pris said, "Now let's talk about home—everything but boarding!" And then proceeded to talk about nothing but boarding. She even talked in her sleep that night.

They all went out and climbed the hills for one last picnic. Joe followed behind his daddy holding his walking stick and pretending they were a train chugging along. Phil rode in a khandi and chattered all the way. Such family outings left beautiful memories, developed closeness, and created appreciation for wildlife, nature, and the wonder of God's great out-of-doors.

Back to the Hot Plains and the Call of Duty

Max, Ruth Ellen, and Bonnie Banker, and Ezra, Frances, Joe, and Phil DeVol went down to the plains together. Arriving in Nowgong at night, they pulled into a veritable fairyland. The school children had been working day and night to tie *diyas* on a frame supported by posts in front of the bungalow. The diyas—little clay dishes with oil and lighted cotton wicks—spelled the word, WELCOME! As they followed the bus up the drive lined on both sides with the same little diyas, the children also each carried one, and sang, "Welcome, Welcome, Our Dear Friends!" The welcome was primarily for the Bankers, but the DeVols were also included as they came to live in the Nowgong bungalow, the DeVols on the left and the Bankers on the right.

Back in Nowgong, the DeVols kept letters going every week to their girls in boarding. The letters coming back to them from Pat and Pris suggested they thoroughly enjoyed boarding school in spite of some nostalgia for America. Other girls crowded into their rooms; sometimes they prayed together. The others felt that Pat and Pris prayed to God as a real person. This was new to some of their friends in Woodstock. The teachers also enjoyed having these vibrant identical twins in their classes, though they sometimes could not tell them apart. The girls enhanced the Woodstock ball games with their enthusiastic cheerleading.

Ezra and Frances, in Nowgong, tried to turn their attention to the study of Hindi, but there was no way of keeping entirely out of medicine even though the hospital was fourteen miles away. Ezra held regular clinics for the schoolchildren on the compound. When the X-ray machine arrived and was set up in Chhatarpur, the DeVols fluoroscoped all the nurses and gave all the missionaries physical examinations. Plague swept through the district, and they were given the responsibility of innoculating the entire Christian community in Chhatarpur and Nowgong. Known as a country demanding only women doctors to treat women, India was changing. High-caste men began bringing their wives to Dr. DeVol for treatment. Officials in high places began to come with offers of rationing favors. In spite of the fact that food was more scarce in Nowgong than in

Landour, the DeVols resisted involvement. They expected to put into effect an equitable fee system and wanted nothing to compromise those plans.

Since the bus was too slow and the truck too expensive, Ezra bought a light motorcycle to facilitate traveling the fourteen miles to Chhatarpur. Frances, sometimes riding on the back of the motorcycle, accompanied him on his weekly visits and helped with the surgery. Increasing demands on the doctor's time caused Frances concern.

"I'm afraid he is going to be overwhelmed with patients before he has a chance to get the language," she said.

Home from Boarding

On December 2, 1949, Pat and Pris came home from boarding. After a glorious reunion, the girls started to unpack, and Frances almost despaired on seeing the condition of their clothes, for the washing methods had sent them into shreds.

Christmas was in the air, however, and Mendel Hodgin's wife, Kathryn, had sent lots of parcels and included dress materials, purses for the girls, a fishing game for Joe, cars for Phil, dozens of pairs of socks, and popcorn, crayons, coloring books, toys, and candy for all.

Even Father's eyes snapped at the sight of O'Henry candy bars, and he said, "Let's eat these in small pieces under the bed covers at night!"

Kathryn sent a beautiful Christmas tree and plenty of ornaments, and the rest of the presents were placed under it. Gifts came from the Junior Christian Endeavor and from the home missionary societies. The Cleveland area sent fourteen parcels to be divided among all the missionaries. Food from the parcels and from the gardens helped the "missionary family" celebrate with a fabulous Christmas dinner followed by a Christ-centered program on December 23 in which everyone, including the children, took part.

Socks hanging from the mantle for all the children were filled by the adults, including the missionary aunties. "Uncle Cliff" Robinson, dressed like Santa, distributed the presents. The extended missionary family became a real one and minimized the pain of being away from one's own relatives on these special occasions.

"The unity which we feel and the interest in each other's problems is really unusual," Dr. DeVol wrote to the people in America. This Friends missionary family, totaling at one time fifteen adults and nineteen children, was often joined at Christmas by visitors and missionaries of nearby missions who also became like family and loved the jokes and laughter.

On Christmas Day, the DeVols participated in the early morning worship service in Nowgong and joined the Christian community afterwards in a feast of goat curry, rice, and *puris*— fried bread—served on a large leaf of a tree. They sat on the ground in a circle with everyone and ate with their fingers. Sweepers gathered around to take the leftovers, and even though the Indian pastor suggested giving them fresh food from the pot for the sake of human dignity, the sweepers insisted that it was their caste right to take away the leftover food, too.

At Home in Chhatarpur

Ezra and Frances completed their first year of Hindi study and passed the examinations with good results. In the fall of 1950 they moved to Chhatarpur, into a newly remodeled bungalow which, though not spacious, was adequate. At times they longed for the quiet remoteness of the Nowgong bungalow, for the Chhatarpur bus stand was practically in their front yard, and at festival times loudspeakers blared from there all night. People waiting to get the bus to go north to the harvest would sprawl out to sleep like cordwood in front of their gate.

Bricks and mortar were strewn over the Christian Hospital compound as expansion was being carried out to turn the women's hospital into a general hospital. Dr. DeVol stepped into his role as medical superintendent and treated Har Charon, a Brahmin, his first male patient, in the new dispensary for men opened on October 30, 1950. Two weeks later, Frances, in full uniform, began work as superintendent of nurses just one week before Alena Calkins departed for the United States. Samson Huri Lal was the first male nurse to join the staff. He helped Dr. DeVol with medical vocabulary and also interpreted his Hindi into the kind of accent the villagers could understand. With the help of Samson, Frances, and Dr. Grace Jones Singh, Dr. DeVol performed his first operation on a male patient in the new general hospital on November 18. Dimina, a recent

Christian convert from Ghuara, got a new glass eye and was pleased. Another village man with a mismatched glass eye came in for an operation. As he recovered, Dr. DeVol hunted through his supply of glass eyes and found an exact match for the man's good eye. Not only the man's physical condition, but also his appearance was greatly improved, and his wife was immensely pleased. The villager sensed he was someone special to a doctor who cared to improve his looks.

As male patients had to be admitted, a ward for men had to be built. The district commissioner loaned the hospital a twelve-bed capacity tent, which was used as the men's ward for five months until brick by brick Williams Ward was completed and dedicated on Easter Sunday, 1951.

"We see so many pathetic cases," Frances wrote. "Many people are brought in as a last resort. There are many abnormal deliveries in which the mothers have been damaged beyond repair by ignorant village midwives. Malaria kills more people than any other disease, and tuberculosis is the second highest killer. Chronic starvation has a lot to do with its inroads. People come with tetanus, typhoid, hepatitis, dysentery, filariasis (commonly called elephantiasis), ulcers, infected eyes, and scabies. How much suffering could be spared with just soap and water!" Most of the people, however, had no soap.

The medical demands nearly crowded out the time they needed for further language study, though they were still required to pass another examination the following year.

Three hard adjustments to the realities of the missionary profession began to shape their lives. The most difficult was separation from children and from one another. These times, impossible to avoid, had to be faced with fortitude and courage. Tearful goodbyes left heartache and sometimes scars. These were not always healed in the high peaks of anticipated reunion and the richness of shared experiences when they were together.

Even yet when Joe remembers the letters he earned for being top man in Woodstock School basketball, he regrets that his parents never got to see him play in a single tournament. Basketball games were always played in the season when his parents were down on the plains and busy in the hospital.

Pris feels the same when she looks into her scrapbook and sees the tickets she bought for the Woodstock Centennial Music

Festival in 1954. All the children were in this festival, Phil for his first appearance in any school program, Joe in the choir, Pat as a majorette, and Pris as a violinist. Playing the violin was a skill not shared with Pat or anyone else in the family. Pris was an excellent player and had learned so quickly that she amazed her teachers. She was appointed as secretary of the orchestra. The first time her father heard her play, he got misty-eyed.

"To think I held that hand when it was a helpless baby's hand," Pris's father said.

Pris prayed that her parents would reach Landour in time to see her perform in her unique way. Though they wanted to be there very much, they were delayed in going because the doctor who was to take charge of the hospital for them returned from vacation a day too late. The disappointment to the children was perhaps keener in that the parents missed the program by only one day.

Another hard adjustment was to discover that even after passing two language examinations with good scores, neither Ezra nor Frances could get sensible answers to their Hindi questions.

"*Khansi ati?* (Do you have a cough?)" (Not *kahanse ati*—where do you come from?)

"*Baragaon se ati.*" (I come from Baragaon.)

"*Ap ka kya nam hai?*" (What is your name?)

"*Mujhae Angrezi nahin ati.*" (I don't speak English.)

During their entire six years in India, Pat and Pris were in an English-medium school for nine months each year, and there was no real pressure on them to learn Hindi, though they did study it some in school. Joe and Phil, however, too young for boarding in the early years, picked up the idiom and accent and chattered away like natives. At such occasions as the first celebration of India's Republic Day on January 26, 1950, Joe and Phil answered questions directed to the family because they were the only ones understanding what was going on—apart from the speeches, that is, which were all in English.

A third major adjustment forced upon the family was the necessity of having servants. Cooking was done with charcoal, and meals were started from scratch with wheat, rice, grain, and raw vegetables from the bazaar. With six to twelve hours of daily duty at the hospital, Frances had no time to shop, cook, or clean. Cleaning ladies came and went, but Dharm Das, a well-trained mission cook, soon joined the DeVols and became like a part of the family. He served as both cook and bearer. When the meal was ready, Dharm Das would ring a bell. When the family members were all nicely seated at the table, he appeared from the kitchen resplendent in white coat and cap, serving each dish with dignity. He began from the left side, circling the table until he stood at last with bowed head at the left of the doctor, who then led the family in the giving of thanks.

Missionaries from all over the area came to the hospital for treatment, and since there were no hotels, they often stayed in the guest room at the DeVols' home and ate at their table.

Cooks had their own ways of doing things. They had ritualistic, but not scientific ideas of cleanliness. It was not Hindi accent that hindered Frances' orders concerning food, accounts, and cleanliness from being carried out.

For example, one evening when Joe and Ethelyn Watson of Lalitpur were present, Frances decided to give the guests a treat of some special Chinese tea. The cook waited patiently as she explained in Hindi how Chinese tea differed from Indian tea, but he did not listen to a word she said. *I've made tea all my life and I don't need a recipe,* he was thinking proudly. He used up every leaf of her precious tea, adding more and more in an attempt to acquire the usual dark color. As a result, the tea went down the drain.

The Children and the Hospital

When home from boarding, Pat and Pris made friends with a few girls who could speak some English. They enjoyed reading Cherry Ames nurses' books and many missionary biographies. They played records. Pris practiced her violin and Pat the piano. Pris liked to slip over to the hospital and watch her dad do surgery. She chose nursing as her career. Pat, though participating some in surgery, liked it less. She chose teaching as her career. Dr. DeVol followed his father's example and taught the children the bones of the body and other lessons from his practice.

One winter as Pat and Pris came home from boarding, their father was about to operate on a man's arch. The operation was called a "triple arthrodesis," and he had cut patterns and taken X-rays to be sure he would do it right.

"I want you girls to see this operation," he said.

The girls, however, were just taking in their beautiful room—a surprise of their mother—with the new green color of the walls and the matching bedspreads. They did not fully realize that the operation of the year was about to take place. Since they had not yet unpacked their suitcases, bathed, shampooed their hair, or changed clothes—which they felt was their next obligation—they missed that opportunity, something they both regretted later.

Both Pat and Pris liked to bake. They usually found plenty of time to do this when the servants were out of the house. They enjoyed each other's company and, as identical twins, often revealed such deep understanding of one another's problems that Frances noted, "They don't really seem to need a mother! They help each other solve their problems."

The twins loved their home in Chhatarpur, and they did not resent the presence of servants or missionary guests, or that their own interests were sometimes secondary. They enjoyed being in on the adult conversations around their table. Dr. DeVol could not help sharing with his guests the news of the dedication of the new Bilwar village church comprised of fifteen adults and fifteen children. These converts out of raw Hinduism had been suffering persecution and were standing true. The building of their little mud church was a breakthrough in the whole area.

Evangelism held priority in the Friends Mission, and missionary guests often marveled at the way the educational, medical, and evangelistic missionaries seemed to keep that goal in focus. Dr. DeVol loved to tell them how the Friends missionaries met about every six weeks for days of prayer and consultation in order to keep their priorities straight and to know how to pass them on to the Indian Christian workers. Joy Ridderhoff of Gospel Recordings was treated like a queen as she brought her equipment in to record Stuti Prakash, the pastor, who preached and sang the Gospel powerfully. This method would extend the work of evangelism.

The missionaries were excited about Dr. DeVol's "milk route" of 110 miles round trip from Chhatarpur through Gulganj to Amarmau. The "milk route" was a public health service that combined medical work and evangelism. Dispensaries were

The "MILK ROUTE"...

When I eat, my stomach aches,...

Then don't eat!

3ION HOSPITAL

M.COMFORT

located at these district headquarters where the Colemans, Robinsons, and later the Hesses and Anna Nixon lived. People all along the way recognized the "Christian Hospital" ambulance and waited by the road for treatment. Frances and the children often went along, and they would stay an extra day in the jungle as the men hunted and brought venison home. Joe reveled in going along with the men. Deer heads on the dining room wall and a panther skin on the floor in the DeVol home bore evidence of their success. Dr. DeVol also went out to hold clinics in the areas where evangelistic camping teams were working and where there was no medical help for miles around. This encouraged the evangelists and opened doors for their message.

For a full week, mealtime conversations centered on Brij Kishor, the Brahmin convert with the opium habit. Dr. DeVol remembered his father's treatment for opium addiction. Clifton Robinson and an evangelist had meals with the DeVols and took turns staying with Brij Kishor as he voluntarily underwent the treatment. He was gloriously delivered, but for becoming a Christian, his wife left him, and he was terribly persecuted by his family.

Hospital patients also were prayed for at the table. The guests and the children were all amazed to hear of Suratiya Bai, who was carried in from a village several miles away. They prayed for her at every mealtime for days. She had a huge tumor which had made her life miserable for months. Her waist measured sixty-five inches. The surgical procedure began with draining off some of the fluid. After three days she could almost lie flat, and Dr. DeVol and his surgical team began their work with the prayer that she would not only get relief from her suffering, but also that she would find peace and know the joy of sins forgiven. She went into severe shock after the operation, and they administered plasma. Everybody prayed, and she came through. From then on, she made rapid improvement. The cyst weighed 20 pounds, and with 44 quarts of fluid drained off, the total weight came to 108 pounds! Afterwards the little woman weighed only 83 pounds, but she gained four pounds before going home. Dharm Das's wife, Bhagwati Bai, told Bible stories to her and led her to faith in Christ. She left saying she would tell her neighbors about Him.

The guests and the children entered heartily into prayer for all these needs, for the spread of the Gospel throughout the villages, and for the patients in the hospital, name by name.

Home from boarding, Pat and Pris at times felt overcome by the pace in Chhatapur.

"It seems I never have a mother anymore," Pris commented one day when guests piled in and the cook was uncooperative. "She's always at the hospital!"

Pat withdrew, sat on the steps of a tomb in the cemetery for untroubled contemplation. There she wrote her thoughts:

> Because I felt no one cared, I pouted . . . for nothing at all. I was trying to get even for their little care. Then Pris turned on, "His Eye Is on the Sparrow." What a blessing to know He cares for me! . . . I was meant to be saved and sanctified to spread God's redemption to others. . . . I must think on the interest of others. What about Brij

Kishor, the camps, Gospel Recordings? Then what happens to me? Well, I don't even know that!

In spite of the hospital needs forever with them, the parents spent cozy evenings around the fireplace at night answering their children's questions, or just being available. Their dad sometimes entertained them with slap-stick beyond anything they had ever witnessed, like demonstrating a way to let the mission board know the condition of the jeep. Or maybe he would just sit there, dozing in his chair, while Mother popped corn and Pris and Pat took turns reading stories to Joe and Phil.

Sometimes their father would take Pat and Pris to a distant, unpopulated area for target practice. One evening as they were returning, a man came running to report an emergency in the hospital.

"Please lock this in the gun cupboard," Pris's father said as he handed her the gun and ran directly to the hospital without entering the house.

Once inside, Pris discovered the gun cupboard was locked and her father had the key. Since Pat, Joe, and Phil were also in the house with her, she decided to make sure the gun was unloaded before putting it down.

"Didn't Dad say there were no bullets in the gun?" Pat asked, looking down the barrel. Pat withdrew just before Pris tested the trigger. Immediately the gun discharged, splintering her violin standing in the corner.

"I was stunned!" Pris recalled later. "The cook ran in to see if we were all okay. He looked worried. I didn't really feel anything but relief that we four were all intact. Afterwards, I had my violin glued together just at the chin rest, but it had lost a lot of its tone. When we returned to Woodstock after vacation, Woodstock School's principal, Canon Sam Burgoyne, sensing my disappointment, replaced my violin with one of his."

On Sundays after church, there was a regular ritual of a family bicycle ride out into the open countryside (except for Mother). Every cool season was dotted with family picnics out to the beautiful lakes, sometimes early morning, sometimes afternoon, depending on how things were in the hospital. Often these were shared with the other missionaries as well. Whether in Chhatarpur during the winter, or in Landour during summer vacation of the parents, such times of being together came to be treasured.

Pris reflected in later years, "A lot of kids don't appreciate their parents because they've never been separated from them."

While the girls were home from boarding in 1951, a cable came announcing the death of Frances' father, Daniel Hodgin, on January 18. The family all felt the loss, for they loved their grandfather, and they comforted their mother.

Joe followed her into the bedroom, and putting his arms around her as she wept, he said, "I know your heart feels bad."

As time drew near for the twins to leave again, Joe also started praying he would have enough money to buy a *bister* (bedding roll) and all the things he would need for boarding at the end of that year. He knelt at his mother's knee and received Christ as his Savior when he was six. How he was growing! He was now over four feet tall and his clothes were being put aside for Phil.

At church, where men sat on one side and women on the other, Joe and Phil usually sat with Frances, Pat, and Pris. Suddenly one day, Joe became restless, wiggled out of his seat, and went across to sit by his father.

Later he explained, "I saw that all the men were on one side."

Phil also was becoming conscious of his size and measured his full three feet and two inches in front of the mirror. Suddenly he turned around with his back to the mirror and asked, "Mother, can you see me backwards?"

Pat and Pris had grown, too. Their dresses were all above their knees and hems were barely wide enough to last another year. Frances called in the tailor and designed new clothes for all of the children. The girls appreciated their mother's choice of patterns. For their junior year, she made them beautiful aqua formals, the most beautiful dresses, they felt, that they had ever worn.

When Joe was admitted to boarding in October 1951, he walked down the path and did not look back. Just a little ways down, he stumbled and came back, for he could cry about that. His father, wearing sunglasses, walked down to school with him.

"I'm having as hard a time as you are, Joe," he confessed. That helped Joe get hold of himself.

In the weekly exchange of letters between each parent and each child, it became evident that once in boarding, Joe, like his sisters, made friends quickly, enjoyed sports, started Bible clubs for his peers, and later became involved in student government. The fact that he could name all the bones in the body put him ahead in his physiology class, and he loved to hear his teachers say, "You're going to be like your father."

Bambi and Homecoming

Back in Chhatarpur, the DeVols were thankful Phil was still with them, but he was very lonely. The husband of a village patient brought him a little deer, and he named it Bambi. Though a cage was built for Bambi, he was still free to roam about the house. To some extent, Bambi filled Phil's lonely hours, but when he heard that his brother and sisters were coming home from boarding the next day, he got so excited he could hardly contain himself. Darkness came quickly, and the cool nights meant cozy sleeping, so Phil went to bed early in order to be in good shape the next day when they arrived. Ezra and Frances had just barely got to sleep when a loud noise at their front gate awakened them.

"Is that shouting and honking at the bus stand?" Frances asked.

"I don't think so. It sounds as if the bus is coming into our front gate!" Ezra commented as he jumped out of bed and pulled on a robe.

Sure enough, the bus had come through their front gate and right up to their front door. Pat, Pris, and Joe were all shouting. They piled out of the bus and smothered their father and mother with kisses as the bus attendant began shoving the bedding rolls off the top of the bus and handing down the tin trunks. Pat and Pris gathered up the lunch baskets and thermos bottles and deposited them on the veranda. The noise brought Phil up from deep sleep, too, and when he saw what was happening, he was determined to be seen and heard.

"Bambi!" he called, as he began chasing his little deer around and around the table. "Look, it's Bambi, look, Bambi!" he shouted as his little deer gathered momentum.

Phil was soon the center of attention and got his share of hugs and kisses as Bambi skidded across the living room floor and asked for petting. It was a long time after midnight before the family got settled down, so happy were they to be together once more.

Bambi grew rapidly, and by the time the older children got ready to return to boarding, Bambi had already begun shoving people around. He got too big for the situation in Chhatarpur and was taken to Gulganj, where there was more roaming space and a fenced-in compound.

One day Phil rode along with his father on his "milk route" to see Bambi. His horns were growing, and he seemed quite wild. When Phil reached out to pet him, Bambi bit him. Slightly wounded but deeply hurt, Phil went crying to his father.

"Oh, Phil, Bambi didn't mean to hurt you. He won't bite you again. Come, I'll show you," his father said. He led Phil gently up to Bambi again and urged Phil to stretch out his hand, but as soon as he did that, Bambi bit him again. Later, Bambi began pushing others around and soon ended up as venison steak on the table in Gulganj.

In due time, Phil got another Bambi and in his concern to feed it well, he gave it *channa* (grain) which had not been soaked long enough in water. As a result, it swelled and made the little deer very sick. Phil's father, knowing how much that little deer meant to his son, brought a syringe and gave Bambi a shot of adrenalin right into its heart. The deer died, but Phil never forgot the effort of his father to save it.

Pulled in Two Directions

As the hospital work expanded, so did the problems. Norma Freer assisted efficiently as business manager, but when she left for furlough in 1951, Frances felt bereft. Strict rationing made it impossible to get enough cloth for sheets. She searched three cities in North India for anything useable. Caring for supplies, ordering drugs, and personally supervising the sterilization of instruments with a pressure cooker over a Primus stove took her time. The staff, she felt, did not have enough experience with pressure cookers and pressure stoves to handle the sterilization.

Many patients burned from these pressure stoves had been treated in the hospital.

Frances, always fearing infections, said, "Our air blew in from the dung hills. God preserved us from infections. Psalm 116:6 was a standby promise for us: 'The Lord preserveth the simple: I was brought low and he helped me.' "

All these responsibilities plus assisting in the operating theater by Ezra's side, the part Frances loved most, kept her more than busy.

"The hospital work rests upon me pretty heavily," Frances wrote, "but I still feel that my first responsibility is to the family. I hate to leave Ezra alone, but the girls have started dating and need guidance. Phil also needs to get into school and is too young yet for boarding. He asks between forty to a hundred questions a day and develops stomach cramps when he thinks he might be left behind. The pull both ways is very hard."

Together, Ezra and Frances prayed and planned for ways to fulfill responsibilities to both family and hospital. God heard their prayers and provided some well qualified nurses, though none were as efficient as Frances. Ezra would miss her greatly. They agreed that Frances should spend an extra month in the hills with the children each summer and return for another month in the fall. This proved to be a good solution, as she had time to get the children's clothes replenished, dental problems cared for, and spiritual problems prayed about before they became major.

Frances later wrote, "I am so happy for the influence of these years on the children. I would not give any amount of money for the years spent here. They get a lot out of their Scripture class—far more than we did in our college course. They are much more aggressive Christians than I have ever been."

During the winter in Bundelkhand, Pat and Pris had spent a week in Gulganj with Betty Robinson, who had told them, "You can be just as close to the Lord as you want to be." They took a new step in committing themselves to Christ, and prayer and Bible study became their daily practice.

Back in Woodstock, they joined other students who wanted to walk close to God. They led an Indian classmate Sunita to Christ. As do missionaries, they tasted the heartache when her parents removed her from school, took away her Bible, and ordered her to quit writing.

Sunita's last letter summed up her struggle: "I have agreed to do what my parents want me to do, but they can't change my heart." Pat and Pris did not hear from her again.

Into Deep Medical Waters

As the hospital staff increased and the work accelerated, the staff members who were used to a slower pace began to resist change. The DeVols felt the problem was basically spiritual. During a very trying period, when Dr. DeVol was ill with hepatitis and Dr. Grace Jones Singh was off with high blood pressure, Frances held the hospital together and started weekly prayer and Bible study with the staff in their home. There was interest and some participation, but all did not respond. Friction in the Christian Hospital was sometimes anything but Christian, and lack of openness—coupled with deep cultural misunderstandings—caused discouragement, which led the DeVols to wonder if they were, in fact, in the right place.

The chief innovator for change was, of course, Dr. DeVol, and his new fee system pinched the rich. The mission from early times had practically given away their medicine. Dr. DeVol wanted to give away medicine to the really poor, but he felt it was morally and spiritually right for people with means to pay.

The medical board, comprised of three Indian leaders and three missionaries, finally understood Dr. DeVol's innovative plans and began to follow him. They agreed to fix fees for medicine, laboratory fees, X rays, hospitalization, and consultations. They also passed Dr. DeVol's suggestion to allow Christians and mission employees to avail themselves of a medical insurance plan by paying a certain percentage of their salaries each month. For people who could not pay, they agreed to build a free ward where both the patient and his relatives could stay without cost as the patient received free medical treatment. Another income-earning plan was the building of family wards. Well-to-do families were willing to pay quite high rent for such private wards where they could also stay with their relatives receiving treatment.

At first, people shunned the free ward where they feared the treatment would be inferior. However, after their operations, patients suddenly pleaded poverty and walked out without paying.

On the operating table under anesthesia, one man said, "*Main dene ka nahin!*" (I'm not going to pay!)

Dr. DeVol felt he had to win through on this. Deep in thought as he went into the tent of men patients, he suddenly thought of a plan. He later explained what happened:

> An idea flashed into my mind. I started in one corner and examined everybody thoroughly, very thoroughly. I stopped by each patient and pounded his chest, palpated his abdomen, and tested his reflexes. When I got to this man, I just took his pulse and went on. I then went over the next man with a fine-tooth comb, and continued this all the way around the ward. I didn't even have a chance to get out of the tent before the man met me at the door with the money in his hand. Everyone in the ward roared with laughter.

Dr. DeVol knew this was no long-term solution, so the war was still on. Heartless as it seemed, he could think of no other way than to order the collection of bills before performing the operation.

"They don't believe us!" Dr. DeVol almost despaired. "The awfulness of not being believed has hit us squarely in the face, and it stings."

One day Ezra said to Frances, "Don't pay that bill to the cloth merchant until he pays us."

Frances knew about the cloth merchant. He also owned houses, lands, and a lucrative bus line. His servant broke an arm cranking one of his buses. Dr. DeVol set the bones and put him in a cast. The day the man broke his arm, the merchant cut off his pay. He also refused to pay his servant's medical bill.

"He is a poor man," the cloth merchant said. "He can't pay!"

Some days later another employee of the same cloth merchant, cranking the same bus, fractured both bones of his forearm. This time before setting the arm, Dr. DeVol asked the cloth merchant to pay the bill. He promised in the presence of others to do so. However, when all was done, he refused to pay. Dr. DeVol was angry with his lies, his arrogance, and his lack of concern for his employees. He was determined to teach the man a lesson he would not forget. He put in a large order for cloth for the hospital and did not pay the bill.

"I'm withholding money from that cloth merchant until he pays us," Ezra explained to Frances.

"That's not right, Ezra," Frances said. "I heard my grand-father tell my uncle always to pay bills, regardless of what others do."

Ezra did not hear her, but later he got the message very powerfully. The merchant raged through the streets of Chhatarpur with threats and accusations. He sent letters to Delhi of how the Christian Hospital was robbing the rich and refusing to treat the poor. A delegation came from Delhi to investigate. The man had instigated a movement in the city to expel the DeVols from India. Patients stopped coming, and the beds in the wards emptied. The man would not pay, and Dr. DeVol would not budge.

"Give me courage to stand firm," he prayed, "and change the heart of the cloth merchant!"

Ezra opened his Bible for a promise to stand on and received instead a rebuke from Jeremiah 7:5,7: "If ye thoroughly amend your ways . . . then I will cause you to dwell in this place."

It took some time for his eyes to open, but as dramatic as on the Damascus road, the light came. Dr. DeVol, like Paul, was not disobedient. Greatly humiliated, he apologized to the cloth merchant, told Frances to pay the bill, related his experience in family prayers, and asked his children to pray for him. He came through this experience having learned a deep lesson from a paraphrase of 1 Peter 5:6: *You bow your neck, and I will fight your battles.*

From that very day, the situation in the hospital changed, and the DeVols began to experience more confidence from the people and a greater understanding of their purpose for being in India.

The agony of not being believed was eased, and Dr. DeVol noted: "Our heavenly Father wants to be depended upon. He wants to be believed."

Very soon the beds in every ward were full again, and some patients, for whom there was no bed, lay on the floor. The free ward also came into full use.

The Healing of a Blind Boy

Chullu, a blind boy of fourteen, was brought penniless to the hospital and admitted to the free ward. Not only blind for many years from bilateral cataracts, but also syphilitic, diabetic, and covered with facial abcesses, he seemed to have lost long ago any expectation of ever experiencing joy in living.

He would make a good Buddha, thought the doctor, *that is, if he were endowed with some adiposity.* Sensing his helplessness to penetrate Chullu's blank apathy, the doctor prayed: *Oh, Lord, help me give sight to this young fellow.*

It took several days to build Chullu up physically to withstand surgery, but through all that time the hopelessness never left Chullu's face. Four days after the operation, the doctor removed the bandages and asked the boy to open his eyes. He waited expectantly.

Chullu took a long time in responding, but when the eyelids finally flickered just a bit, Chullu agreed he could see a glimmer of light.

Encouraging Chullu to open his eyes again, the doctor patiently held his hand in front of the boy's face. Slowly the eyes opened, wider this time, and the boy spoke: "I see your hand."

"How many fingers do you count?" Dr. DeVol asked.

"Two."

"How many now?"

"Three."

"What is this object?"

"An eight anna piece."

"Can you see me?"

"Yes, doctor! I can see you!" Chullu's radiant smile revealed the light had suddenly come, not only to his eyes, but to his mind and heart. After he was released from the hospital, he was fitted with glasses and taught to read.

Added Blessings

An Indo-American Agreement brought in food supplies, hospital equipment, and medical supplies. The United States government paid the ocean freight, and the Indian government charged no duty and paid internal freight. The Christian

Hospital was permitted to import $20,000 worth of instruments. A new four-wheel-drive station wagon jeep also arrived under this plan.

The district medical officer in Chhatarpur invited the Christian Hospital to participate in a medical exhibit, and the staff felt accepted in the community as people came to look at their display of X rays and charts and view their films on the prevention of common diseases like tuberculosis, leprosy, cholera, typhoid, eye diseases, and malaria.

Norma Freer's return as business manager and the coming of Norman Whipple and his wife were valuable additions to the staff. Norman Whipple was an American from Quaker background. He had lived with his missionary parents in another mission until he was seventeen. On his return to India as a missionary in his own right, he married an Indian teacher, and the prejudice of the times caused them to be ostracized. In India, he became a laboratory technician, one of the best, and he raised the efficiency level of the Christian Hospital. Dr. Jones Singh recovered, and Dr. Franklin, a male doctor, arrived. Mary Barton, an English nurse, came for some time to assist. Three Indian ladies joined the staff: Sarah James, in charge of supplies; Phyllis Das, matron of the nurses' home; Rajli Singh, a surgical nurse.

W. Robert and Esther Hess with their daughter Kathy came as new missionaries. Ron was born soon afterwards. The Board sent Chester Stanley and Charles Matti for a visit, and they supported the expansion of the work. The Board gave permission for building a new home in the hills. Pinepoint, and now Pennington, each with two suites, totally furnished even with washing machine, bathtubs, and flush toilets, provided missionary families with housing. Both homes were located just beyond Woodstock School.

Pennington almost immediately became temporary headquarters for the new Evangelical Fellowship of India, an organization drawing together the evangelical leaders and missions throughout India. Revival followed and there was hardly a missionary in North India who was not touched in some way with the flames of revival, spreading through Episcopalian laymen from revival areas in East Africa.

God was blessing on all sides, and the DeVols began to feel at home and accepted in India. Even after another time of severe illness with typhoid, and giardia, Dr. DeVol wrote, "While recovering, the only thing I could think of was Sunnyslope. Well, thank the Lord, that experience is over. I still love the farm, but I don't feel like running away from here."

Saving the Lives of Dear Ones

Missionaries and others from the area were thankful that the DeVols felt like staying in India. For some, their careers depended on it, for they were learning constantly. For others, their lives depended on it. One such was the mission maintenance superintendent, Komal Das Lall, who came down with tuberculosis of the kidney. He was up and back on the job in six months due to the use of a new drug, isonicotinic acid, along with other treatment. This seemed miraculous to the Indian people who had never experienced health being restored to a person with such a serious case of tuberculosis. The miracle continued as others with tuberculosis were treated as outpatients and were well in no time without ever having to go to bed.

Dr. DeVol moved rapidly one day when Everett Cattell was brought in with unusual pain traveling up the leg in which he suffered phlebitis.

"Embolism!" exclaimed the doctor. "We must operate at once!"

He hastily called his operating team. In the tension of that operation, and perhaps to ease his own, Dr. DeVol used the experience to teach the staff as he made the incision.

"Now, note that in the right leg you find this order: nerve, artery, vein, empty space, lymph—easy to remember by their initials spelling NAVEL. We're after the vein."

Everett Cattell was conscious and listening.

"There!" Dr. DeVol exclaimed, "I've got it! Thank the Lord!" He took the clot out just before it passed into the groin.

"You'll never know what it takes out of us to have to operate on those so close to us," Frances remarked after the danger was over.

The Healing of a Crippled Boy

The battle was gradually being won in challenging those who could afford to pay for medical treatment, and Dr. DeVol felt the time had come to awaken the community to the responsibility of caring for others. The opportunity came with Mullen.

Dr. DeVol met Mullen as he was boarding a bus.

"*Baksheesh!*"(alms) the crippled fourteen-year-old begged pathetically. He was unable to walk because of extensive leg burns, which had contracted the muscles until he had to support himself with two half-moon-shaped pieces of wood he carried in his hands.

I think I could help this boy, the doctor thought. *I wonder how he got this way.*

On inquiry, he found that Mullen had sometimes played mean tricks on other boys. To get even, the others found him asleep one day under the shade of a tree, threw gasoline on his legs, and set him on fire. Dr. DeVol talked with people at the bus stand about Mullen.

"If you people can contribute toward the expense, we will try to help Mullen walk again," he said.

A collection of about ten dollars was taken at the bus stand, and Mullen was moved into the hospital. He required a series of operations. When they got to the skin grafting, Dr. DeVol said to Frances, "With both legs to do, this is going to take a lot of time. You do that one, and I'll do this one."

They worked together, and when the job was done, a number of the staff members remarked, "Doctor, hers is even prettier than yours!"

Slowly, Mullen began to get well, his pain disappeared, and he started gaining weight. When he walked out of the hospital, though still with a limp, he looked like a different person. His life had been touched by the healing hands of the love of Christ, and the bus stand people had been a part of that.

The Responsibility of Mission Superintendent

When Everett and Catherine Cattell went home for furlough in 1954, the mission board appointed Dr. DeVol as mission superintendent. By this time, three Indian leaders sat on the policy-making council with the missionaries.

One of the first crises the new superintendent had to handle was a move by the Vindhya Pradesh government to rid their state of all foreign missionaries. Max and Ruth Ellen Banker were the first to be asked to leave. Norma Freer, in bed with hepatitis, was the next. In Delhi, the National Christian Council officials were alerted, and they arranged a meeting with Prime Minister Jawaharlal Nehru. In Chhatarpur, a patient's brother, Congressman Mahendra Kumar, quickly arranged an interview for Dr. DeVol with the governor in the state capital of Rewa.

In Rewa, Dr. DeVol was called into the office of a highly placed government minister, who closed the door and said quietly, "I'm alone in this place, and I'm hungry for Christian fellowship. I'm convinced Christ is the only way."

Pleased to find spiritual hunger instead of hostility, Dr. DeVol shared some thoughts from the Bible and told something of his own spiritual pilgrimage. The minister was no doubt interested, but he kept watching the door and speaking in such a low voice that his fear of taking any open stand was evident, though he seemed to appreciate Dr. DeVol's taking time to pray with him.

The governor, on meeting Dr. DeVol, confronted him: "Why do you persist in making converts?"

Dr. DeVol did not know how to answer this irate official. He sent up a telegraphic prayer and then said, "All of us who are Christians are witnesses."

India's constitution guaranteed each individual the freedom to practice, profess, and propagate his religion, and the governor seemed suddenly to remember that. His mood changed.

"That's absolutely right," he answered. "You have as much right to be a Christian as I have to be a Hindu. I will write the superintendent of police in Chhatarpur and tell him to stop harassing you. No—I'll *telegraph* him, so he will get the message immediately."

The prime minister in Delhi also sent word to Rewa to leave the missionaries alone. It was clear that prayer was being answered on every level.

As superintendent, Dr. DeVol felt a greater sense of responsibility for the evangelistic work. He held clinics in all the camps: with Victor Mangalwadi in Nowgong, with Robert Hess in Kishengarh and Basari, with Stuti Prakash in Satna, and with

Milton Coleman twice in Ghuara. He also checked on the students in the schools in Nowgong and Ghuara.

Looking toward Furlough

Mission staff came and went. Norman Whipple felt he needed to move to the United States for his children's education. The family of Prionath, the head nurse, arranged her marriage. Victor Mangalwadi, one of the outstanding leaders in the church, resigned and moved to a wider field. Dr. Franklin left. Mary Barton, the English nurse, decided to join another mission. Dr. Jones Singh was the only one in sight to take over the hospital as the DeVols prepared to leave for furlough in 1955. Capable as she was, her training had not qualified her for management of a hospital of the present size, and her high blood pressure threatened to put an end to her service altogether.

With only two nurses left, one for night duty and one for day duty, Frances assisted her husband in the surgery. All at one time there were five patients with seven fractures: one with a broken back, paralyzed from the waist down; a boy with a broken arm; a man with an elbow ruined by a passing bus, as he had his arm sticking out the window; two boys with two broken legs each.

One of the boys with two broken legs was named Shankar. He had fallen out of a tree, and the doctor had to perform open reduction on both femurs, straightening and lengthening them to normal length. He then put him in casts. While he was recovering, Shankar read all the Hindi books in the hospital library, including portions of the Bible. His favorite book was *Pilgrim's Progress*. The other boy with two broken legs was illiterate. The hospital evangelist put up literacy charts, and Shankar attempted to teach him to read. With a Bible under his arm, a gift of Dr. DeVol, Shankar left the hospital a believer in the Lord Jesus Christ.

Another patient who brought joy to the DeVols in the final months of their first term was a woman named Durgabai. Dr. DeVol operated on her for intestinal obstruction, but he found so many adhesions that he felt, medically speaking, there was no hope for her. Her husband, an orthodox Hindu, asked the doctor to pray.

"If you want us to pray in the name of the Lord Jesus," Dr. DeVol told him, "then please ask the Hindu priest whom you have praying outside her door to leave."

The man went out and dismissed the priest, and the doctor, nurse, and relatives gathered around Durgabai's bed and prayed. She recovered, and before leaving the hospital, she and her husband went to the church. Pastor Stuti Prakash allowed her husband to speak in the service, and he said, "Durgabai is alive because the Lord Jesus Christ had mercy on her as a result of Christians' prayers."

Durgabai lived for many more years.

Graduation of Pat and Pris

Before Pat and Pris went to boarding for the last time, they visited some of their nearby Woodstock friends in another mission. While they were away, Dr. DeVol was called by the Maharaja to Panna, fifty miles from Chhatarpur. The Maharaja's brother was ill and needed a doctor. Ezra took Frances, Joe, and Phil with him for the trip. When they got to the palace, they were invited in for tea before being introduced to the patient. The palace was fabulous. In the entrance room they were confronted with a glass cage holding a ten-foot mounted lion. In the forty-foot dining room, skins and heads of eight tigers were on display. The huge living room was furnished with luxurious Persian carpets and crystal candelabra.

After tea, Dr. DeVol was taken to see the patient and found him at that very moment having a heart attack. He prayed that the man would not die. He felt the Lord led him to give just the right treatment, and all went well.

A month later on Joe's eleventh birthday, the whole DeVol family drove seventy-five miles to the diamond mines beyond Panna. The weather was beautiful, sunny, and cool. The flame of the forest trees brightened the jungle with their beautiful deep orange blossoms. The mine they visited was huge and had produced one of the largest diamonds in the world. For one thousand tons of dirt, the miners would find fifty or sixty diamonds a day.

On some of their family trips, Ezra took along a gun, and they stopped now and then as he took aim to get a peacock, a bear, a wild boar, or a deer. Pat and Phil would hope he would miss, and Pris and Joe would hope he would hit. Joe enjoyed taking his turn, too, and they all enjoyed venison steak when they got it.

In early March 1955, the children left Chhatarpur. Two months later, with the work placed in charge of Dr. Jones Singh, and with the promise of the return of Mary Barton for the time they would be on furlough, Ezra and Frances said goodbye to Chhatarpur. Not only the people of the church, but the municipal board of Chhatarpur honored them and warmly invited them to return. They had every intention of doing so.

Proceeding on to Landour, the DeVols stayed for daughters Patricia and Priscilla's graduation from Woodstock High School. The girls looked beautiful in their new clothes—blue suits Aunt Kathryn Hodgin had sent, along with lovely material for graduation formals. Their mother designed these and an Indian tailor made them. Saying goodbye to the some four hundred students who attended this unique school, Pat and Pris turned their eyes eagerly homeward to college and their future.

Their six years in India had been significant ones. They would always remember the children of missionaries in India, who would remain their friends through life. The missionaries of Bundelkhand, whom they called "aunt" and "uncle," also would remain close. The Woodstock School teachers from various countries, skilled and interested in the students as persons, were outstanding. To this day, Pris remembers Principal Sam and Mary Esther Burgoyne of England, who replaced her damaged violin with their own. She still has that violin.

The beauty of the snow-capped Himalayas, the fantastic sunsets over the plains, the constant changing panorama of sunshine, clouds, and shadow, which made up the setting of their daily life in Woodstock School—these and many other memories would go with them always.

The family reached Delhi June 12, 1955, and transferred to the Frontier Mail train to Bombay. For the next twenty-four hours as they sped through the Rajasthan desert with a big block of ice in the middle of their compartment to help make the trip bearable, Ezra's thoughts returned to his first such trip in 1949 and God's promise of His presence in Exodus 33:14.

He then recalled the special promise for his last year in India as superintendent of the mission—Joshua 1:5: "There shall not any man be able to stand before thee all the days of thy life."

"This has seemed like too big a promise for me," Ezra commented. "I have been neither a Moses, nor a Joshua—nor have I any resembling characteristics—but I recognize in this verse a promise that the Lord intends for anyone who will answer God's call, lean on His strength, and trust in His faithfulness. I look back on this term of service and see that this promise has been true. Thus far, of those who have opposed me, no one has succeeded in preventing what was the will of God for me. God has turned their opposition into a demonstration of His power in every circumstance."

As the train sped along, Ezra shared these thoughts with his family. Together they sang, "Great Is Thy Faithfulness, Lord, Unto Me," and were assured of God's presence as they ended this first chapter of their ministry in India.

The DeVols arrived in India for a six-year term
April 1949—June 1955

Phil with his father and pet deer—Bambi

Phil and Joe camping

Pat and Pris going to Woodstock

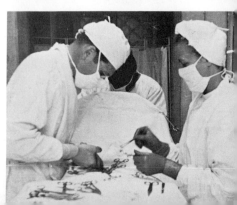

Dr. Ezra and Frances operating

Pat, Kusum, and Pris (above)

Joe, Hirawanti (with fawn), Jiwan, and Phil

In Chhatarpur Pris supervises as Pat teaches Sunday school to the missionary children—Bonnie and Mary Evelyn Banker, Ron Hess, Phil DeVol, Mary Cattell, and Carol Jean Coleman.

Violin—Pris
Piano—Pat

Frances hosts orphans brought up by the mission. Dharm Das, the cook and bearer, was also one of them.

Frances, Pris, and Pat camping in the Himalayas

Patricia and Priscilla DeVol graduated from Woodstock High School, 1955.

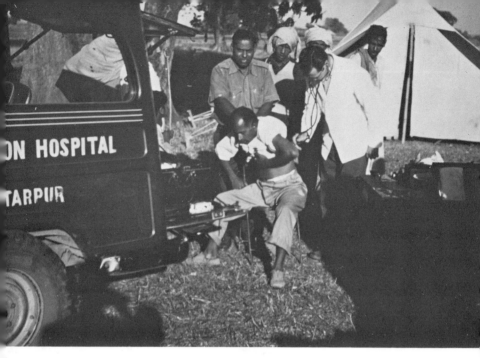

The ambulance that made the "milk route." Male nurse Samson H. Lal assists Dr. DeVol.

Three superintendents "back from the hunt"—Everett, Bob, and Ezra with Joe and Phil

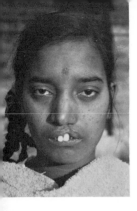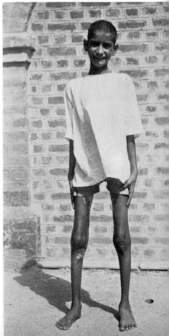

Young woman with hairlip, before and after   Chullu, the blind boy

Suratiya Bai with 108-lb. tumor and after
surgery with Nurse Priobala

Mullen, the cripple, before and after

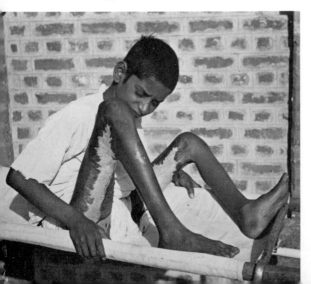

8 "...For My Sake⁀ and the Gospel's..."

Everyone who has left houses or brothers or sisters or father or mother or children or fields for my sake will receive a hundred times as much and will inherit eternal life.

Matthew 19:29 NIV

Return to Chhatarpur

Mullen, the last person to say goodbye to the DeVols as they left Chhatarpur in 1955, was the first on October 26, 1956, to reach the toll barrier into the city to welcome them back. He stood expectantly gazing down the road. A huge crowd gathered, each jostling for a good position to see the truck as it came into sight. Mullen, who had survived the burning and the operations on his legs, defended his place and guarded his garland lest it be crushed. He had made it himself with flowers from the DeVols' bungalow garden.

"There they come!" someone shouted.

Before the man at the toll gate could lift the barrier, the excited mob surged forward and brought the truck to a dead stop. In spite of his limp, Mullen was the first to reach the vehicle, and smiling from ear to ear, he slipped up and put his garland around Dr. DeVol's neck as he got out of the truck.

"Salaam, Doctor Sahib," he said, his eyes beaming.

The doctor's heart was deeply touched.

Milton Coleman, the driver, waited while Frances, Joe, and Phil also got out of the truck and stood in the middle of the road with Dr. DeVol as the people surrounded them. In no time, the four DeVols were loaded with garlands up to their ears. Some had brought garlands for Pat and Pris, too, forgetting that

141

they were now in college in America and would not return to India.

Back to Work

That very day, after a bite of lunch but before unpacking, the DeVols went to the dispensary to see patients who were already lined up and waiting. The hospital—almost empty when they arrived—began to fill up again.

While the DeVols were away, the friction in the staff had increased, and Dr. Grace Jones Singh had resigned and opened her own clinic in the bazaar. No other doctor had been found to take her place. Only three Indian nurses remained. The only way the hospital had been kept open was through the loan of an American nurse from the Woman's Union Missionary Society in Jhansi. Norma Freer was in bed with hepatitis, and Mary Barton, the English nurse, was ill. So Beth Brunemier came to keep the dispensary open and hold the remaining staff together.

In no time, Dr. DeVol, with Frances by his side, was in the operating theater battling for the lives of seriously ill patients. Parwat Kunwar, a Christian with severe cardiac decompensation, was the first to get attention. Then came a missionary who had a very difficult delivery. The baby boy seemed fine, but he died most suddenly and unexpectedly. It was a shock to everyone.

A Tragic Accident

Joe and Phil, too late for the fall term in Woodstock, stayed on in Chhatarpur until March. They had many Indian friends, and Phil became a favorite of all the tonga drivers in the city because of his love for their horses. He spent a lot of time at the bus stand, drumming up business for them, and received the special reward of being allowed to drive the tongas.

Both boys understood the heavy responsibilities on their parents' shoulders, and Joe liked nothing better than to go to the hospital and lend a helping hand or go on rounds with his father. Because of the shortage of staff, he found a lot to do, and especially the day a boy was admitted after a very bad car and bus accident.

The accident had taken place on Sunday, but the unconscious fourteen-year-old Baldeo was not brought into the hospital until Wednesday, deeply comatose, his pulse failing, and from every indication with only a short time to live. Frances ached as she assessed the skill needed to save this boy's life and compared it with the limitations of the available supporting staff.

In America there would be at least two to four doctors and several nurses, she was thinking as they began work, *but here we will have to use even twelve-year-old Joe's help.*

The X ray revealed a depressed fracture of the skull and the shadow of a blood clot, causing pressure on the brain. With his small staff gathered around him, Dr. DeVol led in prayer. Frances was taking the role as the assistant to the doctor, and trying also to supervise the scrub nurse and the circulating nurse. Joe steadily held the flashlight as the doctor with deft fingers began to cut open the cranium, remove the clot, and ligate the bleeding vessels. Just as soon as the skull was opened and the blood clot removed, Baldeo's condition improved, but blood was flooding the scene. The hospital lacked the equipment needed for this procedure, but even as he worked, Dr. DeVol kept praying aloud for God's help and guidance in what to do next.

"Thank You, Lord!" he said as he located the spurting artery, ligated it, and with gelfoam controlled the venous bleeding. Everyone relaxed a bit as they noticed the lad's respiration becoming regular and his pulse returning to nearly normal.

Baldeo was put to bed and given all available supportive measures. In thirty-six hours, he responded a little and answered to the call of his name. In forty-eight hours, he was conscious and able to talk, but he had double vision, could not coordinate his eye muscles, and was afflicted with partial facial paralysis. Steady improvement continued over the next three weeks as facial paralysis practically disappeared and he began to read with both eyes focusing properly. All the relatives knew that Baldeo had been saved because of prayer, and as he returned to his village, the news spread far and wide.

"Ezra can't keep up this pace indefinitely," Frances wrote with concern. She also thought of the cook, Dharm Das, who patiently waited far into the night to serve their supper.

"You are working all the time," she said to him.

"But you are working all the time, too," he said, as at 11:00 p.m. he donned his white coat and cap and, in his dignified way, proceeded to serve the warmed-over meal.

On the Amarmau Milk Route Again

Even though the hospital was already nearly full, Dr. DeVol felt he should keep open his once-a-week 110-mile "milk route" to Gulganj and Amarmau, and, on his first trip, he took care of eighty people in the two dispensaries and along the road. He saw another thirty patients at Bob Hess's camp in Bamori village. Frances and the boys went along to assist. The dull weight of poverty and the drabness of the starved lives of so many of the village people living far below the minimum standard for health stirred their compassion. The pathetic patients bore the useless marks of idolatry, showing their futile attempts to gain help and health by the only means they had known.

"Their condition is perfectly awful," Frances wrote. She held her breath to avoid the odors as they treated burns, boils, infected eyes, gangrenous feet, and abscesses.

Back to Chhatarpur, the DeVols met the daily surgery demand for as long as their energy held out.

Turn Ye Northward

Just weeks before the DeVols returned from furlough, the state of Vindhya Pradesh with Rewa as capital was absorbed into Madhya Pradesh, India's largest state, with Bhopal as its capital. Also there were profound changes in the church.

Some Christian converts had returned to Hinduism in the Bilwar and Dhamora areas, including Khub Chand, who had been a Christian for eighteen years. God had used him to open up village after village, and his reversion shook the evangelistic policy of the mission to its very foundations, sending the missionaries to their knees. They were in the process of devising a five-year plan, which would set the church free from the mission and allow some of the missionary personnel to answer calls for all-India work. The Robinsons were already in Delhi and Anna Nixon in Jhansi. When the United Mission to Nepal was inaugurated March 18, 1954, Everett Cattell, mission superintendent, had taken an active part in the formation of its constitution, and the mission council supported this move both in prayer and with finances.

These changes dominated table conversations at the end of 1956 as, on December 9, Ezra in his morning devotions read

Deuteronomy 2:3: "Ye have compassed this mountain long enough: turn you *northward*."

"Does this mean we should go to Nepal?" Ezra wrote in his diary that day.

A "Sambar" Feast and a Time of Remembering at Christmas

Three letters from Priscilla and one from Patricia in the United States had awaited the DeVols on their arrival, and every week another letter came from each of them. In spite of the busy days in the hospital, both Ezra and Frances found time to answer each of the girls' letters every week, giving special attention to problems they mentioned, and sharing spiritual insights from their daily devotions and concerns about the work.

At Christmas, with Linden Cole of Oregon and mission board representatives Chester Stanley and Ralph Comfort present to help in the formation of the new five-year plan, the DeVols were kept busy entertaining guests. To get meat for a Christmas feast, the men went for a hunt. Forty village "beaters" agreed to go through the jungle making subdued noises so that the animals would come out into an open clearing where the hunters could see them.

Joe and Phil went along with the men, for they already were schooled in the laws of the jungle. They were alert to the sound of rustling grass, the snap of a twig, or a low growl. They could identify pug marks on the river bank and the distant "whoop-whoop" of monkeys. They knew enough to look out for a tiger, leopard, or bear when birds began to flit about and chirp in a certain way, or when they heard a frightened bark of a deer.

The guests watched with fascination as the black bucks and *sambars* (elk) came out into the open, and Ezra, Milton Coleman, and Joe had chances to use their hunting skills. They brought home enough elk meat to feed the community.

After the usual Christmas feast and program with all the missionaries and guests present, the DeVols spent a quiet Christmas Eve at home, missing Patricia and Priscilla more than ever. Letters would soon come telling them that Pat and Pris in the U.S.A. were having a wonderful Christmas with their Uncle Charles and Aunt Leora DeVol and family. Meanwhile in India, the DeVol family felt the need of doing something to bring Pat and Pris close. So they got out the pictures they had taken on the trip home from India and on their recent furlough in the U.S.A.

There was a picture of the SS *Arcadia*, on which they had sailed out of Bombay on June 18, 1955, past Aden, and through the Red Sea to Cairo. As they walked around the Pyramids, a beggar pestered them for bakshish until Ezra tried to brush him aside.

"I'll put a curse on you!" he shouted.

Ezra turned his back and then suddenly dropped and broke his movie camera.

The pictures the DeVols showed from that point on were slides. There was the Sphynx, the Rock of Gibraltar, and sights up the coast to England.

Only one thing marred that part of a beautiful trip—a confused definition of worldliness as expressed in two of its symbols. The first was lipstick. Pat and Pris, who had been away from home in boarding school for six years, had been in the habit of making their own decisions on many such issues.

"I really don't think lipstick has anything to do with salvation, and I don't think it says I'm a wild person," said Pris.

Pat looked on the use of lipstick as a mere symbol of joining her generation as a woman.

"Dad wears his mustache, and I also want to look well-groomed," she reasoned.

On shipboard this matter became an issue as Dr. DeVol, an Ohio Quaker, visualized the reaction of church members in America as they met his daughters wearing lipstick—a thing he himself did not approve. He requested Pat and Pris to remove it, and this caused tension between the generations.

The other issue was dancing. One day as Pat and Pris were in the lounge enjoying the band, they noticed when the tempo of the music changed and people moved onto the dance floor. Knowing the family attitude toward dancing, Pat and Pris moved toward the door to go out, and as they did so, Pat looked back at the dancers, thinking: *I don't need that in my life. Those dancers don't look all that happy. Their faces look like masks.*

Just then their father came by. He assumed that Pat and Pris had been attending the dance, and fearing that they might be tempted to turn their backs on all that he held dear—the

Bible, prayer, and commitment to God—he put his foot down. Aware of what they would see in the U.S.A. where they would soon have to face life entirely on their own, he felt he owed it to them now to hold up standards. So he took each of them by an arm and walked them to their cabin.

"You are not going to dance!" he ordered.

Pat was so angry that she wept and went back out on deck and stood looking out over the dark waves. Feeling deeply misunderstood and frustrated with no opportunity to explain, she ached for a sense of her father's trust which she felt she deserved. She stayed out so long that she caught a cold that ruined her sight-seeing tour of Westminster Abbey, the Tower of London, Windsor Castle, and other sights during their four-day stopover in England.

"I don't think your father understood you," Frances explained as she talked the incident over with the girls later. "But you know he wants the right thing for you, and you know what that is."

This comforted Pat not at all. "Yes," she agreed, "he wants what is right, but taking time to understand would have helped."

Reflecting on the evening later, Pris said, "For the time being it made a difference in our relationship."

By the time they reached the U.S.A., they found cultural changes that rendered these issues insignificant. The hurt, however, took time to heal. Unfortunately, the father was not aware of his daughters' feelings or of the struggle of Pat to make her father feel proud of her. She kept listening for expressions of love and trust she did not hear. Twelve years later, when her father came home with the threat of blindness, Pat determined to put all resentment behind her, forgive him, and tell him how much she loved him. When she did that, she felt a new sense of peace. Complete release, however, came years later when the father was made aware of his misunderstanding and was able to talk it out with his daughter.

From London, the DeVols sailed on the 82,000-ton *SS Queen Elizabeth*, the largest ship in the world at that time, and arrived in New York July 12.

Settling in Marion, Indiana, for furlough, Patricia and Priscilla entered Marion College, Joe and Phil attended a nearby school, and Ezra and Frances began deputation tours as time allowed. Ezra also was given the opportunity to spend six months at Mayo Clinic learning new surgical techniques. He attended seminars and lectures, observed operations and diagnostic procedures, and spent most of his time in orthopedic, plastic, and genitourinary surgery. He shared his India experience with other visiting doctors from all parts of the world. A group of Christian doctors also met regularly for prayer and Bible study and challenged each other spiritually.

Dr. DeVol faithfully attended the meetings of the American College of Surgeons, and, while in New York at a meeting in 1956, he was made a Fellow of the International College of Surgeons.

Having to be away from home for these courses and for deputation work, Ezra's furlough time with his family was limited, but he finally did get home in time to hear Pris play her violin in the area performance of the *Messiah* at Huntington, and to celebrate Christmas together. They were all keenly aware that it would be the last such opportunity for a long time.

As pictures of Colorado and Wyoming flashed on the screen, the DeVols recalled their last few months with Pat and Pris in America. That summer Dr. DeVol attended a meeting of the Evangelical Friends Alliance in Denver and visited the Navigators in Colorado Springs. The whole family went along and enjoyed the beauties of the Rocky Mountains. They celebrated Phil's birthday in Towgotee, Wyoming, where they listened to the wind in the pines and the roar of the mountain stream under a brilliant, starry sky. They visited Yellowstone Park, and the pictures of the bear, deer, elk, and the geysers were fantastic. They showed pictures of Dragon's Mouth, Mud Volcanos, Yellowstone Lake, and Cleopatra's Needles, where they stopped for family prayer, reading Psalm 36.

Visas to return to India came at the end of August, and travel was booked on the world's second largest ship at that time, the *SS Queen Mary*. Pris started her nurses' training at White Cross Hospital in Columbus; Ezra, Frances, Joe, and Phil went to Sunnyslope to pack; and Pat, on her father's 47th birthday, left the family for Marion College to continue her teacher's training.

Before they all separated, the father had good advice for his daughters: "Remember if you date someone who is not a Christian and you think it's your duty to win him to the Lord, it's a trap. God loves him more than you do, and it's not your duty to do that."

This was the saddest separation the DeVol family had experienced, even sadder than 1940 in China. There was something so final about this one as all at once Pat and Pris, who had not been separated throughout the first nineteen years of their lives, dressing alike, sharing life together, were now going their separate ways from each other, and also from their parents, who in just a few days would be on the other side of the world.

"The Escolmes are your guardians," Father explained as they all drove Pris to Columbus, "but that does not change anything, for a letter will reach us in seven days and get back to you in seven days. We are not giving up our parenthood."

They were all misty-eyed when they said goodbye. Had it not been for friends, the Escolmes especially, and Uncle Charles and Aunt Leora DeVol to fill the gaps, it would have been even more difficult.

In the DeVols' Chhatarpur living room that Christmas night of 1956, the memories of that last year together came to an end with the pictures, but they had brought Pat and Pris very near. Ezra and Frances took time to write to the girls to tell them about the Christmas evening.

When Frances wrote her mother about it, she added, "If I think ahead to six years without them, it hurts too deeply."

The next six years of the DeVols' second term as missionaries in India would see the girls through their training and into their professions—Pris as nurse and Pat as teacher. There would be many times when they would long for the privilege of running home. They did run to each other, and on meeting the first time after their separation, they wept as they realized they each had bought and were wearing a dress of the same rust color. Yet how their lives were changing! Before the DeVols could get home again, Priscilla would be married to Tom Cox and be the mother of two children, Stephenie Ann and William Walter. Patricia would have taught school three years in Greenford, Ohio.

A stopover at Windsor
Castle on the way
home—Joe, Pat, and
Frances, 1955

The first furlough—in
Indian dress

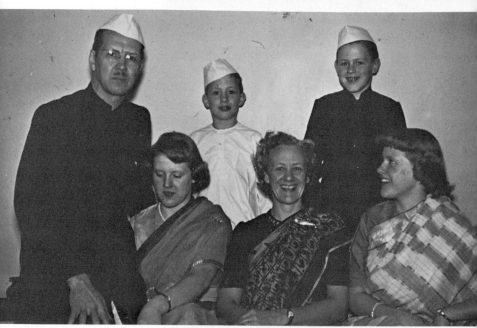

Pat and Pris, freshmen in
Marion College, 1955-1956

Furlough 1955-1956—reunited with Hodgin relatives (top) in Michigan and DeVol relatives in Ohio. DeVol brothers and families (below) near Sunnyslope.

Learning to walk again after polio. Vishal (above right) finds home and food at the Christian Hospital.

Joe held the flashlight for Baldeo's (right) operation. Philip takes Kathy Hess for a ride in a tonga.

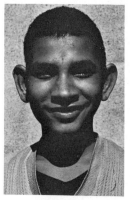

Dr. Grace Jones Singh, who opened a bazaar clinic after serving 25 years at the Christian Hospital, returned to help in emergencies, as here with Sosan Mategaonker.

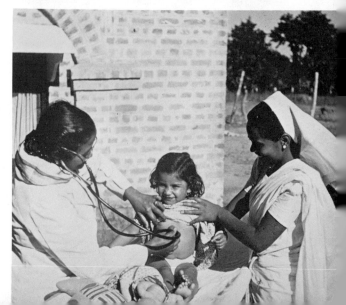

Thakur Singh and his wife, Sikhs in Chhatarpur, welcome the DeVols' return to India even though the weather is unusually warm.

Early morning picnics at a nearby lake were refreshing.

With skills learned from their father, Joe and Phil brought back a *nilgay*, enough meat to feed the community.

9 "Some through the Fire"

"They will fight against you but will not overcome you, for I am with you and will rescue you," declares the LORD.
Jeremiah 1:19 NIV

More Staff Needed

For seven months, Dr. DeVol was the only physician in the Chhatarpur Christian Hospital. As the number of patients increased, he had to give up his weekly Amarmau "milk route" clinics. The beds in the wards were filled, and cots were added, increasing the bed capacity from fifty-eight to sixty-five. In addition, some patients spread their blankets on the floor.

From miles around, missionary patients crowded into the DeVol home. At times Frances felt overcome trying to keep up with family responsibilities and a house full of guests, in addition to the hospital demands. Her hours on duty were inflexible because there were only three other nurses to care for both day and night duty.

"Once you begin the practice of medicine, there is no way to stop it," Frances observed.

In spite of the heavy schedule, Ezra still found time for his Sunday-after-church bicycle ride with the boys, and one day when the sky was clear and the air cool and brisk, they took off through the jungle to a beautiful lake.

"I still remember Dad showing us how to build a lean-to," Phil commented years later. "He showed us the types and shapes of sticks to use and how to place them together to make a solid little house on the shore of the lake. I have done that with my own kids since."

155

Woodstock School in Landour opened again in February 1957, and Joe and Phil had to pack their trunks. Joe was going into the eighth grade and Phil into fourth. They had been out of boarding school for two years and dreaded leaving home again. They both felt it unmanly to cry and determined not to do so, but their resolutions were washed away in a torrent of tears as they left their parents, Indian friends, and the horses in Chhatarpur. Woodstock School's food and unheated buildings in wintry Landour momentarily obliterated the memories of the happier side of boarding life.

"It hurts to send them off," commented Frances. "They've been so helpful."

Letters from boarding soon arrived, bringing happy news that Joe was president of the Christian Endeavor and Phil had been elected to serve on the elementary school senate.

If the DeVols wondered who would hold the flashlight during operations in Joe's place, they did not have long to wait. Their house was again filled with missionary patients from different areas, and they found another "Joe."

Dr. DeVol, not feeling so well himself, stopped one evening at Norma Freer's house to see some missionary patients as he came home from the hospital. The two missionaries were sitting hunched over on the sofa, their hands folded tightly across their stomachs. As the doctor leaned wearily against the mantle of the fireplace for support while he listened to their symptoms, one of the patients said, "We can't seem to get on top of this intestinal trouble, Doc."

The doctor groaned and, after a brief silence, answered, "Well, if I knew what to give you, I'd take it myself!"

Healing began with a good laugh.

Joseph (Joe) and Ethelyn Watson came 120 miles whenever they needed a physical check-up. They knew Dr. DeVol not only as a loyal friend but also as an excellent surgeon. More than once, he had performed surgery in the nick of time and saved them from serious problems. Joe Watson wrote about one of these visits to the hospital in Chhatarpur:

> I was staying overnight in Chhatarpur planning to leave before daylight. Doc was working late on a problem operation scheduled for the next morning. He was drawing diagrams, cutting paper, fitting for the skin transplant and

grafting. There was a sudden rush of footsteps. Emergency!

A patient, a young woman recovering from an operation, was slipping away fast. Doc grabbed two flashlights, his emergency bag, and ran across the hospital grounds. I followed closely. I had to; he had the flashlights!

She has gone, died, is all I could think. No reflex, no eye movement, no pulse. Doc's orders were exact. I held the flashlights, keeping the lights on wherever he ordered— the syringe, the bottle— then to that spot where Doc placed his finger. Doc injected right into the heart, praying aloud, calling the patient to respond, calling me to direct the light here, there!

As he injected the needle, he said, "This will raise the dead."

A split second of intense silence, then a flicker, a response, a pulse, and finally a strong healthy beat!

Doc gave a few orders to the nurses, and we walked back to the house. He went back to planning for tomorrow's operation on a young boy who had fallen into a fire a few years earlier. His badly burned neck had healed over, but his chin was pulled to his chest. Now, years later, they brought him to Doc to do what the family called the impossible. To release the skin so the boy could raise his head, live, speak, laugh, and play involved surgery, skin transplants, and preparing for countless unanticipated problems.

Doc was up long before dawn. It was five a.m. when I heard his low whistle. That meant he had already finished his devotions and more research in his medical journals and was ready to go into the work of the day, and that urgent operation.

Dr. Grace Jones Singh, more than anyone, seemed to realize the pressure on the DeVols as they carried the hospital on alone. She came to express her concern. She might even have consented to come back to work, but she had already started her own clinic, and since she could control the hours, her blood pressure had returned to normal. It seemed clear that the Lord's answer for the Christian Hospital lay elsewhere, and the whole mission became involved in the search.

A Flood of Light

Working without proper light added to the strain of every operation in the Christian Hospital, but even this was used toward a miraculous end. One day a critically wounded man was brought into the hospital by the superintendent of police. The patient, shot through the shoulder with a shotgun, was badly torn up and very frightened. The whole staff flew into action. The operating room was soon in order with an Aladdin lamp and two flashlights. As usual, Dr. DeVol, ready to operate, bowed his head and prayed. The superintendent of police, standing there to watch the whole procedure, gasped.

After the tense drama was over and the patient was wheeled to his room, the superintendent of police grasped the hand of Samson Huri Lal, the male nurse.

"When the doctor prayed, did you see that light?" he asked.

"What light?"

"Didn't you notice, when he bowed his head?"

"He always prays before he operates," Samson explained.

"But, didn't you see it? As he prayed, the whole room was flooded with light!"

"I guess I had my eyes shut," Samson said politely.

"Oh, Sir, you should have seen it anyway. It was a brilliant light, and it filled the room. I felt the presence of the Lord there!"

Samson thought about this for a long time afterwards. *Surely the Lord is with us*, he thought, *and may He protect me from thinking of this prayer as a routine ritual.*

Quite literally, the whole hospital compound was flooded with light on May 1, 1957, when the electric current was switched on at noon and stayed on until 11:00 p.m. That night, alone in the bungalow since Frances had just gone to the hills to be with the boys, Ezra stayed up late enjoying the fans, playing the phonograph, and reading.

"Adequate light has changed the whole atmosphere," he commented. "It's lifted my spirits amazingly. I suppose when we get to heaven it will be something like this when we will look back and recall how we had spent our lives in shadows with occasional illuminated periods."

One of the shadows of this period had been the lack of adequate staff, but this situation also was suddenly lighted up as Dr. D. W. Mategaonker, a young graduate of Vellore Medical College, arrived the same day as the electricity. During the next two months, five more nurses and another Vellore Medical College graduate joined the staff. Dr. Shrisunder, a classmate of Dr. Mategaonker, was also a committed Christian and eager to learn.

This increase and stabilization of the hospital staff could have come at no better time, for the mission's five-year-plan had just gone into effect through which the work in Bundelkhand was shifted from a mission-centered to a church-centered strategy. The American Friends Mission was planning to deploy educational and evangelistic missionary personnel elsewhere, allowing Indian leadership to take over. The medical work, however, was to remain in charge of the mission and was considered a "listening post" in Bundelkhand to give encouragement to the Indian church as it progressed to becoming indigenous.

Everett Cattell had been called home to be general superintendent of his denomination, and in his place the mission board appointed Dr. W. E. DeVol as mission superintendent of the India mission. The Cattells moved in with the DeVols to spend the last few days of their stay in Chhatarpur, and Milton and Rebecca Coleman moved from Amarmau to Chhatarpur into the house vacated by the Cattells.

The Court Case and Other Trials

There was expectancy in the air and all seemed ready for advance as Indian leaders accepted the challenge of responsibility, as the hospital—in better condition than it had ever been—demonstrated the love of Christ to an increasingly larger community, as the Cattells—assuming the leadership in the United States—would be in a position to interpret India to the mission board, and as Ezra picked up the reins of leadership in the American Friends Mission.

On July 29 as formal farewells for the Cattells came to an end, the people went home anticipating one last chance to honor them for their more than twenty years in India on their departure from Chhatarpur on July 31. All the people had departed from the farewell tea, and darkness had settled over the city, when there was an insistent knock on the door, and Everett Cattell, answering it, looked into the face of an anxious court official. Once inside, he spoke in a hushed voice.

"Cattell Sahib, a warrant has been issued for your arrest. I urge you to leave tonight before it is served on you. No one must ever know that I told you."

Piece by piece the story came to light. A disgruntled Christian, Pyare Lal Brown, hurt in his childhood by a rather harsh judgment against his father, had allowed bitterness to twist the whole focus of his life on harassing the mission. There had been times when prayer for that man seemed almost prevailing, but he managed somehow to resist the conviction and end up more opposed than ever. Like flies attracted to honey, other disgruntled people sought him for leadership, and he used them, as convenient, to embarrass and attack the mission. His most recent victory had been won through threats as he bullied the Christians in Nowgong into giving him a large church wedding. He had chosen an evangelist's daughter as his bride. This evangelist, Itwari Lal, had been dismissed from mission service and brought under church discipline for distortion of the Christian message in his preaching in Hindu villages. Called to account for his actions by the ministry and oversight body—consisting of Everett Cattell, Stuti Prakash, and Samson Huri Lal—Itwari Lal refused to appear and consequently was dropped from church membership. This gave Pyare Lal the golden opportunity for which he had been looking. Just as his chief target, the mission superintendent, was about to escape from India, Pyare Lal incited his father-in-law to sue the ministry and oversight body for defamation of character. This was a criminal offense.

"You know our Indian courts," the official reasoned with Everett Cattell. "Who knows how long you will be held here to deal with these false charges! I urge you to flee."

Everett Cattell did not take long to decide. Thinking of his twenty years of ministry in India and of the two men charged with him, he said, "I believe it is right that I leave at the time I have set. If the warrant has not come by then, I will proceed, but I will not run away."

The next morning, another official knocked at the same door and delivered the warrant.

Homeless and packed, but unable to leave, Everett Cattell proceeded as far as Jhansi. Catherine and Mary stayed there with Anna Nixon, and Everett returned to Chhatarpur to stand trial with the other men. After the second hearing of August 6, he took a quick trip to Allahabad for a meeting he had scheduled earlier. He had hardly boarded the train when a cablegram reached the DeVols from Chester Stanley about the tragic death of the Cattells' son, daughter-in-law, and baby granddaughter: "David, Jane, and baby killed in auto accident."

Ezra jumped in the ambulance and tried to pursue the train, but he was too late. The next day, he and Frances met the returning train in Harpalpur, and taking Everett to Jhansi, they broke the news to Catherine and Mary and brought them back to Chhatarpur.

The church mourned with them for David, Jane, and Lisa, but those of the opposition in the trial stayed away.

Khub Chand, a convert of eighteen years, had reverted to Hinduism and had agreed to be one of Pyare Lal Brown's chief witnesses. He, too, stayed away at first, but as he recalled the wonderful days he had shared in the jungle with David, he could not bear to be quiet and finally went to see Catherine. When he saw the tears and heartache of the woman who had taught him to read the Bible and mark the promises with red and the warnings with blue, he also wept.

"I'm coming back, Memsahib," he promised, "and I'll do the work of your son here in Bundelkhand."

Later, on the witness stand, as Khub Chand was called to speak, he told the truth.

"Whatever happened to you?" one of the women asked him afterwards.

He replied: "Do you remember Balaam? He wanted to curse God's people but he could not. It was the same with me. God shut my mouth and I had to tell the truth."

Pyare Lal Brown had lost his chief witness, but he had others, and the church was lacerated, humiliated, and heart-broken as the wounds went deep. The judge decided to hear the case in full. Ezra laid claim to the promise of the Lord in Exodus 23:7: "I will not justify the wicked."

Other trials besides the one in court added to the distress of these days. First Rebecca Coleman, and then Frances DeVol came down with typhoid fever, and grief weighed heavily upon everyone.

"You must continue moving," Ezra urged Everett as he treated him for hives. "You already have your tickets to For-mosa [Taiwan], and whether you can go or not, surely Catherine and Mary should proceed. The minute you get free from this trial, you can follow."

The whole mission council agreed, and on August 26, Catherine and Mary left for Taiwan.

In their beds, Frances and Rebecca prayed and encouraged others to pray.

"We cannot depend upon Hindu lawyers or the Hindu judges for victory," Frances noted. "We can only trust the Lord to use them for His purposes. Should the case go against us, the church is doomed, for how can they ever again discipline a member?"

As the court hearings came to an end, those on trial and the missionaries with them shared promises.

Ezra said, "I feel as if the pavement under me is solid rock as I read, 'I am with thee to deliver thee.' " (Jeremiah 1:19)

Frances from her bed read 2 Chronicles 20:17: "You will not have to fight this battle. Take up your positions; stand firm and see the deliverance the LORD will give you .... Do not be afraid; do not be discouraged. Go out to face them *tomorrow*, and the LORD will be with you."

The next day was the day of decision. Everett Cattell came to morning prayer with Jeremiah 40:4 as his verse for the day: "*This day* I am freeing you from the chains on your wrists . . . . Go wherever you please."

Samson Huri Lal came in followed by Stuti Prakash, both eager to share their promises. Samson's was Psalm 31:8: "You have not handed me over to the enemy but have set my feet in a spacious place."

Stuti Prakash's was Psalm 55:18: "He ransoms me unharmed from the battle waged against me, even though many oppose me."

Ezra accompanied the three men to the court to hear the final decision. Judge Goswami took plenty of time to appear, and when he finally came into the court room, Ezra anxiously noted it would be close to impossible that day, over the kind of roads they would have to travel, to catch the 5:00 p.m. Calcutta train at Satna, ninety-two miles from Chhatarpur. At 2:00 p.m., in the exasperating leisurely pace of the Orient, the judge entered and went through the usual formalities. In due course, he announced that the case was dismissed.

As soon as courtesy allowed, Ezra and Everett left the courtroom, dashed back to pick up Everett's suitcase, and praising the Lord for the fulfillment of every promise He had given them, made the train.

Negotiating the twists and turns of the dusty road on the way back home, Ezra, alone, suddenly felt the weight of the load that had been left on his shoulders.

"Moses my servant is dead. Now then you . . . . No one will be able to stand up against you all the days of your life. As I was with Moses, so I will be with you; I will never leave you or forsake you." (Joshua 1:1,5)

How Ezra needed those words of encouragement as he returned to Chhatarpur! Almost immediately he had to put Rebecca Coleman in the hospital with a very high white count and vague pain that suggested perforation of the bowel following her typhoid fever. Resolutely he fought for her life and saved her.

Next came Esther Hess, whose baby was already overdue. Her blood pressure shot up, and he could not hear any heartbeat of the baby. Inducing labor, he and Frances fought and prayed to save the life of Esther, as she nearly died on delivering her stillborn son. Would tragedies never cease in 1957?

As everyone expected, the court case was not over. Before the month had ended, the opposition appealed it to the sessions court. Though he was in no way chargeable, Ezra appeared along with the two men at the first hearing.

"Why are you here?" asked the man on the bench. "You are not involved in this case."

"I stand with the accused," said the doctor, and he continued to stand there as the case dragged on from court to court.

The opposition's nine lawyers who sought to sabotage the church and mission were frustrated by the keen defense of the Hindu lawyer who took up the cause of the church. Shiv Narain Khare was impressed with the strong, decisive character of Dr. DeVol and began to understand the power of the promises in the Bible. Born on Christmas day, Mr. Khare was drawn to a study of the life of the Lord Jesus Christ. He began to read the Bible himself and bring promises to bear on the case he had undertaken.

"The LORD knoweth the way of the righteous; but the way of the wicked shall perish" (Psalm 1:6), Mr. Khare wrote to Dr. DeVol on May 30, 1959, when it appeared that the end had come and that the church had won. The case was appealed again, this time to the High Court in Jabalpur, and there for many more months it proceeded until November 21, 1960, when the oppositions' money was exhausted. By that time the falseness of their charges was thoroughly exposed, and the church throughout India rejoiced as the judge's decision in favor of Stuti Prakash and Samson Huri Lal became final.

The Death of a Cow

Because of the tremendous victory won in court by the Friends church in Chhatarpur and the fame of the lawyer, Shiv Narain Khare, a nearby mission came to Dr. DeVol for help when one of their missionaries was jailed because of the death of a cow. The Kratofil family in Guna daily breathed the anti-Christian hostility of that town, but not until the day the cow ran into the missionary bungalow gate and broke its neck did they know the depth of the Hindu animosity toward Christians.

An ugly crowd gathered, shouting, "Cow slaughter!" and the few Christians living in small homes ran into the larger home of the missionaries for safety. The Indian evangelist failed to get inside, and the crowd beat him mercilessly, injuring him for life, and then set fire to his house.

With all doors locked, the people in the missionaries' house took refuge on the second floor, and Paul Kratofil, to frighten away the mob, fired two shots into the air. The police came and did some firing, too, and a boy was wounded. They rescued the missionaries in a van, but Paul Kratofil was charged with cruelty to animals under Section 428 and was accused of attempting to murder the boy.

Dr. DeVol and Shiv Narain Khare went to Guna, praying and searching the Bible for promises as they went. In the charge of attempted murder, the lawyer caught the false witnesses immediately, as there was no possible way the boy could have been shot from the window of the missionaries' home.

The cow slaughter charge was more difficult and more serious. Lawyer Khare took time to study it. The gate was broken in such a way as to suggest the cow had caught its horns in it. Two eyewitnesses had gone on record that the cow died instantly. A veterinarian surgeon, however, supported the charges that the missionary had beaten the cow to death with bamboo rods.

"He is lying, but how can I prove it?" Lawyer Khare pondered.

Dr. DeVol supplied the evidence he needed. "Instant death must be caused by brain damage or a broken neck," the doctor explained. "Even when a larger animal is shot and mortally wounded, it may run hundreds of yards and live a long time. A tiger shot through the heart was able to jump up in front of a *machan* (platform in a tree) three times before he collapsed. It seems clear that the cause of the cow's instant death had to be either direct brain injury or a neck injury damaging the medulla oblongata."

"Which could not be caused by bamboo rods!" commented Lawyer Khare.

Back in court, Lawyer Khare's questions were so direct that the veterinarian surgeon was forced to change his testimony. The judge, a clever and honest man, immediately saw the situation for exactly what it was and dropped the charges.

"I congratulate you," Dr. DeVol said to his friend as they walked away.

"I don't deserve the credit," Lawyer Khare said. "Your God helped me today."

New Experiences in Surgery for New Doctors

Dr. Mategaonker and Dr. Shrisunder, Indian young men born in the homes of Anglican deacons, were born again under the influence of the Union of Evangelical Students in Vellore. Clifton Robinson, in Vellore to speak at UESI meetings, met these eager young doctors who wanted internship under a surgeon in a place where they could witness for Christ. They had never heard of Chhatarpur far to the north, with different language and culture, but when Cliff told them of Dr. DeVol, they located Chhatarpur on the map and moved there a few months later.

Eager to learn and live, these two young doctors found Dr. DeVol exactly what they wanted as a surgeon and as a Christian. The operating theater became a room for high drama, where their medical understanding expanded through every operation as they drank in knowledge from this experienced son of Drs. George and Isabella DeVol, a man after his parents' own heart in his eagerness to teach what he knew.

Frances did her share of teaching, too, mostly to the nurses, but also to the people. They could not understand her aversion to flies.

"Why do you bother?" they asked. "They don't eat much."

With three doctors and more nurses, the plant was expanded and new operating, sterilizing, and work rooms were added. The hospital received relief supplies to distribute through the dispensaries, including thousands of pounds of dried milk and 150 pounds of cheese. The milk had to be mixed and the cheese given like medicine, cut in finger-size squares, and placed in the mouth. A grateful patient contributed an incubator; the Indo-American agreement made possible the importing of $4,000 worth of new medicines; the mission board and friends sent a new sterilizer, vaporizer, and instruments; a widow of a doctor in Massillon, Ohio, sent instruments for eye operations. This latter gift seemed most providential, as Dr. Mategaonker was sent to Mungeli to take special courses in ophthalmology from a student of Dr. Rambo, the famous doctor written about in *The Apostle of Sight.*

For the first few months, as the young doctors assisted in the surgery scheduled three times a week, they observed a variety of procedures and became aware of facts they had not previously learned.

Miss Leela Cherian, sister of the nurses' matron, Phyllis Das, came from Jabalpur for treatment. Dr. DeVol discovered a tumor about the size and shape of a football. Though there was no blood bank and no time to arrange for a transfusion, the patient was prepared for the operation. After the incision was made, Dr. DeVol realized that he was in for trouble. There was a great deal of bleeding and it seemed impossible to get hold of the large tumor in the pelvis.

Though there had been prayer at the beginning of the operation, the young doctors heard Dr. DeVol praying aloud, "Oh, Lord, show us what to do! Please help us!"

Dr. DeVol quickly walked around to the other side of the operating table, and as soon as he did this, he saw that there was a line of cleavage around the tumor that could be separated. Within five minutes, he had peeled the tumor out of its coverings as one would peel a section out of an orange. The bleeding stopped, and the danger was over.

"When I prayed, the Lord put it in my mind to walk around the table," Dr. DeVol explained.

The two young doctors learned that dependency on the Lord was a very real thing, not just something to talk about. In this case, it not only saved Leela Cherian's life, but renewed her faith and trust in the Lord Jesus Christ.

Parwati was another patient whose life had been saved in 1957 by a cesarean section. She had been torn by a village midwife, was infected, and lost her baby. Dr. DeVol advised her to return to the hospital for her next baby, and she did come but arrived late. Her uterus was already ruptured, and she was in critical condition. The operating room was quickly set in order, and the staff scrubbed and hurried in. In spite of intravenous fluids and plasma, Parwati's blood pressure dropped to zero and the pulse was not palpable at the wrist. She had been typed for transfusion on admission, but in the forty-five minutes that it took to get ready for the operation, a suitable donor could not be found. Needless to say, the situation was desperate.

Dr. DeVol moved fast, delivered the baby, and controlled the bleeding with clamps, preparatory to removing the uterus. Before this was done, however, a large accumulation of blood had to be removed from the abdominal cavity.

"Here is blood," Dr. DeVol exclaimed with sudden insight, "and it's the right type. Let's try citrating it to prevent clotting and then filter it."

A team got busy carrying out his orders and brought back about two pints (1000 cc) of blood. Parwati was immediately auto-transfused, and as the operation proceeded, her blood pressure came up to seventy, then to eighty, and by the end of the operation, it was up to ninety over seventy.

The next day Parwati was sitting up in bed, holding her baby boy. She proceeded to make a rapid recovery. The operating team, including the young doctors, felt that they had witnessed a miracle. Parwati openly confessed her faith in Christ to the nurses, to the hospital evangelist, to other patients, and to her relatives. When she returned home, she began attending church in another mission at Mahoba.

In 1986, Joe Watson in Florida, reading a medical article telling of an unusual and very complicated and involved procedure for reusing a patient's own blood in surgery, commented: "In the 1960s in India, my friend Dr. DeVol used this method in a much simpler way, I am sure, but he saved a life."

Lawyer Shiv Narain Khare came to the hospital for help when his beloved four-year-old daughter was dying. Dr. DeVol, at the little girl's bedside, found her chest tightly bound. He ripped the bandages off and injected intercardiac adrenalin and coramine, and then gave artificial respiration. As he suspected, it was already too late. Lawyer Khare was overcome with grief. Having come to love him through his masterful handling of the trial, Dr. DeVol grieved with him. Suddenly he felt a strong urge to kneel down and pray for the little girl. *This is useless; I do not have faith for a resurrection*, he argued within himself. The conviction became overpowering, however, and not wanting to hinder God's will in any way, he knelt down by her bedside and prayed.

Nothing changed, and as Dr. DeVol left the home, he felt frustrated and foolish. He later learned that Lawyer Khare regarded this act as a demonstration of great faith, and even more than that, as a symbol of genuine love for his little girl and for his family.

The relationship of Dr. DeVol and Lawyer Khare was no longer just lawyer-client, or doctor-patient. A friendship resulted and a channel of deep Christian witness flowed from this obedience. The young doctors were impressed with this depth of caring.

It was not surprising that Shiv Narain Khare sought help from Dr. DeVol, but what surprised everyone was the appearance of the opposition lawyer with his nephew Dinesh, who had been hit in the head with a stone thrown by the lawyer's own son. The doctors in the Christian Hospital appreciated this opportunity to graciously hold out healing hands to this relative of a man who had in court thoroughly denounced missions and Christian institutions.

Another surprise came when the government hospital surgeon in Nowgong chose the Christian Hospital as the place for his own surgery. He had not been friendly with Christians, but the Christian Hospital doctors hoped they might be able to meet his physical needs and also minister to him spiritually. The operation went well, but afterwards, to their horror, infection set in and there were complications such as were common in other hospitals.

The government hospital surgeon, half delirious with a temperature of 104, said, "If I had wanted to get an infection, I could have gone to a lot of other places, but I came here because I hoped I would not have any complications."

Dr. DeVol was overcome with shame and anxiety. As he worried over this, Philippians 4:6 came to his mind: "In nothing be anxious." He found himself resisting this with the thought, *How can I help being on edge when so much is at stake?*

The still, small voice that he recognized as the voice of the Lord said, "All right, then, worry about everything. Yes, everything."

"No, Lord, I don't want to worry about everything. I just want your help in worrying about this."

His ludicrous logic was not only convicting but amusing, and turning the whole thing over to the Lord, he went for breakfast and whistled his way over to the hospital for rounds. He went first to the room of the government surgeon.

"Good morning, Dr. DeVol," greeted the cheerful patient, normal in temperature and greatly improved in both health and disposition.

Dr. DeVol shared this whole experience with Drs. Mategaonker and Shrisunder, and, laughing heartily, they were drawn into deeper kinship.

The new doctors appreciated Dr. DeVol's openness as he shared from his rich and varied experiences. They listened well as he taught them:

> Harmony is not a luxury in the operating room; it is an absolute essential. Wholehearted teamwork—between surgeon and anesthetist, scrub nurse and circulating nurse, the nurse in charge of the operating room and others in responsible positions—gives security to the patient.
>
> In emergencies, speed is sometimes essential, but usually the best results come from good, thorough work. I have visited Mayo Clinic in America, and I have been impressed with the leisurely way operations are performed there. They do not put emphasis on speed, but give meticulous attention to detail and make adequate incisions to care for the problem. One of the doctors there told me, "We make speed when that is not our primary aim."
>
> We try not to be too insistent on patients' staying in the hospital or having necessary operations or treatments. We explain the situation fully and let them be absolutely free to decide their course of action without persuasion beyond helpful encouragement from us.
>
> We want patients to see the love of God in us and not a coldly scientific health organization. I frequently ask the Lord to help me smile at my patients. I don't want to ever regard them as problems. I want to see them as personalities who want love and understanding, and as people who deep in their hearts want to see Jesus.
>
> Another point I would like to make is the importance of keeping good records. I don't know how to emphasize this, but I hope you will never forget it.

Dr. DeVol did not have to wait long to find a way of emphasizing the importance of keeping records. One day, he was called into court to give witness in a case where serious charges were made against a Mohammedan girl on whom he had operated. Her relatives were hounding her out of their society with the strong accusation that she had been in the hospital for an abortion. Dr. DeVol had good records and was able to trace her problem to cervical polyps. There was no evidence of the products of conception. When this record was presented to the judge, the young woman was cleared of the false charges and restored to her family with honor.

The two young doctors were married in 1958. Dr. Shrisunder's wedding took place January 10, and his bride came from his own language area. Dr. Mategaonker chose a Chhatarpur nurse, Sosan Singh, daughter of Lachhman Singh, who had worked in Bundelkhand dispensaries for many years. They were married May 12. A new house was built for each of these new families.

As operations increased and the hospital expanded and the younger doctors began to take turns at surgery, Dr. DeVol's work grew lighter. Regular staff prayer meetings and Bible study became very lively, and Dr. Mategaonker began another such study on Saturday night for patients and workers in the hospital. With the staff becoming more professional, Dr. DeVol added a staff medical meeting in which they discussed operative cases and studied the latest developments in medicine. This challenged the new doctors also to have something to share. Together, they agreed that the purpose of the Christian Hospital should be to set a standard of loving personal care and a more specialized service than could be found generally, especially in rural areas. They agreed: "To give medicine without giving encouragement is to give but half a dose."

Pressure from his father to come back home caused Dr. Shrisunder to put in his resignation. He did not leave, however, until late 1959 after Dr. Mategaonker had finished his first three months' training in ophthalmology and his wife Sosan had completed a special graduate course in nursing. It seemed quite clear that Dr. Mategaonker purposed to stay for many years. He did, in fact, stay twenty-six. He became a strong support not only in the hospital but in the church as well.

"Now Turn North"

Water shortage was so severe in 1958 that the hospital was closed in June. All except the dispensary staff took vacations, and then came back in full force to begin work July 1. Later that year, an electric pump was installed and for the first time there was enough power coming through to run it.

The DeVols went to the hills early as Joe was graduating from the eighth grade on May 30 and his father was the commencement speaker. That year had started off well for the boys, who had accompanied their parents and others to Vellore in South India for the annual Evangelical Fellowship of India conference where Corrie ten Boom, Dr. Akbar Haqq, and Clifton Robinson were among the speakers. Joe, followed by Phil, had gone forward in one night meeting and made a public commitment to the Lord. This had made a difference in their school life as they took a lead in spiritual things as well as in sports and student government. They did well in their school work and were proud to be among Woodstock's 450 students representing fourteen nationalities.

Taking time to attend the annual Landour Medical Conference, the DeVols heard Jonathan Lindell of the United Mission to Nepal speak of their need for a surgeon. Later, on November 16, 1958, two telegrams came followed by an official letter requesting them to come to Kathmandu.

As Ezra pondered the implications of this invitation, he opened his Bible and turned first to Deuteronomy 2:3: "Turn ye northward." This verse, marked and dated December 9, 1956, had impressed him deeply when he first heard of the missionary challenge to Nepal. Since that time, concern for Nepal had grown in the hearts of both Ezra and Frances, and the invitation to Kathmandu seemed providential. However, in his regular reading that morning, Ezra got quite a different message from Jeremiah 2:36: "Why gaddest thou about so much to change thy way?" He felt confused and realized he needed the help of the mission council. Previously, he had prayed for the solution to a problem coming up in the council, and the still, small voice had said: *I'm not going to reveal the solution to you alone. I'm going to reveal it to the council tomorrow.* The same seemed to be true at this time, and in ten days, the DeVols had received written approval from all the Friends missionaries on the field to go to Kathmandu for a month.

The need in Nepal was tremendous. All the missionaries had heard of the people who came for treatment, finding their way over rugged mountains, traveling ten or fifteen days, only to be turned back because there was no qualified surgeon in the country. They all felt that Dr. Mategaonker and Dr. Shrisunder could manage the Christian Hospital for a month.

Joe and Phil, home from boarding, dreaded leaving Chhatarpur.

"My best friends are here, and we play tennis together," Joe complained. He also liked working in the hospital, watching operations, typing reports, and developing the X rays.

As for Phil, he had a *dhobi*'s light brown horse for a pet. Its tail was whacked off, its back legs knocked together, and its back was too weak to support a rider, but Phil greeted it each morning and said good night to it each evening. He paid for its food from his allowance and was faithful in rubbing it down. He hated to leave his borrowed friend.

Nevertheless, on January 18, 1959, all the DeVols took the train to Patna and flew the next afternoon to Kathmandu, arriving at 4:00 p.m. in chilly zero centigrade weather.

"It's so much like China," Ezra commented, feeling instantly at home.

The DeVols felt the tremendous challenge in this Kathmandu Valley where missionary work had been started less than five years earlier and where converts were still threatened with a six-year jail term for changing their religion. As they wended their way through the temple-lined streets, the driver suddenly slammed on his brakes to miss a woman who darted out in front of them.

"She's trying to shake the evil spirit she thinks is following her," the driver explained. "Hopefully, we hit him."

"This will be your home," the DeVols were informed as they were ushered into the hospital compound to the former playhouse for the king's children. They kindled a small fire in the stove—which had a chimney poking through the window—and warmed themselves before proceeding to the hospital dining room for supper with the hospital staff.

The next day, they looked out at the surrounding snow-capped ranges up to 20,000 feet.

"Imagine operating and looking up to these snowcapped peaks!" commented Frances.

That morning with Drs. Edgar and Elizabeth Miller, he a cardiologist and she a pediatrician, Dr. DeVol made rounds in the Shanta Bhawan Hospital occupying a former palace. After getting an idea of the scope of the work, Ezra and Frances both went on duty in the operating room. That month they worked all day long, doing five or six operations a day, three days a week, helping some 105 people gain a new lease on life through major and minor surgeries. Even Joe found a challenge in typing reports, and both he and Phil painted the X-ray room.

"The Lord helped us in the ministry in Nepal, and we saw several definite answers to prayer," Ezra noted.

The most vivid answer to prayer that month came for Ram Ratna, who had been thrown to the pavement in a bicycle collision and suffered severe damage to his head. He had been taken to the government hospital where they applied some iodine and sent him home. Four days later, thinking he was going to die, his relatives were taking him to the Bhagmati River so that he could put his feet in the sacred waters on his way to eternity. Someone stopped them and suggested they first take him to Shanta Bhawan Hospital. The fact that they listened and took him was amazing, for they were known to be anti-Christian, anti-American, and pro-Communist. However, as a last resort, they came. Dr. Miller met them in the emergency room and immediately called Dr. DeVol, who, on examining the man, found he was already cyanotic and had no pulse and no blood pressure. Dr. DeVol felt that any attempt to help this dying man probably would only push him over the brink. This might give these people the idea that he had killed the man, and thus might increase their hostility toward the mission.

"What are you going to do for him?" Dr. Miller asked.

"Do for him?" Dr. DeVol replied in amazement. "You can see that he's dying. Anything we would do for him would just finish him off."

"Aren't you going to do *anything*?"

The note of desperation in Dr. Miller's voice started Dr. DeVol praying silently. *Lord, what shall I do?*

Clear guidance came: *Do a lumbar puncture.*

Fully aware of the danger of this procedure for this dying patient, Dr. DeVol acted in obedience to what he felt was God's leading. Immediately he saw color return to the man's face and his blood pressure go up.

Excitedly, Dr. DeVol said to Dr. Miller, "Yes! This man has a reversible condition! Help me find the instruments for surgery and get the team together!"

In the hospital, instruments needed for this kind of surgery were scarce and in poor condition, as such an operation had never before been performed in Nepal. However, the team went to work. They did not wait for much anesthesia, as the man was already unconscious. Dr. DeVol lost no time getting through the skull of the man with a hard, steel Trephine instrument used to bore holes in the skull and a gentle hair-like Gigoli saw used to cut through the bone between the holes in order to do the least possible damage. There, pressing on the brain, he found a blood clot about half the size of an orange, gently took it out, and replaced the portion of the skull that had been removed.

Even while the man was on the operating table, he began to improve. His condition remained critical, and Dr. DeVol stayed by his side for many hours as he teeter-tottered between life and death. Before leaving him for the night at 11:00 p.m., Joe joined him in prayer at the man's bedside. The staff in the dining room also prayed for him.

At home that night, the thought kept coming to the doctor, *What are you going to do if you go over in the morning and find that man dead?* He turned to Habakkuk 3:17 and strengthened his faith:

> Though the fig tree does not bud and there are no grapes on the vines, though the olive crop fails and the fields produce no food, though there are no sheep in the pen and no cattle in the stalls, yet I will rejoice in the LORD, I will be joyful in God my Savior.

The next morning as Dr. DeVol returned to the hospital to check the patient, he found him with normal blood pressure, calling for his family.

The male nurse on duty for the night was so thrilled with this answer to prayer that he kept saying, "What God can do! What God can do!"

The surgical healing was indeed a marvelous demonstration of God's love. It permanently changed this man's and his relatives' attitude toward Christianity and toward those bringing it to their country.

The thrill of seeing a girl with a tubercular spine rise up and walk in eleven days, of relieving the suffering of royalty as well as of a poor woman carried over the mountains in a basket, of witnessing pageantry with cavalry, drummers, and band with King Mahendra in celebration of the first day of spring, of joining in worship on the mission compound with fearless new Christians, of visiting a Christian in jail—all these things made this first month in Nepal one of the happiest of Ezra and Frances' missionary career. As they left, forty-two names appeared on the farewell note of gratitude Shanta Bhawan staff presented to them.

This was the beginning of the DeVol's increasing involvement in the United Mission to Nepal. Though the mission council recommended that they be seconded to UMN for six months each year, the DeVols found it impossible to spare more than a month at a time and not more than three months a year. Dr. DeVol explained:

> We feel a tremendous pull both ways. On the Nepal side of the ledger, we see a land recently opened to the Gospel with one-fifth the number of doctors per capita as India, a lovely climate, and a more aggressive people—a land, to be sure, with different problems from Bundelkhand.
>
> On the Bundelkhand side, we see our own responsibility to the mission board: a hospital needing to be operated on income from fees, depending partly on our presence; a church still to be firmly rooted; and the need yet to build sufficient staff of high-grade professional skill to carry on.

Building Up the Christian Hospital

Trips to Nepal over the next three years were possible because of the steadiness of Dr. D. W. Mategaonker and his willingness to assume responsibility. Sosan, his wife, assisted in the hospital as a nurse. Dr. Shrisunder reluctantly left in late 1959, but Dr.

Mategaonker staggered his training in ophthalmology with the DeVols' trips to Nepal so that one or the other was always present.

When Dr. Mategaonker did his first cataract operation, the patient, wearing her new glasses, was just like a little girl with a new doll. Since one in every five blind people in the world is Indian, Dr. Mategaonker had many eye operations lined up. It was a thrill to Dr. DeVol to see old Hannah, mother of the first converts in Ghuara, looking wise in her new glasses even though she could not read a word. As Dr. Mategaonker's successful operations multiplied, word spread through the villages that there was a doctor in the Christian Hospital who could give sight to the blind.

A number of nurses, pharmacists, and laboratory technicians—trained through mission scholarships—returned to strengthen the staff. One of these was Gabriel Massey, who had been trained as a pharmacist by Drs. DeVol and Grace Jones Singh. He also took training for Christian ministry in Union Biblical Seminary. He returned to Chhatarpur for double duty in the church and in the hospital, and supported himself as well as his father, mother, and one brother. In the hospital, Gabriel assumed responsibility for the X-ray room, gave anesthesia, and compounded medicines. He cared for the communication system and book room. As chaplain, he gave evangelistic messages and arranged for the showing of medical and biblical filmstrips on the hospital veranda every Saturday night. In the church, he coordinated Christian education, preached, presided as clerk of the yearly meeting, and served on the executive committee.

Eventually Gabriel married a nurse who also worked in the hospital and, like Dr. Mategaonker, was one of the steady ones who stayed on even when the government hospital raised its salary scale above the mission's and drained off five nurses and one pharmacist.

This exodus added to Frances' already heavy burden, as did Norma Freer's furlough. The year she was away, Frances also had to act as business manager and secretary to her husband in his capacity as mission superintendent.

After Norma Freer returned in 1960, the DeVols were able to secure more staff, some from nearby mission hospitals, and the last year of their second term proved to be the busiest the

Christian Hospital in Chhatarpur had ever experienced. There was an increase in all branches of the work. The number of out-patients increased by 18 percent; the number of treatments, 26 percent; the total number of patients, 12 percent; major operations, 22 percent; deliveries, 25 percent. All operations for the year totalled 675, an increase of 45 percent.

The work of the Christian Hospital was progressing, and Nepal was beckoning. With Dr. Mategaonker, a better staff, and others in training, the future for medical work in the mission looked bright. There was, however, another burden on Ezra's shoulders—the care of the churches—which during this term took the heart out of both him and Frances and hindered their giving the time to Nepal that the mission had allotted.

Troubles in the Church

A church member employed in the hospital and office, who was caught embezzling funds and stealing drugs, was dismissed from service. Though he was a member of a large and reputable family, he lied, and with his family's support, began proceedings to sue Dr. DeVol. At the same time, a teacher who had lost his job was encouraged by Pyare Lal Brown to sue Dr. DeVol, Milton Coleman, and George Masih. The first court case was still going on, and the "suing" disease became so rampant in Chhatarpur that it seemed out of hand.

If there was any temptation for Ezra to turn his back on this hopeless situation and flee to Nepal where opportunities beckoned, it never came to light, though he was very discouraged.

"I don't understand why, in spite of all our efforts to reach the Hindu public in Chhatarpur for Christ, our own people, men from our own Christian community, attack us," he confided to Frances. "You know, I have been disturbed in my sleep recently by awful dreams about running from some horrible creature that persists in pursuing me."

Frances suggested having their evening quiet time on the rooftop above the noise and dirt of the nearby bus stand. A cool breeze and a beautiful sunset soothed their wounded spirits. They watched the muted tones of lavender, gray, and pink become more brilliant with gold and red, and then increase in intensity until the whole heavenly canopy seemed to burst with glory. Clouds piled up around the horizon, and the silhouette of palm trees and temples outlined against the sky gradually grew dark and faded into night. Calmness settled down upon them as they lifted their hearts to God in thanksgiving, confidence, and trust. In such regular times of prayer, the Lord gave them guidance.

Quietly, Ezra said to Frances as they went down the stairs, "The Lord just showed me that my fear is not only dishonoring to God's power but also to His integrity. He will send none of His servants on a useless errand, and He has sent us here."

"And He is holding us here," commented Frances, "though I cannot understand why."

"I now feel I have the right answer if they should come to take me to jail," Ezra continued. "I will not accept bail, but will just take along my medical journals and get caught up on my reading."

Fortunately, these two cases came to nothing and the only embarrassment was to the opposition. Pyare Lal Brown, in a final attempt to get the upper hand, had spoken so irresponsibly in the church that Dr. DeVol had to rebuke him publicly.

As they walked out of the church, Pyare Lal confronted Dr. DeVol: "Doctor Sahib, you're not the person you used to be. You've lost all your power. There was a time when God heard your prayers, but not anymore."

"Is that true?" the doctor asked him. "Well then, Brother, I need you to pray for me."

In full view of the passersby on the Mahoba Road, Dr. DeVol took Pyare Lal by the hand and pulled him down by his side as he knelt on the ground in front of the church. Others, watching, were amused and astonished, mostly astonished, but in actual fact, before the confrontation was over, Pyare Lal Brown confessed he was not a real Christian.

"I know if I come to the Lord," he said, "it must be all the way, and I can't do it because there is too much to make right."

Prayers continued to ascend for Pyare Lal Brown, that he would yet experience the rich grace of God and "come all the way." Dorothy Chambers of Westerville, Ohio, prayed daily for him for thirty years. He finally repented and made his peace with God just before he died August 3, 1986. However, at this time he continued to oppose the mission, and particularly the sale of mission properties in Amarmau, Gulganj, and Nowgong, the transfer of churches and parsonages to the new yearly meeting, and the developing of leadership according to the five-year plan.

With the sale of the Nowgong property, the church's annual meeting was moved to Chhatarpur in 1960. All seemed to go well until July, when Pastor Stuti Prakash's daughter married a Hindu. Opposition gained momentum in this volatile situation, and a campaign was launched to put Stuti Prakash out of leadership in the church. The DeVols and Norma Freer were the only missionaries in Chhatarpur at the time, and they felt the attack on this spiritual leader in the church was so vicious that there was hardly any hope of continuing. They went to prayer, feeling the time had come to close the mission.

Ezra cabled the mission board: "Pray for us, that the message of the Lord may spread rapidly and be honored, just as it was with you. And pray that we may be delivered from wicked and evil men, for not everyone has faith." (2 Thessalonians 3:1,2)

When the vote was taken as to whether or not Stuti Prakash should be retained as pastor, sensible and godly people took a stand, and the opposition lost.

Ezra said with gratitude, "I realize I was praying for victory but planning for defeat. But the Lord had everything in control, and since we are three praying together, He has given us power through His promises in Matthew 18:18-20."

Troubles in the church were, of course, not over, but in late 1960 the Hess family returned to India and stopped in Chhatarpur for six months before proceeding to their new assignment in the Union Biblical Seminary in Yavatmal. Bob Hess helped draft a three-year plan of continued help to the Indian Church, which took effect in April 1961 as the Bundelkhand Masihi Mitra Samaj (Bundelkhand Friends Church) was set apart as an independent yearly meeting. They were now self-governing, and hopefully, self-propagating, but not yet self-supporting; therefore, the mission budgeted to give them aid on the ratio of seven rupees to one raised by the church.

There was great expectancy in the air as the new BMMS's first elections were scheduled for Saturday afternoon. But just as the delegates were being seated, Pyare Lal Brown—determined to put Stuti Prakash entirely out of leadership—

arrived with a busload of his supporters from Nowgong. He did succeed in putting Stuti Prakash off every committee and then in stirring up the people to raise the question again about his daughter's marriage.

When some of the hospital staff also voted with Pyare Lal in this campaign, Dr. DeVol felt the end had come. This turn of events had made Pyare Lal Brown virtually the leader of the new BMMS Yearly Meeting, and as superintendent of the mission, Dr. DeVol was determined to have no part in watching the church die under such onslaughts.

"The time has come to amputate," he said, recalling how God had spoken to him during an operation when he had to decide whether it was better to amputate or reconstruct. "When the situation is hopeless, there must be amputation; if there are any signs of life, there is a challenge to the surgeon to try reconstruction," he had learned.

The operation had been on a boy with eyes, legs, arms, and chest badly burned in an explosion. The right hand especially was badly lacerated, all the fingers were torn off, and the thumb was so severely damaged that it was only hanging by one tendon, a little skin, and subcutaneous tissue containing some blood vessels. The bones in the thumb were shattered, muscles were shredded, and penetrating bits of debris were all through the tissues of the hand. Because of the extreme importance of the thumb, and since he could see evidence of a continued blood supply, Dr. DeVol and the staff spent three hours that night attempting to restore this hand as nearly complete as possible. The cut edges bled a little, indicating that there was life in the dangling appendage. He stabilized the bone that was fractured in the thumb with Kirshner wire and another bone with stainless steel wire. Then he closed up the wound and finally applied a plaster cast for protection. Eventually the thumb was saved.

The situation in the church was so life-threatening to real spirituality that Dr. DeVol had the full support of the missionaries for taking drastic measures against the Nowgong threat. The decision was to stop all future financial aid to the church in Bundelkhand and to begin steps to close the mission unless some action was taken by the new church to "amputate" from their body that part in which there was no evidence of spiritual life.

The result was that the Nowgong Church refused to abide by the discipline of the government-registered *Bundelkhand Masihi Mitra Samaj* Yearly Meeting, and insisted on following Pyare Lal Brown's lead. Therefore, they were "amputated" from the membership of the new BMMS. This meant the new independent yearly meeting lost seventy-one members and was left struggling for life with a total membership of only 176.

This drastic discipline of the body, the church, proved in the end to bring genuine healing. During the next year, one by one, most of the members from the Nowgong Church repented, were forgiven, and were received again as a part of the new independent body whose members all had a deeper understanding of and commitment to the spiritual nature of the Body of Christ.

The End of a Second Term of Service in India

As the DeVols' second term as missionaries came to an end in Chhatarpur on May 3, 1962, the farewells were deep and tender. There was strong evidence that after this furlough they would go to Nepal instead of returning to Chhatarpur. Even the people who had opposed Dr. DeVol did not want that to happen.

For the DeVols, the pull both ways was still strong as after farewell teas, garlands, tears, and goodbyes they boarded the train and headed for Delhi. The train chugged its steaming, smoky, and dusty way around a new corner in their obedience to God, and on the way they recalled the victories of their second term:

• The right of the Church to discipline its members was upheld in the courts.

• The Church had survived and had been revived.

• The hospital, with Dr. Mategaonker as the new medical superintendent and Norma as the acting general superintendent and business manager, was equipped for its healing and witnessing role in strengthening the Church in Bundelkhand.

• The mission's five-year plan had been completed.

• Properties no longer needed by the mission in Bundelkhand had been sold and reinvested in Union Biblical Seminary, in the Evangelical Fellowship of India, and in the stabilization of the new BMMS.

Thinking back even further to their college days, Ezra and Frances remembered a lesson they had learned from Hudson Taylor: "Move men through God by prayer alone." They had often been brought back to the practice of this principle, and now, having said goodbye to the men and women in Bundelkhand who had become so much a part of their lives, they turned again to God in prayer that in the future as in the past they would know the truth of the promise in Isaiah 43:2: "When you walk through the fire, you will not be burned."

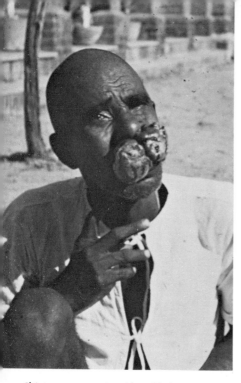
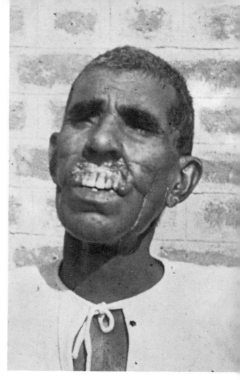

Chintaman came in with epithelioma (cancer) of his upper lip. Dr. DeVol operated and removed the cancerous lip. He then did a skin graft from in front of his ears and below his chin. Chintaman was one happy man, healed, with a new lip and mustache.

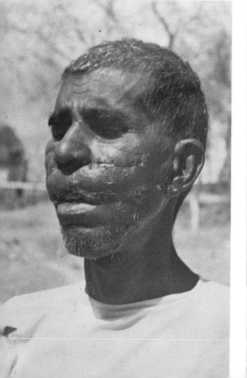

Parwati lived and went home with her baby after auto-transfusion. Ganshyam Das (above), after an operation, also lived because of having an auto-transfusion.

Suffering from tetanus and given up as hopeless, Sheila's life was saved through prayer.

Durga Bai and Nurse Sarah Nath. Hospitalized with intestinal obstruction due to massive peritoneal adhesions, she was saved by post-operative prayer of Christians.

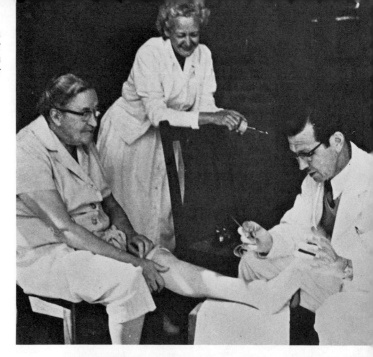

Corrie ten Boom sprained her ankle in Chhatarpur

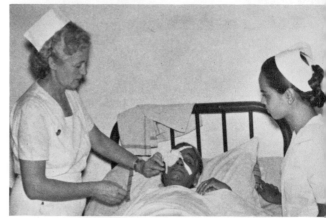

Frances training a nurse in surgical nursing

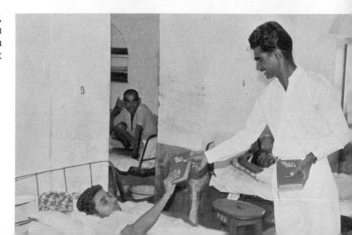

Gabriel Massey, hospital chaplain has a Bible for a patient

American Friends Mission Council: Superintendent Ezra DeVol, Milton Coleman, Robert Hess, Clifton Robinson, Frances DeVol, Norma Freer, Rebecca Coleman, Anna Nixon, Esther Hess, Elizabeth "Betty" Robinson

The High Court in Jabalpur recognized the Church's right to discipline its own members, November 21, 1960. Left to right: Komal Das Lall, Stuti Prakash, Shiv Narain Khare, and Samson Huri Lal. Lawyer Khare stood against nine lawyers of the opposition—"The LORD knoweth the way of the righteous," he quoted.

Vellore Medical College-trained
Dr. D. W. Mategaonker came to
Chhatarpur and stayed
twenty-six years.

"Turn North"—The DeVols with
Joe and Phil go to Nepal for a
month of surgery, 1959.

10 Memories that Bless and Burn

> *May the God who gives endurance and encouragement give you a spirit of unity among yourselves as you follow Christ Jesus, so that with one heart and mouth you may glorify the God and Father of our Lord Jesus Christ.*
> *Romans 15:5, 6 NIV*

Graduation of Joe and Phil

"Look, Joe! There they are!" Phil said as he caught sight of his parents waving at them through the window of the bus just arriving at the station opposite Picture Palace in Landour, Mussoorie.

Joe reached for the bedding rolls being handed down from the top of the bus as Ezra and Frances emerged—hot, dusty, and thirsty—into the hustle and bustle of coolies grasping to take their bags while vendors shouted out their wares. After the warm greetings were over, the coolies—with bedding rolls, suitcases, lunch baskets, and thermos bottles firmly strapped to their backs—started the long climb through Mussoorie Bazaar to Tehri Road and past Woodstock School to the Friends Mission house, Pennington. Following them, the four DeVols were stopped along the way from time to time.

"*Salaam*, Dr. DeVol *Sahib, Memsahib! Ap ka kya hal hai?*" (Hello, how are you?) shouted Chandra Prakash, the shopkeeper on whom Dr. DeVol had operated when he first came to India.

"*Achchhi tarah! Aur Ap?*" (Fine, and you?)

The doctor was immediately brought up to date on the state of health of the shopkeeper and his family, and Chandra Prakash learned that the DeVols were soon leaving for furlough.

"But you're coming back to India again, aren't you?"

189

"Oh, yes, we plan to come back," Dr. DeVol answered.

"Me, too," said Joe, "but not right away. I graduate from high school this year, but as soon as I finish college, look for me!"

"I'll be back to graduate from Woodstock High School four years from now," Phil said. "My folks may go to Nepal, but they'll still come to Landour in the summers."

"*Ek taraf, ek taraf*" (Out of our way!), shouted the coolies, pushing a ricksha up the narrow street.

A bejeweled raja riding high past the DeVols suddenly exclaimed, "Dr. DeVol!" It was the Raja of Sarila. Dr. DeVol had operated on his wife.

"Hello, Your Highness! How is the Rani of Sarila?" asked the doctor.

"Oh, she is fine, fine! Thanks to your treatment and your prayers! You must bring Mrs. DeVol to visit her before you go to America. We live in Happy Valley."

Other missionaries shopping in the bazaar also stopped them on the way. Dr. Carl Friedricks from Nepal was among them.

"Betty and I want you to come for dinner before you leave. What about Saturday?"

Ezra deferred to Frances, who replied, "That would be great. You can bring us up to date on the latest happenings in Nepal."

"The news isn't all good. Permits to open work in Okaldunga are slow in coming, but the hope of your returning to Kathmandu after your furlough is the best news we've had for a long time."

"We're not sure yet, but the pull is surely in that direction," Ezra said.

"We'll talk more about it at dinner," said Carl as he went on his way.

"You're late!" Bob Hess shouted as he saw the DeVols coming up the path toward Pennington. "Your house is in order, but come over on our side for supper."

The evening was filled with laughter, shared news, jokes, and future plans. Mission leadership had passed from Ezra to Bob Hess, and there were policies and problems needing discussion and prayer. However, the excitement of graduation, the ship trip home, and the anticipated reunion as a family in America took precedence that first night.

During the brief time the DeVols were in Landour, Frances, amid farewells, tried to wind up household affairs in preparation for leaving. She gathered up the household things she would replace on furlough and sorted out the boys' clothes they would not wear again to sell in the annual Landour Barter Sale. More than 5,000 articles changed hands among the missionaries and their servants that year.

The whole family was caught up in a round of Woodstock School events and graduation. Phil had excelled in scholastic endeavors, student government, track meets, and, surprisingly, in art. He had won first place in the poster contest. Joe was a leader in spiritual activities and school government, on the honor roll, and high-point man in basketball.

Phil was thrilled that his father had been chosen to give his graduation address and proud that he chose an up-to-date topic: "Countdown," referring to the astronauts. That same evening Joe graduated from high school, and the final big event of the year was a banquet given in the seniors' honor and attended by their parents.

Leaving India for the Second Furlough

By June 4, 1962, with all farewells over and all luggage again loaded on the backs of coolies for the trek downward, the DeVols left Landour via Dehra Dun and Delhi for Bombay. Income Tax Clearance, "No Objection to Return" certificates, tickets, luggage, exchange of money, passports, health certificates, and the many other details needing attention in transporting a family across the world were cared for, and time was even found, on the eve of departure, to view at the United States Information Service Center the documentary of John Glenn's *Friendship 7* earth orbit.

That night the monsoon washed over Bombay, and as they awakened early to get to the dock by 8:00 a.m., they found the whole area completely flooded and taxis unable to travel. Ezra called the Salvation Army and found a truck to take him and the luggage. He arranged for the rest of the family to come—to Phil's utter delight—in a horse-drawn victoria, a large black buggy. There was a temptation to panic, for time was limited, and they had a long way to go through flooded streets, but they made it on time.

The DeVols, with all their luggage, happily boarded the rather small SS *Asia* in time to get to the first sitting for lunch. That was their last meal for about three days, for the seas were rough. Nothing, however, clouded the peak of anticipated reunion of the family when they would arrive in New York. All the excitement of stops along the way did not lessen that hope.

The Trip Home

At Naples, the DeVols got off the ship and went overland by train and bus to see the ruins of Pompeii, cathedrals, works of art in Rome and Florence, the high snowcapped peaks of Switzerland, Germany's Black Forest, and the intriguing canals and art museums in Amsterdam. There they boarded the SS *Nieu Amsterdam*, a 36,000-ton vessel of 1,200 passenger and 700 crew capacity, and headed home.

Just six more days of refreshing ocean travel to New York! The time passed quickly, and on July 11 at early dawn, the Statue of Liberty welcomed them home. The sun rose red and gold back of lower Manhattan, and Brooklyn was beautiful as they left the ship. Once into the waiting room among milling crowds, they strained their eyes to see a familiar face. Suddenly there they were—two beautiful, red-haired, vibrant young women, looking very much alike, accompanied by a tall and handsome man. Tom wore white, Pat wore green, and Pris wore peach, to represent the white, green, and saffron color of the Indian flag. They also carried folding seats of the same colors to sit on as they waited.

Oh, what rejoicing! The meeting could not have been happier. They packed themselves like sardines into Tom Cox's car and rode to the Hilton Hotel to spend the next three days away from everyone, just to get acquainted with one another and share the happenings of the past six years.

Family Reunion

"It has been so hard to miss your graduations," Frances told the twins, "and your wedding, Priscilla, and the birth of Stephenie and Billie. I can hardly wait to see them. Tom! I can't get over the fact that we now have a son in the family who tops us all!"

Pat was bubbling. "I tried for days to get you on the phone when I had some snow holidays, but for a long time I couldn't get past Delhi. I just had to talk with you and hear your voices. When finally I heard you speak, I couldn't think of a thing to say to you. I just couldn't talk! I laughed after I had hung up. You must have thought I was crazy!

"By the time I graduated, the Escolmes had moved to Damascus. They have been wonderful. I have spent every summer with them. I felt God helped me get a place to teach near them. The man who hired me was W. C. Smith, an acquaintance of Dad's and Uncle Charles' from Marion College days."

After discussing life with the Escolmes and the joys and sorrows she had encountered in the classroom, Pat continued: "I realize I was blessed, being in Damascus Friends Church where I often saw our missionaries as they returned from furlough.

"Last Yearly Meeting was just great! They called me and told me they were showing a film about the Chhatarpur hospital. I went over and saw both of you in the film Waldo Johnson had taken while visiting you in India in 1960. You know—the one in the operating room where you were doing the cesarean section. It was so exciting to watch you save that mother's and baby's lives. The people asked a lot of questions and I was able to answer some of them. I really felt a part of you all and of the mission in India again."

Joe spoke up. "You should have been there when Waldo Johnson visited us. We went on fantastic hunts. He wanted to get a tiger, and we reserved a forest block near Amarmau. Uncle Milton had seen many tigers in that area. Well, we saw everything but tigers. There were elk, antelope, deer, wild boars, hyenas, wolves, bears, and leopards. Dad shot a leopard."

"You should have seen it!" Phil interrupted. "The biggest leopard I ever saw! We still have the skin with the head. We had it on our living room floor."

"Yes," interjected Frances, "and all of us—even our dog Prince—walked around the edge of it, not wanting to step on it. Having seen these majestic animals in their natural habitat leaves you with a certain awe of them."

"Dad," Joe urged, "tell them about the time the leopard nearly got you!"

"Well, one evening after sunset, I happened to be leading a column of men in a hunt when suddenly a large leopard exploded out of the shrub and charged with a roar straight at me! I just had time to think, *This is it!* It was too dark to sight through the scope, so I fired from the hip. The flame from the barrel teetered just above the leopard's head. He rocketted toward me, but the blast and the flash of the 30-06 'Gamemaster' diverted the big brute just enough to the left so that I could have patted his back as he flashed by. You can be sure I didn't return to the attack, nor did I follow him into the jungle!"

"Talk about scary experiences in hunting," Phil contributed, "one was with Uncle Bob when the brakes on the jeep failed as we headed down the bank into a deep river. There were two Indian guys in the back. Dad was driving, Uncle Bob was on the passenger side, and I was in the middle. It was night, and the lights went out. Dad was yelling, 'Brake fail, brake fail!' The two Indian guys yelled, 'Ram! Ram!' Uncle Bob reached over and grabbed the steering wheel as he saw we were headed for the deep part of the river. He pulled us back into line and we made our way across the narrow bridge, which was covered with water."

"Remember, Phil," said Joe, "that time we went hunting with Dad and we all took off in different directions, and I happened to look up and see you aiming your gun in Dad's direction? I could see him, but you couldn't, and I yelled at you, 'Phil, you're aiming at Dad!' You turned white as a sheet, lowered your gun and fell to the ground. You said, 'Oh, I thought I was aiming at a peacock!' "

"What?" exclaimed their father. "You never told me about this! Is that true, Phil?"

Phil shuddered. "It's true! Wow! I get cold chills now thinking about it! We agreed not to tell you, Dad, because we were afraid you might never take us hunting again."

Everyone laughed.

"But I don't care much for hunting," Phil continued with a grin, "and Joe's in the United States now, so it's okay for you to know."

"Enough of your hunting stories now," Frances spoke up. "I've been longing to hear from Pris and Tom. It was so hard to miss your wedding."

Pris, who had missed her parents on August 8, 1959, when she married Tom, gave her mother an understanding pat. She was so excited that she was given a sedative and slept most of the afternoon while everyone else went sightseeing. However, they talked about her work at the mental hospital on the hilltop and the many decisions at the time of the wedding. Pris had borrowed her wedding dress and veil. Her Uncle Everett and her pastor Leonard Wines had performed the ceremony in Westgate Friends Church, and Edward Escolme had given her away. Martha Langdon and others in the church helped with the reception—150 people came. They had sent a recording of it to India, but they discussed it all again. After the wedding, Tom and Pris moved to Chillicothe, and Pris drove two hours to work each day.

Then Stephenie was born, and Tom did not want Pris to work after that. He was preaching at a couple of churches and selling insurance, and they were able to get along all right.

"There is so much joy in getting to know you at last, Tom," Frances said, "and just being together again. I can hardly wait to see your children!"

"It is so special, just being together," said Pris.

They quoted verses in unison that had special meaning, sang some of their favorite choruses, and prayed. Then they said good night.

The next day, the girls took their mother shopping. Afterward they all went sightseeing.

On July 12, the happy reunion came to an end. Tom, Pris, and Pat returned to Chillicothe, and the DeVols went by train to Salem. A host of friends met them and escorted them to the missionary home in Damascus where they were to live throughout their furlough.

The Ramblings of the Rambler

The DeVols could hardly wait to unpack, pick up their Rambler, ordered earlier, and drive to Brighton. Mendel's wife, Kathryn, made room for everyone, including Mother Hodgin and the other brothers and their wives. Two days later, after celebrating

Mendel's birthday on July 15 and Phil's on the 16th, the DeVols left for Sunnyslope and Chillicothe where at last they saw and held in their arms their first two grandchildren, Stephenie Ann, born June 1, 1960, and William Walter (Bill), born March 10, 1962.

Pat rode back in the Rambler to Damascus and slept on the sofa just to be near her parents as long as she could. The whole family got together again at Yearly Meeting for the very special sesquicentennial celebration of the Quaker Church in the eastern region of the United States.

Family times during this furlough, however, were all too rare. Heavy deputation work put thousands of miles on the Rambler as both Ezra and Frances worked with the churches in encouraging interest and prayer support for missions.

The firm invitation to return to Nepal as medical director of Shanta Bhawan Hospital in Kathmandu came to Dr. DeVol and was approved by the mission board in November. In accepting this, Dr. DeVol became aware of his need of training in administration. He signed up for a medical administration course at the University of Pittsburgh from January 3 to April 20, 1963. This took him away from home during the week, and deputation work continued to keep him busy every weekend.

Life's Pulls on the Family

Joe entered Malone College at Canton, and though it was only thirty miles from home and not four hundred, everyone knew the DeVol family had turned another major "corner" and things would never be the same again.

Joe had to face some tough decisions after getting on his own. Shortly after entering college, he had to deal with the draft. He took a stand as a conscientious objector.

Financial realities surprised Joe. As the son of a missionary, he had never been aware of lacking things that were really important. Suddenly he began to measure himself by the standards of his classmates and realized his father's salary was pitifully low. For example, the son of the surgeon who had taken over his father's practice in Marengo was driving a Corvette, and Joe was tempted to think: *Wouldn't it have been nice if Dad had been a surgeon here in the United States so that I wouldn't have to get a summer job, and so that I could go to any college I wanted to, and have a swimming pool and all that?*

When the first snow blanketed the campus, Joe had to pick up the shovel and clean the sidewalks to earn some extra pocket money.

"I'm doing the work of a sweeper here," he wrote one of his Indian friends. "You'd never believe the amount of snow I can handle in one scoop! I know you've never seen snow, but you have seen pictures of what I'm talking about. I'm not complaining, for I wouldn't trade my experiences in India for any amount of money. I don't have a car or a bank account, but I have rich memories of the joy we had in India as a family and of the friends I still have there."

In the fall, Pat went back to her teaching, this time in Canton, and often went out with Russell Haynes, a former student of Virginia Polytechnic Institute and William and Mary College, who worked as a designer for Babcock and Wilcox in Barberton, Ohio. He soon became her fiance, and at Christmas she went to Martinsville, Virginia, to meet his family.

Phil could not have avoided feelings of loneliness when he came home from school to an empty house, even though the Escolmes filled in to see that he had good meals at their house. His father was away in training, his mother in deputation work, Joe in college, and Pat busy teaching. Though he had many friends, none took the place of Joe. The parents felt deep concern as they noticed his interest in family prayer and church attendance diminish and saw by his report card that his grade point average had gone down.

Called for an interview about their experiences as "missionary kids," both Phil and Joe answered their questions from the surface and became aware of having grown cold spiritually.

Around a campfire one evening, Joe heard another boy saying, "I wish I could be like Joe DeVol."

Oh, no! thought Joe. *I know I'm not the kind of a guy he thinks I am.* Phil did not let anyone know what he was thinking, but his parents sensed the needs in the hearts of both their sons.

Frances prayed: "Lord, help us be the parents we ought to be to our children. Let us talk more often to them about their personal walk with Thee."

Joe was soon at the altar, renewing his Christian commitment. His inner peace was restored, but he was mentally confused.

"Dad," he said, "it just seems like—Well, why should a Christian have to do this so often—I mean, this going forward and asking forgiveness?"

"Well, Joe, even yet I have to go back to the Lord and ask Him to forgive me when I'm wrong. That has happened many times, for the Lord convicts me. When He does, I have to ask His forgiveness and apologize to people before I get peace."

"But you always try to do right," Joe reasoned.

"Yes, but I don't always know what is right, and sometimes I think I'm right and don't take time to pray. Then the Lord shows me I must repent and confess what I have done. To confess means to say the same thing God says about what I've done. Do you remember the time that rich man came into the hospital and demanded that I treat his servant free?"

"You mean that cloth merchant?"

"No, this was another fellow. He was the richest man in Chhatarpur, and he argued with me right in the ward in front of his friends, our staff, and the patients."

Joe laughed. "Oh, yes! You said to him, 'Okay! If you won't pay, then I'll pay!' And you reached into your pocket and took out Rs. 100 and handed it to the cashier."

"That's right, Joe, and everyone roared with laughter. Everyone, that is, except the rich man. He became livid with anger, and pulling Rs. 1,500 out of his pocket, he slammed it down on the desk and walked out. The onlookers seemed thrilled about having the privilege of seeing that miserly fellow put in his place, but I lost my peace of heart. I argued with myself quite awhile, saying I'd just taught him a lesson, but the Lord convicted me. I had to go back and apologize to the man in the presence of those in the ward for my action, which had been an insult to the man. I also asked the Lord to forgive me."

"I remember," said Joe. "I know that was hard, Dad."

"Obedience, not human perfection, is the secret to spiritual victory, Joe. Your mother and I always try to obey God no matter what it costs us."

A Grandchild, a Wedding, and Plans for Nepal

Pat and Russell moved rapidly into their wedding plans after their engagement so that Pat's parents could be present. Though Pat's would be the only wedding of their four children they would be privileged to attend, even for this one there were many complications in setting the date. Pris, Pat's matron of honor, was pregnant and would deliver about mid-May. The DeVols were returning to India and Nepal about mid-June. Meanwhile, both Ezra and Frances were on the road in answer to the demands of the churches wanting information concerning the challenging new mission field of Nepal.

"Just this one more," the mission board was tempted to say as the calls piled up.

"I am disappointed," Pris wrote the board. "It seems that the only way we can arrange to see our parents is to have a baby or get married! I want my parents with me when my baby is born."

Geoffrey Marshall Cox cooperated beautifully by being born May 13, 1963, in time to let his mother take her place in the Alum Creek Friends church as matron of honor for her twin sister, Patricia Lee DeVol, who was given in marriage by her parents to Russell R. Haynes, Jr., on Saturday, June 8, 1963. Pat was radiant in a bridal gown of white lace over organdy, complemented by an organza veil and bouquet of lily-of-the-valley and orchids. The church was beautifully decorated with gladioli, chrysanthemums, and candelabra. Pris wore a dress of lace over yellow taffeta and carried a bouquet of yellow roses. Stephenie, age three, was the flower girl in white and green organdy. Joe and Phil served as ushers, and afterward at the reception for some three hundred guests, they ate their fill of wedding cake and goodies. Later, the family and their relatives went to Sunnyslope for a lot of remembering of the joys they had so often experienced there.

The next week, after tender goodbyes to two daughters, two sons-in-law, three grandchildren, a son, and at least one hundred other people gathered at the Canton airport to see them off. Ezra, Frances, and Phil, along with another Woodstock student, Suzie McCullough, flew off to Delhi with a one-day stopover in the Holy Land. The DeVols were glad to note that

Phil seemed impressed with the beauty and sense of reverence in the Garden Tomb. They also enjoyed seeing his pleasure as he swam in the Dead Sea and found he could not sink.

On arriving in Delhi, the DeVols rented a car for the 130-mile trip to Landour and stayed on in Pinepoint until after Phil entered Woodstock High School on June 22, 1963, for his sophomore year. Before leaving, they longed for a more certain word of spiritual victory from Phil, the only one of their children still with them, but they could do nothing except pray and wait. He was a loving son and was happy and excited to be back.

"It's harder than ever to leave Phil," Frances said, "and the assignment in Nepal seems like such a tremendous undertaking. We have no might and no power; it has to be of the Holy Spirit. I've had some real fears, but this morning Psalm 34:4 spoke to me: 'I sought the Lord and he heard me, and delivered me from all my fears.' "

Reluctantly, the DeVols left Phil standing and waving on the brink of the hill as their car turned a sharp corner in its descent, taking them on toward the new and challenging mission in Nepal.

Sam and Mary Esther
Burgoyne with the DeVols.
Sam Burgoyne was
principal of Woodstock
High School.

Landour—where the DeVol
children went to school
and where Dr. DeVol
performed his first
operation in India on
shopkeeper Chandra
Prakash.

A photo taken
by Ezra from
the back of an
elephant

The Gate of India, New Delhi. Bundelkhand fort—and a trek through the jungles with Joe, Phil, and their dog Prince. The Taj Mahal visited by Cousin Ethel DeVol Imel and husband.

Priscilla Ann DeVol Cox, Woodstock High School graduate of 1955, Nurses' Training 1959, married Tom Cox 1959.

"Fish stories" documented by Joseph Edward DeVol, Woodstock High School graduate of 1962.

Patricia Lee DeVol (far right), teacher in Greenford elementary school, Ohio, 1962. Pat graduated from Woodstock High School in 1955 and Marion College in 1959.

11 Life in Kathmandu Valley

*I will go before you and will level the mountains; I will break
down gates of bronze and cut through bars of iron. I will
give you the treasures of darkness, riches stored in secret
places, so that you may know that I am the LORD, the God
of Israel, who calls you by name.*   Isaiah 45:2, 3 NIV

Delays in Reaching Nepal

After saying goodbye to Phil, the DeVols went to Chhatarpur to
relieve Dr. Mategaonker for a few weeks' vacation. They found
Norma Freer just recovering from hepatitis and the people of
the city disturbed to hear of their leaving Chhatarpur so soon.
Ezra went to work the next morning, but Frances went to bed
because she was ill. She soon recovered, and they celebrated
Phil's birthday, July 16, by performing four operations and
scheduling five more for the following day.

On July 23, the DeVols proceeded to Nepal via Calcutta to
pick up their luggage, but it had not yet arrived.

During many days of waiting, Dr. DeVol recorded in his
diary: "My schedule is in Thy hands, Lord—each incident—
including the interruptions, delays, and unexpected developments. Why should I not allow the peace of God to rule (completely control and master) my heart?"

Together, Ezra and Frances read Isaiah 45 over and over,
claiming the promises. "I am the LORD, and there is none else,
there is no God beside me." They encouraged one another, saying, "We are in His will, and He is helping us."

When the ship arrived and they went through customs, Ezra
commented: "Count it all joy when ye go through customs!"
Six weeks later he would be "blessed" with the same "joy" as

the luggage arrived in Kathmandu, and customs on the same items would have to be paid to the Nepali government.

Challenges of the United Mission to Nepal

As the DeVols flew into Kathmandu on August 13, 1963, they looked down on the world's highest mountain range—the beautiful, rugged, snowcapped Himalayas. About the size of England, this small country's 56,000 square miles were nestled between India and China-occupied Tibet. About 93 percent of her 10,000,000 people were scattered throughout the hills and lower plains, and about 500,000 were clustered in the Kathmandu Valley. This lush area lay at the level of 4,500 feet surrounded by scenic grandeur. Hindu wooden temples outlined the city. On the outskirts stood the Buddhist Bodnath Temple with eyes on each side of the pinnacle watching in all directions.

In 1951 the government changed from a one-hundred-year rule of the Ranas to the restoration of King Tribhuvan Bikram Shah. By 1953 the ruler was his son, King Mahendra Bir Bikram Shah Deb, who opened Nepal's doors to the light of science, education, and commerce. On March 18, 1954, he permitted the United Mission to Nepal (UMN) to come in. They agreed to be subject to the laws of Nepal, and the new government accepted their clearly stated purpose:

• To minister to the needs of the people in Nepal in the Name and Spirit of Christ, and to make Christ known to them by word and life;

• To care for the sick, educate, develop agriculture and industry;

• To train the people of Nepal in professional skills and leadership.

In 1955 Nepal became a member of the United Nations and launched a five-year plan to improve transportation, agriculture, industry, and education. Their new constitution, announced on February 12, 1959, proclaimed religious freedom but allowed no conversions. By August 17, 1963, just four days after the DeVols arrived, a new set of laws came into effect concerning conversion which directly affected the UMN: There was to be no conversion to or propagation of Christianity, Islam, or any other faith so as to disrupt the traditional religion of the Hindu community of Nepal or disturb the mind of a

Hindu. Penalties attached were (a) three-year imprisonment for anyone seeking to convert another; (b) six years to one who converts another, and expulsion of any foreigner doing so; (c) one year to a person who converts himself; (d) a fine of Rs. 100 if anyone attempts to convert himself.

Probably to camouflage the anti-Christian intent of this law, the government first applied it to a Mohammaden who had married a Hindu woman eight years previously. The man was jailed for eight years and the woman for two. Meanwhile, Prem Pradhan, a Christian, was in his third year of a six-year sentence for baptizing one or two people.

Under the agreement by which they came in, the United Mission to Nepal understood that they were allowed to teach and witness (propagate) in limited forms but were not allowed to baptize or lead in forming a church. The officials clearly understood that Christians by nature witnessed to the Bible and to Christ and that though they would confine this witness to their places of living and work, still in all probability there would be some conversions. The missionaries realized Nepal was in a period of social revolution and hoped that enlightenment would eventually bring more religious freedom. The new law, however, seemed severe, and if it were enforced, the UMN would have to leave or compromise their commitment "to make Christ known by word and life."

Just at this juncture, the American Friends Mission became the twenty-third denominational member of the UMN now made up of one hundred missionaries from a dozen different countries.

Medical Director of the United Mission Medical Center

One week after arriving in Nepal and settling into a home of three unpainted rooms and a hallway, Dr. DeVol began his work as the medical director of the United Mission Medical Center (UMMC) in Shanta Bhawan Hospital. The UMN (United Mission to Nepal) soon secured Surendra Bhawan, another small palace just five minutes walk from Shanta Bhawan. This increased the UMN's Medical Center (UMMC) bed capacity to 135, which was 26 percent of all available hospital beds in the entire Kathmandu Valley.

This was still not enough. The beds were filled, and additional patients were put on pallets in the halls and between the beds in the wards. One night a man had to remain on the emergency room table because there was no bed space.

People had very little knowledge of sanitation and in many cases shared their homes with the animals, drank water from polluted wells, walked down streets with open sewers, and ate food not properly washed. Tuberculosis was rampant, as was leprosy, goiter, elephantiasis, rabies, malaria, dysentery, worms, and malnutrition. Immunization and sanitation programs were just being developed, and as yet there was little understanding of the germ theory.

"The medical need in Nepal is five times greater than in India," noted Dr. DeVol. Therefore, to more adequately meet the need, the UMN began plans to build a new 250-bed hospital in Kathmandu.

Back Into Surgery

Dr. DeVol was no longer the only surgeon in the UMN or in Nepal. A number of doctors had been trained and had returned to the government hospital, and Dr. Berry, a younger surgeon, was on the UMMC staff. The two Dr. Millers were there for cardiology and pediatrics. Dr. DeVol was expected to do the orthopedic and urological surgery, but cataracts developing in both eyes hindered him in both administration and surgery. He had to replace his glasses from time to time with stronger and stronger lenses. Nevertheless, he and Frances continued working together. Thursday was their operation day.

Ezra and Frances were thrilled and amused as they saw two boys happily walking out of the hospital. When they came in, one had been so knock-kneed he could not walk, and the other so bowlegged he could barely walk. When they were well enough to have the casts removed, they almost split their faces with smiles as they stood tall on their straight legs.

Little Bibi Maya was brought in with tuberculosis of the spine. She was paralyzed from her waist down. For many days before coming to the hospital, she had received no care, and her matted hair was crawling with lice. The DeVols and their surgical team cleaned her up, and Dr. DeVol operated on her spine. During the next few weeks, they prayed her through many dark moments and much suffering. To everyone's amazement, Bibi Maya walked again.

"This is an absolute miracle," said Mr. Barnes, First Officer of the U.S. Embassy in Nepal. He had seen not only Bibi Maya but many others walk again who were brought into the Shanta Bhawan Hospital in hopeless condition, not expected to live.

Dirgiman was another of those miracles of healing. He had a broken back, was paralyzed in the right leg, and could barely move his left leg when the men brought him in. After Dr. DeVol operated on his spine and removed a piece of bone pressing on the spinal cord, he began to improve. A week later, he was able to move the paralyzed leg, and from that time on he made steady improvement. One Sunday morning, a month later, he sat up on the edge of the bed.

"I want to put my feet on the floor," he said. As soon as he did that, he stood up and started walking! People came running to see him and began praising God with him.

The Medical Needs of Royalty

When members of the royal family were patients in the Shanta Bhawan Hospital, His Majesty Mahendra Bir Bikram Shah Dev and Her Majesty Queen Ratna would sometimes come to visit them. This required advance notice and proper security measures.

One such occasion was when the King's uncle was there with a fractured hip. The King and Queen stayed on after the visit to see Dr. DeVol in his office. They demonstrated great friendliness, assuring Dr. DeVol of their interest in increasing the United Mission Medical Center's facilities in Kathmandu.

Over a period of six weeks, the UMMC cared for the Queen Mother, who was suffering from severe back pain. On arrival at the palace, Dr. DeVol, a lady Indian anesthesiologist, and a nurse were kept waiting at the gate. After asking a series of questions, the guard finally allowed them into the grounds.

When they reached the palace, the guard said, "Take off your shoes here before you enter the palace."

They were escorted into the Queen Mother's richly curtained room where she lay, suffering, on a heavily padded and rolly-top bed. The royal physician translated Dr. DeVol's questions to the Queen Mother in Royal Nepali. This took a lot of time as Dr. DeVol did not want to make a wrong diagnosis. Finally he pinpointed her problem, and the team proceeded to give the needed injection. Since the bed was slippery, the Queen Mother overweight, and the Nepali doctor and nurse overawed at the thought of touching royalty, they were not able to hold her sufficiently steady to give an intrathecal spinal anesthetic.

"We can't do it, doctor," the Indian anesthesiologist said. "You'll have to hold the patient."

As Dr. DeVol took hold of the Queen Mother, she slipped on the bed, and he lost his balance.

"Why don't you sit on the bed, Doctor?" the Queen Mother suggested in very clear English.

On the next visit, the UMMC team did not have to wait so long at the gate and were allowed to take off their shoes at the top of the stairs. By the fourth visit, they were not stopped at the gate, and no one asked them to remove their shoes until they reached the Queen Mother's bedroom. As they chatted away in English, King Mahendra also stepped into the room from behind the curtains and joined in the conversation.

On the last visit, they were not asked to remove their shoes at all. His Majesty King Mahendra and the Queen Mother, in gratitude, welcomed them royally and served them coffee. His Majesty then requested Dr. DeVol to examine his sister, Her Royal Highness Laxmi Devi.

After completing the examination, Dr. DeVol found His Majesty's sister suffering from a poorly functioning gall bladder.

"Please operate," His Majesty urged, confident in light of the healing of the Queen Mother that Dr. DeVol could perform miracles.

What shall I say to him? Dr. DeVol began to ponder.

When his aide de camp had been operated on, His Majesty himself had sent word to Dr. DeVol, "Don't open the gall bladder. Send it to me."

Later he had telephoned back to the doctor: "When I opened it, I found 288 stones!"

When the king's personal secretary had come in for an operation, His Majesty again had sent the same message: "Don't open the gall bladder. Send it to me."

He had telephoned again: "I found 44 stones!"

Her Royal Highness Laxmi Devi had no stones. What would His Majesty say when the operation was finished and he had nothing to count?

"I wish it were as simple as that," Dr. DeVol said after thinking for a long time, "but surgery is not the answer to your sister's problem. However, we will treat her medically."

The Challenge of Administration

Administration was Dr. DeVol's main responsibility, though not his first love. As Director of the United Mission Medical Center, he had more administration and less surgery than he wanted.

"Surgery has been my pride and joy for years (to not operate would be a sort of death)," he confessed. "But now I have more time to do a more important—though less spectacular—work, the expediting of the service of the whole hospital team. Someone should do this and do it well, and since it has fallen to me to do, may I do it with all my heart and mind and unto the Lord for His glory, which means I must be 'hidden in Christ.' " (John 12:24)

Frances prayed for her husband: "Lord, place Your hand on Ezra's shoulder. Let him hear the whisper of Your voice in his ear. Put Your love in his heart. Help him fulfill Your plan for his life."

Then she prayed for herself: "Lord, temper with tranquility my manifold activity, that I may do my work for Thee in very great simplicity."

As administrator, Dr. DeVol set about to clarify lines of responsibility, giving more power to appointed committees. Workers who had been less than professional in their work were challenged to be more punctual and alert so that a staff person through all working hours was always on duty in every department, including the reception desk, business office, X ray, laboratory, and pharmacy. With good cooperation of the Nepali policemen, security was tightened and new gatemen employed to cut down trespassing and thievery.

With the help of a newly formed advisory finance committee, made up of the UMN treasurer, the UMMC business manager, a Ford Foundation economist, and three other members of the staff, Dr. DeVol held many long consultations in order to establish policies for UMN and UMMC covering employment qualifications and contracts, severance pay, retirement, provident fund, increments, and salary scale. The implementation of these policies contributed significantly toward the smooth working of the institution.

A German secretary Renate Wagner, an American medical technologist Jamie Sandoz, a Canadian superintendent of maintenance Tom Haggerty, a German electrician Wolfgang Kruse, and an English business manager Dorothy Broom helped increase the hospital's efficiency. Results from their work included improved transportation, a new kitchen and dining room, the installation of a 75 kw generator, a completed laundry unit, and a rewired hospital. The American Industrial Development program of the United States (US AID) was generous in loaning equipment, and friends from America sent donations to underwrite the expense of added facilities. Before the end of that year, the UMMC had treated some 50,000 patients, and the following year the census went up 13 percent.

As in India, the idea was prevalent among some of the leaders that mission hospitals existed to give away medicine. Dr. DeVol had begun his campaign against this theory as far back as 1959 when he first visited Nepal. As in Chhatarpur, he determined to raise the income, to develop a medical insurance plan, and to get support for opening a free medical ward.

"We insult and pauperize the patient by giving him free treatment when he is able to pay," Dr. DeVol argued. "I agree with the theory that the whole community is exploited when a patient who is able to pay all or part of his hospital cost is given free treatment. He will ultimately receive the greatest benefit if he is treated justly and honestly, rather than sentimentally."

At that time, out-patient department collections totalled less than 25 percent of the total cost, excluding donated missionary personnel. His success in convincing those in charge to raise this amount had been a factor in the board's inviting him to return as an administrator.

Having been through this battle before in Chhatarpur, Dr. DeVol knew he would face opposition from a few of the UMN leaders and also from the populace at large. He was adamant, however, and for a very good reason. Back in 1940-1942 in the University Hospital in Nanking, China, he had observed that patients were paying about 85 percent of the cost of running the hospital. When the war came, the hospital continued even though help from outside was cut off.

With China pressing down on Tibet to Nepal's borders, there was no way of knowing how long the doors would be open to western aid, or on the other hand, how long western aid would continue to flow to the Orient. So Dr. DeVol was determined to build a solid foundation with financial responsibility shared on a wide basis.

A test came one day as several well-dressed Nepalese men brought a communist agitator into the hospital emergency ward. Because they came in taxis and were all well-dressed and wearing shoes, Dr. DeVol shrewdly guessed they could not be poor. Realizing that collecting fees from these men was a critical issue for the success of his new policy, he decided to oversee the process himself. Failure at this stage, he felt, would make the future establishment of the right to charge for treatment an impossibility. The men insisted on free treatment, and there was an impasse. The spokesman for the group would not give in, and Dr. DeVol would not budge, though he was sweating, as he could imagine what the headlines in the Nepali paper would be if they did not get their way: *Dr. DeVol Refuses to Treat the Poor!* In such tight spots he had long since found there was only one way to turn. He went to his office and prayed, asking God what to do.

Still uncertain but prepared to follow God's leading in the next step, he returned and found that the communist agitator had already collected the money and was ready to pay the bill. This set a precedent for the hospital to collect from those who could pay.

The battle was not over, however, and during the holidays when the OPD census slumped and criticism rose, Dr. DeVol asked the Lord for assurance that he was pursuing the right course.

"I need to know for sure," he prayed, "so let me put out this fleece. If we are going in the right direction, please send two hundred patients into the OPD by twelve o'clock."

He became restless at eleven-thirty and went to check on how things stood. Already 196 patients had been registered.

He returned at twelve o'clock, just as registration closed, and found that exactly two hundred had registered, no more and no less.

He thanked God as he prayed, "Oh, Lord God, lead on; continue to guide!"

Social Obligations

Frances assisted her husband in the operating room not only every Thursday, but any time Dr. Berry or the resident surgeon was absent. She taught surgical nursing to the nurses taking their training under UMN. Her main responsibility, however, was serving as hostess for the United Mission Medical Center. The following year when a full-time person came for this job, there was still enough work to keep both of them busy.

Social obligations far exceeded those in Chhatarpur. Nearly every week, the DeVols were expected to attend important government and mission functions.

Invitations came from the American Embassy and other embassies for celebration of their special days. On July 4, American Ambassador Stebbins and his wife saw to it that Independence Day was celebrated properly. They offered free hot dogs and coffee, provided rare treats of hamburgers, beef, Coca-Colas, and ice cream, and gave the children helicopter and elephant rides. The DeVols enjoyed the luncheon and the ambassador's speech.

When the Ranas were overthrown, King Tribhubvan, and later in 1955, his son King Mahendra worked to bring national consciousness to the new country. Glamorous festivals aided him in this as Gurkhas, Sherpas, Lepchas, Newars, and other racial groups became less conscious of their tribal identity and felt more like Nepalese. One such occasion was the celebration of the twenty-first birthday of the Crown Prince Birendra Bir Bikram Shah Dev when he became the Colonel of the Nepalese Army.

The Nepali guests proudly wore embroidered caps, jodphurs, and tightly fitting black coats. The DeVols, dressed for the occasion, were seated with honor among other dignitaries of which there were many foreigners. The American community alone in Kathmandu numbered four hundred.

The guests had been seated only a short time when the band marched onto the field with trumpets blaring. From the front entrance, they circled the red carpet covered podium. The King's Lancers followed, taking their places, dressed in black helmets, trousers, and boots in contrast to their bright red jackets decorated with medals and white stripes criss-crossing their chests and backs. Their *kukuris* (swords) were smartly fastened to their belts. The army generals came mounted on prancing black horses, two by two, and followed their commander on a white horse, until they all stood in formation around the podium.

A loud crescendo of the band brought the guests to their feet as the Crown Prince—resembling Lord Mountbatten in his resplendent white uniform and cap with gold braid and medals—came riding in a Cadillac to take his place on the podium.

The band ceased playing for a moment as the Nepali flag was hoisted. The red background edged with blue, with a white emblem of the sun god on one pennant and the moon god on the other, unfolded as the band began the national anthem and the singing followed:

> Hail to His Majesty
> Gracious and noble King
> Of the Nepalese!
> May God Almighty
> Bestow long life on him
> And grant his people
> Prosperity and success.

When the Crown Prince, now the Colonel of the Nepalese Army, finally stood before his people, the Nepali army marched sharply past him, giving their salute. They were dressed in simple khaki hats, shirts, and shorts, with matching knee-length socks and sturdy brown shoes, their two matched kukuris in holsters on their belts.

Afterward, the DeVols mingled with the Americans, Britishers, Russians, Indians, Japanese, Chinese, Germans, and other Europeans who joined the Nepalis in their great celebration. To all people the DeVols reached out, building bridges for greater and more meaningful relationships in later opportunities.

The Queen came to the biennial meeting at Surendra Bhawan for the Trained Nurses Association of Nepal. She accepted the invitation to open the convention, and Frances had the responsibility of seeing that invitations were printed and sent to 150 ministers of government, and to the doctors. A program had to be arranged, tea planned, and the room prepared with proper seating for the Queen and her sister-in-law, Princess Helen. Nurses from the government nursing school, people from the World Health Organization, and the students and staff of the UMN were present.

Opportunities came through the Nepal Council of World Affairs for contact with the Russians. They requested Dr. DeVol to attend a meeting with the Soviet Cosmonauts, Major Andrian Nikolayev, Capt. (Mrs.) Valentine Nikolayev, Lt. Col. Valory Bykovsky. Thereafter, when the Russians visited Dr. DeVol's office, they found a Russian Bible on his desk, available for them to read. Russian patients admitted to the hospital found Russian Bibles at their bedside and were free to take them home.

Dr. DeVol received the mandate to open a chapter for the Fellows of the International College of Surgeons to encourage fellowship and the exchange of medical knowledge among all the surgeons now in the valley. On May 17, 1965, seven doctors from the UMN and the government hospital met and formally became members of the FICS, another "first" in the country of Nepal.

Workers' conferences were an annual affair. All the missionaries and Christian workers living in outstations who could arrange to have a few days free would come to Kathmandu to give reports of their work and be renewed spiritually. Frances had the task of finding enough sleeping space for them through the use of air mattresses on the floor and cots in the halls.

Not only outstation missionaries, but guests from India and around the world, including mountain climbers, tourists, and mission executives, made their way to Frances' door in search of accommodation. In 1965 alone, 494 guests visited in the DeVol home. Some stayed to work, like Dr. Betty Milledge, an excellent anesthesiologist whose husband was a physiologist on the Hillary team of mountain climbers. She greatly facilitated the surgical team. She was the first to make it possible for Dr. DeVol to relax from the concern for the anesthetization of his patients. What a relief!

Participation in Spiritual Activities

The DeVols, as always, attended church services on Sundays, sometimes at the Mar Thoma English services, which had been started by Union Biblical Seminary graduates of India who came up and supported themselves to get a work going in Kathmandu. Another English service for the international community attracted them, though it seemed too foreign and often too liberal to be effective. Sometimes Ezra was asked to speak at this service.

In addition to these English services, a foreign group, made up mostly of U.S. AID workers, formed a Bible study and requested Ezra to teach it. They had their own pastor who did not seem very interested in Bible study, and he was happy to be relieved of the responsibility. At first Ezra chose his own topics for teaching, but when the formal study book they had chosen was put into his hands, he was amazed at the higher criticism. Not being a theologian, he was, nevertheless, schooled in the Bible from his youth and was appalled at the number of factual errors on which the teaching was based. He convinced the Presbyterians, Mormons, Methodists, Evangelicals, Agnostics, Quakers, and other denominations represented in the study that the book had been written by an immature person on a flimsy foundation whose conclusions could not be trusted. Dipping into his own rich experience with the Bible, Ezra shared the ways God spoke to him through it and why he believed it to be the Word of God. He dealt with deep and controversial issues, quoting freely from the writings of well-known theologians.

"It is not only our right to ask questions," Ezra explained, "it is also our human responsibility. But in doing so, let us not fail to recognize the genuine mystery in the activity of God. As David Wallace says, 'The mystery of the Virgin Birth is only a part of the larger mystery and incomprehensibility of the Incarnation of God in Christ.' "

The result in the lives of people from these lessons was not measurable, but at least one doctor of the American Embassy and a professed skeptic who attended regularly was convinced that the Bible was true.

More than these foreign groups, the DeVols enjoyed the Nepali services. In the home of Rajendra Rongong, a teacher who also did the preaching, many Nepalis came to listen, learn, and believe. Rajendra was the only Christian up to that time who had been sent out of Nepal for advanced education. He studied at the University of Delhi in India and at Rutgers in the U.S.A., and had returned to Kathmandu as a government teacher, purposely to witness for Christ.

Most often the DeVols went to the Nepali Christian Congregation attended by hospital staff and many others, and pastored by Robert Kartak. Under the new law, pastors had to decide what they would do about baptisms. Two nurses in the hospital had been converted after the DeVols' arrival, and Robert Kartak decided to perform the ceremony in Nepal and face the consequences.

Prem Pradhan was in the midst of a six-year prison term for his faith, and the DeVols often took gifts to him and sought to encourage him to stand true. Such gifts included the illustrated "Good News" magazine containing the Gospels and Acts, which he shared with his cell mates. They often took him food items, and at Christmas they provided him with a full dinner from their table. To guarantee that it contained no poison, the guards insisted on Dr. DeVol's tasting every item in front of them before they allowed it to come inside the gates.

Ezra helped Prem Pradhan arrange for his two children's education. Most of the time when he visited Prem Pradhan, they talked about the other prisoners being converted through his testimony. He had even led the man in the next cell to Christ while both of them were in solitary confinement in adjacent cells. They paced their walk across the cell floor to meet at the wall through which they could hear one another. By alternate sentences, they communicated, and the man was led to Christ. Prem Pradhan spent lonely hours embroidering maps of Nepal and then gave them to people who visited him. He gave one to Ezra, with the caption embroidered at the bottom, "Pray for Nepal."

In April 1964, the wife of the officer who had jailed Prem Pradhan was converted. She bought a Bible and started family prayer in her home. On the king's birthday in 1965, Prem Pradhan received the surprise of his life when the guards unlocked his door and led him out to freedom. Thus with other prisoners pardoned that day, he had the happy experience of being united with his family after four-and-a-half years.

To encourage more prayer for these Nepali leaders and out-station workers, the DeVols started weekly Wednesday evening prayer meetings in their home. These meetings were attended by many of the Christian hospital staff members. They prayed for converts such as the young man who out in the fields near Pokhara had become so convicted of sin that he asked a man working beside him, "What can I do to be rid of my sin?"

The man said, "Go to the mission people. They say their God has a remedy for sin."

The man went to the mission, learned about Jesus Christ, and received Him as Lord. He stayed to learn more and then returned to his village to win six families. Eventually that village came to be known as "Antioch." In similar ways, many other villages heard the good news and responded. Once a year at a center such as Pokhara or Kathmandu, a Bible school was held for these new converts. One who attended and gave his tes-timony was Durga Singh, a former political prisoner led to Christ while in jail with Prem Pradhan.

The DeVols were aggressive evangelicals, and though they respected and sought to abide by Nepal's laws, in both work and witness, they tried to let no outward restraint hamper their heartfelt sharing of the reality of Jesus Christ's love and their faith in His ability to turn lives around. They identified with the longing of people to know God, but the inward pain they felt was poignant as they watched people seek contact with Deity through the bow of their heads to an idol, the spin of a prayer wheel, or the wave of a prayer flag. Their own worship of the Creator included a welling up of love and praise as they watched the moon shine through the clouds above the sparkling snowcapped Himalayas at night and listened in wonder at dawn to the song of the magpie robin while looking down on the lush, green paddy fields with heaps of drying red chilies and yel-low corn here and there. In stark contrast to the silent and spo-ken prayers in family worship and in church and the inspiring sermons and hymns that made up the worship they had expe-rienced since childhood, there was the frenzied participation of the masses, including royalty, in the glitter and noise of the festival honoring the "living goddess."

The DeVols watched the Durga Puja worship from a balcony. Spears with red flags attached were placed throughout the area, and clarified-butter lamps were ablaze. As the band played with rising crescendos and soldiers fired into the air sporadically, important and very tall military Nepalis in civilian dress picked up the ceremonial swords and at a given signal raised them and shouted in unison. Then one among them, appointed for the task, marched forward to the place where a buffalo calf was tied with its head against a stake. At the shout of his comrades, he raised his exceedingly large kukuri and with one stroke cut off the animal's head. The DeVols watched this awesome sight as some twenty-five buffaloes and fifty goats were sacrificed.

A goldsmith's daughter was chosen for the role of the "living goddess" at the age of three. If she did not cry when put into a room with the bleeding heads of these animals killed for sacrifice, she was identified as an incarnation of *Kali*, the goddess who demanded blood. Each year until she reached the age of twelve, she would be paraded through the streets during the ten-day Dassara Hindu festival. On reaching puberty, she would be replaced by another young girl, and her future years likely would be spent as a temple prostitute.

"If Dassara Festival can go on for ten days," Dr. DeVol challenged his staff, "what should hinder our celebration of Christmas for ten days in the confines of our Christian hospital compound?"

Enthusiasm was contagious. The hospital compound took on a festive appearance. Christmas-related pictures, posters, and texts decorated the walls of wards, halls, and foyers. Taped Christmas carols rang through the hospital compound. The Nepali Church prepared and presented a tableau of the biblical account of Christ's birth as the pastor read the relevant Scriptures. Live animals—sheep, lambs, and doves—enlivened the scenes. Word spread, and outsiders came in to see and hear. On Christmas Eve the whole staff participated in a candlelight procession, singing for the patients while going through all the wards, stopping in each one as a staff member gave a short Christmas message and led in prayer. In one ward, Dr. DeVol shared his songbook with a member of the royal family. To this celebration no one objected, and the hospital was filled with joy. That is, neither the government, nor the patients, nor outsiders crowding in—no Nepali objected. One or two timid missionaries, however, expressed fear that such an aggressive evangelical approach might endanger the delicate balance of agreement between UMN and the government.

Continuing Supervision in Chhatarpur

One condition of the mission board on seconding the DeVols to work in the UMN was that at least twice a year they would spend a month in Chhatarpur. Travel and permits to cross national borders could be sticky, but Major General Padam Bahadur Khatri, the Nepali Minister of Defense and in Charge of Foreign Affairs, was helpful.

"You don't need to come to my office to get my help," he said. "You can come to my house."

Major General Padam Bahadur Khatri arranged for the DeVols to obtain a multiple entry visa into Nepal. This was a way of showing his gratitude for a cholecystectomy operation Dr. DeVol had performed on his wife in 1960. He had already shown his gratitude by paying Rs. 1,000 instead of Rs. 500 for the operation. Later he became the Nepali Ambassador to the U.S.A.

Ezra and Frances DeVol's first return visit to Chhatarpur was on January 26, 1964, in order to give Dr. Mategaonker a month's needed vacation. Dr. Mategaonker, however, had the day scheduled with six cataract operations and other procedures to complete before he could leave. The hospital was full and overflowing, and two other young doctors were expected to join the staff soon.

"With such a team, what cannot God do through this hospital!" exclaimed Frances. During the month, the DeVols scheduled operations five and even six days a week.

Before returning to Nepal, Dr. DeVol was requested by the UMN Board to visit Lahore to see the United Christian Hospital's million-dollar building project. He was commissioned to get ideas from there for the new medical center proposed to His Majesty's Government in Kathmandu. He talked with the engineers constructing the building, and one of them, Dan

Bavington, later came to Kathmandu to survey the situation. His Majesty's Government informed UMN in April that he had granted their request but had not yet given exemption from custom duty on materials they needed from outside.

On his next trip to Chhatarpur, Dr. DeVol delivered by cesarean section the Mategaonkers' first of three children, a little girl, Mala, born May 7, 1964.

Phil's Love of Life

While Ezra spent the month of May in Chhatarpur, Frances went to Landour to spend the time with Phil. Now topping six feet, Phil seemed very happy in Woodstock, almost happy-go-lucky. In his junior year, he was vice-president of the student body and worked on a committee to plan social activities for the school. He loved his Chinese roommate, Larry Pao, and got along well with the international students in the student body. He continued to be popular and was a leader throughout his senior year. His grades were better than average, but he was willing to accept himself as being no "brain," though the results of his work when he put forth effort belied that fact. He received an award in drama and got his "W" for basketball.

As editor of the Woodstock yearbook, Phil with his friend Richard Friedricks stayed in India through the Christmas holidays to get the best printing job possible done on the *Whispering Pine* in Lucknow. He returned to Delhi for his Standard Achievement Test exams. Following that, he traveled south, spent all his money, and was robbed of his suitcase. He finally met his parents on December 28 in Chhatarpur, where he and twenty other guests and Friends missionaries celebrated a late Christmas together.

Phil cared little for Nepal, but he reveled in being in Chhatarpur.

"No place I have been is as beautiful as Chhatarpur and Bundelkhand," he said. He called it home, no matter where the family lived.

However, Phil adored his parents, and after Christmas he went to Nepal to be near them for as long as he could. The parents felt concern that Phil seemed willing to settle for less than "all out" for the Lord, but they did not find him rebellious. He was a thoughtful and loving son.

Phil's own assessment of this period of his life was more stern.

"In high school," he said, "I got really cynical. I think I was more cynical than my parents were aware, about the church, Christians, and patriotism, but never about my parents. They were consistent, always seeking God's will and really trying, and I couldn't fault them for that. I can't imagine what would have happened to me if they had been any less than what they were. The basis of our struggles, which began then, was that I rebelled against their spiritual discipline, though never against them. I began to look on Christianity as a crutch that I did not need. I wanted to taste life, be uncommitted, and feast on seeing, smelling, and hearing the world."

Phil's cultivation of detachment and desire to remain uncommitted was no doubt partly a protective covering of a very sensitive spirit, for from the first year of his life he had lived among India's poor and suffering and experienced the pain of it as something too massive and severe to manage. His parents' efforts to cope with it had often taken them away from him. He felt no bitterness about this, for the outcastes and beggars were his friends. So was every stray dog and knock-kneed horse. Though he loved the sport of being on a hunt with his father and relished venison steak as much as anyone, he did not enjoy the kill. The bloody bit of skinning and cutting up the meat to divide among the people of the community would never have been completed except that he had early learned from his father that when he came up against a tough job, he had to go through with it whether he wanted to or not. He must have sensed that commitment would lead him to the "all out" discipleship he saw in his parents, and he was not ready for it yet. Therefore, their concern for him was deep and their prayers constant.

The Strain of Cataracts

Dr. DeVol required stronger and stronger lenses to keep functioning in the operating room. In the summer of 1965, Dr. Rambo confirmed that his right eye was ripe for surgery. In consultation with Dr. Rambo, the DeVols decided to go to the Christian Medical College Hospital in Ludhiana for the operation from a Dutch ophthalmologist, Dr. Franken.

Phil wrote from Woodstock urging his parents to consider going to America.

"As I see it," he wrote, "there are three reasons why you should go now: (1) To attend Joe's wedding this summer. (2) To get your eyes fixed. (3) To be able to get back to run the mission while everyone else is away in 1966. KEEP THE BANNER HIGH!"

The DeVols wanted to heed Phil's advice. Oil had been discovered on Sunnyslope, which made his plan economically feasible. They longed to see Joe, who had made them proud by his strong Christian witness, his achievement in athletics, and his becoming a top book salesman in an effort in his second year of college to take responsibility for his expenses. They were more than anxious to meet the nurse he had chosen as his bride, Judith Anne Chapin, a Malone College classmate from Bell, California. The wedding on June 19, 1965, would take place in Bell Friends Church. However, after consideration with prayer, they felt no liberty of spirit at that time to leave Nepal or India.

National events, however, had also added fuel to Phil's fire, because Pakistan went to war with India and temporarily cut off any possibility of the DeVols' getting to Ludhiana for the cataract operation. The tense atmosphere in Kathmandu was exacerbated with the making of specific evacuation plans for all the missionaries. In Landour and throughout North India the government ordered blackouts and the building of air-raid shelters.

"I had a dream about you the other night," Stuti Prakash, the pastor in Chhatarpur wrote to the DeVols at this time. "I saw you sitting on a rock surrounded by deep water."

His prayerful concern lifted their spirits as did also the promise from Isaiah 43:5: "When you pass through the rivers, they will not sweep over you."

Less than two weeks before they were to leave, China as well as Pakistan became involved in the war with India. Finally, September 20, 1965, the United Nations ordered a cease-fire, and the way cleared to Ludhiana just in time to proceed with the operation. On October 9, 1965, the date previously set, Dr. Franken operated and Dr. Rambo stood by to encourage and to pray.

The following week as Ezra was kept flat on his back, Phil came from Woodstock to help his mother with the nursing care. Frances and Phil by turns read to him, and as he recovered, father and son had some deep and candid talks about his finishing high school, his enrolling in college, the draft, finances, and spiritual life.

"Be God's man, Phil," his father admonished tenderly as Phil returned to Woodstock.

The operation on the right eye was considered successful though recuperation took longer than expected. The left eye was deteriorating rapidly, but before the operation on it could take place, he was advised to get a contact lens for his right eye.

"If Ezra gets good vision which we fully expect with refraction," Frances wrote, "he wants to get back into surgery full time. He does not like administration, and the multiplication of serious problems plus the added eyestrain has made the past few months almost too much at times. Do remember us in prayer about this matter."

As soon as he was able to travel, Ezra and Frances took the train to Harpalpur, where they were met with the hospital car and were taken on to Chhatarpur for rest and recuperation. The rest did not last long, for in spite of his inability to use both eyes at once, Dr. DeVol insisted that Dr. Mategaonker get a few days off. With the help of a new Indian doctor, Dr. DeVol scheduled a few operations, and, though everything went all right, it was evident that he would not be able to take on much surgery until he had a contact lens, which he hoped to get in January.

Valley of Decision

"I've discovered I'm really a surgeon at heart," Ezra said to Frances as they talked over some of the problems in the work facing them on their return to Nepal in early November. "Perhaps sometime in the future someone whose first love is administration can be found as director of the UMMC in Nepal."

The problems that tried the souls of missionaries were not primarily the big ones of banned conversion and restriction of Christian witnessing. There were fairly clear guidelines for handling them. Nor were they the strains of living in a foreign culture with inadequate communication and inability to speak the language, or the corruption, or the problems related to health, sanitation, or inadequate living arrangements. The real hurts came from inside, in breakdown of relationships, or in the loss of spiritual vision, causing staff members to bend the mission to serve their individual interests rather than to serve the people.

One such thrust came from the Indian staff who predominated in the laboratory, X ray, and pharmacy. They wanted to be considered the heads of departments. At the drop of a hat, however, they took time off for picnics without regard to who would remain on duty. They seemed not yet to have learned the inseparable relationship of responsibility and authority.

The Nepali staff, on the other hand, tried to unionize. The ambassador was sure they had communist backing, and he informed Dr. DeVol that Nepali law made such action illegal. Political involvement was beyond his ken, but Dr. DeVol decided to consult Shri Nir Kumar, a lawyer who had been courageous enough to defend Christians four years earlier. The lawyer proved to be very helpful in this tough battle, which continued vigorously for two months. In an effort to keep the matter out of the courts, Dr. DeVol called a meeting of all employees and presented them with the reasons why he felt their action was wrong. As a charitable institution, he pointed out, they were not even paying the running expenses to say nothing of the salaries and capital expenses. As a hospital, they had to keep open twenty-four hours a day, 365 days a year. As a mission, they should be prepared at times to go beyond the call of duty. As a united mission including twelve nations, unions would clearly result in division, not cooperation. There was no precedent for unionism in Nepal, and surely professionals would lose status on joining a labor union. The meeting had some effect but did not keep the matter from dragging on for a long time. Finally there was victory.

When the kitchen crew including the cook walked off the job with demands beyond the ability of the mission to pay, the problem was centered in disgruntled leaders who needed discipline. Finding who they were took two months, but again peace finally came to the kitchen when they were replaced.

The DeVols never lost sight of the fact that real victory was measured by changed lives and a clear witness to Christ in the land of Nepal. At times difficulties seemed to cloud the purpose for which the mission existed.

"How to live in constant victory, no matter what, is part of the everyday walk, and it is a battle with the unseen," they concluded.

No battle was as difficult, however, as the one involving a few leaders in the mission who opposed the new fee system in the hospital and the efforts to increase vocal Christian witness. Struggles with unions, nationalities, disgruntled employees, and even with the frustration of deteriorating eyesight paled before the seeming loss of ground gained in these fields.

Shortly after the first cataract operation as the DeVols returned to Nepal, the executive committee of the UMN met to discuss the opposition to these policies, and their conclusion was to replace Dr. DeVol and transfer him to another mission hospital in Tansen on the grounds that the building program needed more attention. This decision came as a shock, not only to the DeVols, but to nearly everyone on the staff. It resulted in an examination of the decision-making body, for there had been only three voting members in the meeting representing twenty-four member bodies. A strong request went in for changes in the makeup of the executive committee and for reconsideration of the decision.

The DeVols, however, under no circumstance would allow their position to be brought up again. Dr. Carl Friedricks, a friend and colleague whom they respected, had been appointed in their place, and they began to make plans to leave as soon as he could come. Dr. Friedricks, however, requested them to stay out their term until the end of June, while he worked on building plans. They agreed to this, but waited for guidance from the mission council and the mission board before giving word on the move to Tansen.

Four months before this development, Dr. Mategaonker had expressed his desire to study for his master's degree in surgery, and the mission council had already noted that for this to happen, the DeVols should plan to return to Chhatarpur after their next furlough.

"There is no doubt about it," the DeVols admitted, "this assignment in Kathmandu is the hardest one we've ever had. We do not feel inclined to move on to Tansen unless that is what the board wants. Our hearts are very much drawn to Chhatarpur to help Dr. Mategaonker."

While they waited, two cables arrived, the first with news of the death of Frances' uncle, Erwin Hyne, and the second of the death of her mother, Frieda Hodgin, a woman of prayer. As Frances tried to grasp what had happened, her emotions seemed to wall off the grief for a later time. She prepared for the coming of Dr. Carl Friedricks and family, who had to move into very small quarters. Their son roomed with Phil until they left together for Woodstock school for their final few months before graduation. Dr. Carl Friedricks took up the plans for building but soon ran into the same temporarily immovable roadblocks with the government that had brought Dr. DeVol to a standstill. The hospital was indeed built, but not until sixteen years later.

The UMN board remained firm on the new fee system, and though Nepali law against conversions did not change, the witness for Christ continued to spread, just like the corn Dr. DeVol had heard about from Mr. Johnson of U.S. AID.

Traveling in the country, Mr. Johnson had noticed a fine field of corn and had asked the Nepali farmer his secret.

"There were three strange grains in some of the American wheat that I received," he explained. "I planted those grains and got some ears of corn. The next year I planted that corn and reaped an abundant harvest. This is the fruit of those three grains. Since then, I've given seed to my neighbors, too."

The witness for Christ had not come to Nepal by accident, as did the corn. It was brought through sacrifice and disciplined obedience and was nurtured with prayers and tears of caring Christians. By 1987 it had multiplied to more than 25,000.

Fishtail Peak, Annapurna Range, Nepal and Kathmandu Valley Temples (below).

Frances DeVol, entertaining Her Royal Highness, Queen Ratna (above). Harry Barnes (and wife), First Officer of the American Embassy. Major General Padam Bahadur Khatri (and wife) Minister of Defense and in charge of Foreign Affairs.

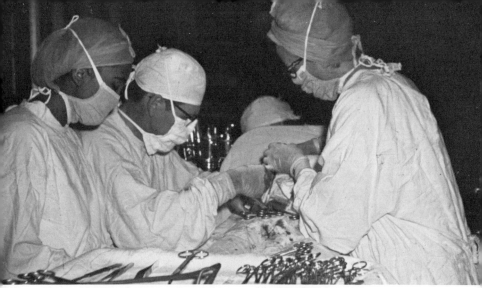

Dr. DeVol (top), assisted by Frances as nurse, was the first surgeon in the United Mission to Nepal.

Shobha (left center with her baby), a tetanus patient of Dr. DeVol's, was healed and became a Christian and a nurse in Nepal.

Bibi Maya (above), a victim of Pott's Disease (tuberculosis of spine) and a paraplegic, walked again!

This woman was carried eighty miles over the hills to the hospital.

An indigenous church in Pokhra, Nepal

Pastor Robert Karthak (with his wife) did not hesitate in baptizing converts in Kathmandu in spite of threat of prison.

In Kathmandu the eyes of Bodnath temple never blink or cry or see!

Crown Prince Birendra Bir Bikram Shah Dev became the Colonel of the Nepalese Army on his twenty-first birthday.

A boy (center), who before surgery, was so bowlegged he could barely walk.

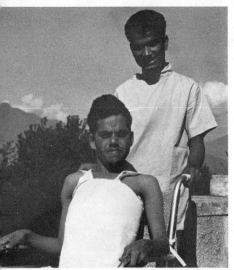

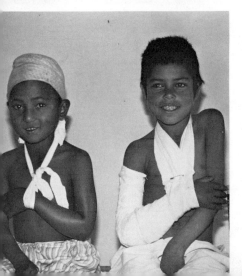

A teacher (above left) fell from a tree and broke his back.

Ram Ratan, who had a fractured skull, with Dr. DeVol.

Supra-condylar fracture of the humerus (left).

Paul Rees and Bob Pierce with the DeVols

Jamie Sandoz of Oregon with the DeVols at the UMN Hospital in Nepal.

Dr. Sharma, Dr. Bethel Fleming, and Major General Padam Bahadur Khatri (above right). Dr. Fleming opened the medical work in Nepal for the UMN and was the first UMMC Director.

Dr. DeVol, front left, met with UMN missionaries from six stations at a workers' conference in Kathmandu.

12 The Battle for Sight

The eternal God is your refuge, and underneath are the everlasting arms.   *Deuteronomy 33:27*

Three Weeks of Darkness

The DeVols' service in Nepal came to an abrupt end on Sunday, March 6, 1966.

"Ezra's eyes seem to be bothering him," Frances noted. "He keeps testing them."

Both Ezra and Frances were so worried by evening that they called the only eye specialist in Kathmandu, even though it was a holiday and he was not in his office. Dr. Laxmi Narayan Prasad of the government hospital agreed to see them at once and discovered retinal detachment in the right eye. To prevent further separation, he ordered Dr. DeVol to bed for five days with both eyes bandaged. Knowing of no laser beam equipment in either Nepal or India, Dr. Prasad recommended their going immediately to the U.S.A.

Friends from every direction came to help pack and secure the necessary income tax clearance, permits to leave and return, and the plane reservations. Dr. Carl Friedricks cabled Phil in Woodstock, the mission in India, the families, and the mission board in the U.S.A., requesting arrangements for hospital admittance.

On their last day in Kathmandu, Ezra was strengthened as Frances read to him a promise sent by a colleague, Dr. Eleanor Knox:

I have chosen you and have not rejected you.
So do not fear, for I am with you;
Do not be dismayed, for I am your God.
I will strengthen you and help you;
I will uphold you with my righteous right hand . . . .
For I am the LORD, your God
Who takes hold of your right hand
And says to you, Do not fear;
I will help you. (Isaiah 41:9b, 10, 13)

Frances wrote in her diary that day: "God wants us to be so dependent and so sure of Him that if He beckoned us to step right out into space from a mountaintop we would do it. I want to honor Him with just such faith."

A host of friends in Kathmandu waved goodbye as the DeVols "stepped off the mountaintop" of Nepal. Phil came down from Woodstock to meet them in the Delhi airport and help transfer them from the small plane to a Boeing 707. One can only imagine Phil's feelings as he waved goodbye to his surgeon father with bandaged eyes and his gentle mother now in charge. They would not see him graduate from Woodstock, and he would have to find his own way home.

Between Zurich and London, Dr. DeVol began to see the convoluted retina peeling off the eyeball as the detachment increased, and he sensed a point had been reached beyond which there would be no hope.

"Oh, Lord, that I may receive my sight!" he cried out in the darkness from the depths of his being. The first step in answer to this cry was the provision of a stretcher on changing planes in London, making it possible for him to lie flat the rest of the way to New York.

As soon as possible after landing in New York, Frances called the Cattells, who had contacted the ophthalmologist, Dr. Claire King, and confirmed plans for their consulting Dr. Roscoe Kennedy in Cleveland Clinic. It was night when they arrived in Cleveland. The twins and their families, the Cattells, the Escolmes, and other relatives and friends met them and arranged for them to spend the night in a motel across the street from the clinic.

In spite of the cables and phone calls, the need for emergency care had not penetrated the understanding of the people on duty in the clinic, and the next morning the hospital sent a wheelchair—not a stretcher—across the street to pick up the patient. He was kept sitting while the routine red tape for admission was cared for. In the midst of these anxious and helpless moments, Ezra heard God's promise: "Be strong, do not fear; your God will come.... Then will the eyes of the blind be opened." (Isaiah 35:4, 5) *No matter what happens*, he felt assured as faith took hold, *God is in charge, and He will overrule all circumstances*. His anxiety left him.

The children came to see and encourage their father. Patricia came with her boy, Michael Irwin Haynes, who would be two years old on July 4. His grandfather had never seen him. The family stood by as Frances took the bandage off Ezra's eyes, conscious of the fact that this might be his only chance ever to see his grandson. Priscilla brought Stephenie, Bill, and Geoffrey.

As soon as Dr. Kennedy came to know what had taken place, he was alarmed, for he discovered a seventy-five percent detachment. It was too late to use the laser beam. He had to perform surgery.

"This is the worst detachment I have ever operated on," he admitted.

For the next ten days, bandaged and with his head wedged between two sandbags, Ezra continued to lie in darkness. The hours crept by, but Frances was constantly by his side caring for him, telling him all about what was going on around him, reading to him, or playing tapes of long stories to keep his mind occupied. She encouraged visitors to come, and the children and grandchildren came time after time.

Earl Smith, a friend and a Friends pastor in the city, came daily to shave Ezra and crack jokes that penetrated the panic and brought the warmth of friendship at a time he was fighting to hang on to sanity. At times Ezra teeter-tottered between delirium and consciousness as he felt he was nailed to Sunnyslope barn floor with spikes in each shoulder and with hay in the loft falling down on him.

Healing

Light flooded the room the day the bandages came off, and the surgeon threatened with blindness could see! In the days that followed, Frances went through all the accounts in the New Testament of the healing of the blind, reading them aloud.

A few days later, the DeVols left the hospital and had a smooth ride in Russell Haynes's Cadillac to the Cattells' home in Canton. Joe and Judy arrived from California the next day, and the DeVols were thrilled to see their new daughter-in-law. Pat, Pris, and their families all joined them for a family reunion, and Ezra was delighted not only to hear the voices of his grandchildren, but also to see them and hold them on his lap. As his vision improved, Russell and Pat took their parents for a drive, and they all enjoyed the delight Ezra expressed on seeing the blue sky, green grass, tulips, hyacinths, and daffodils. These were rich family days, but they missed Phil, still in India.

Healing continued steadily. Though there was some loss of peripheral vision, by the end of June Ezra was reading with his right eye, driving the car, making plans for the second cataract operation, and preparing to return to India.

Dr. Dan Weidenthall at St. Lukes Hospital in Cleveland, after giving Dr. DeVol a very thorough examination, advised him that cataract removal from his left eye carried with it a one-hundred percent higher risk for him than for the average person.

"I'd recommend that you not have an operation at all if you could be content to clip coupons for the rest of your life," Dr. Weidenthall remarked, knowing very well about Dr. DeVol's burning desire to get back into surgery.

The cataract operation on the left eye was scheduled for July 12, 1966, and was performed by Dr. Craig George in Alliance, Ohio. Using an advanced technique, he operated under local anesthesia, and in five days Ezra was discharged and back home in Damascus. In one month's time, eyesight in both eyes had greatly improved (20/15 left eye; 20/50 right eye), and he was able to read small print with the use of his new glasses.

Reunion with Philip

Phil, having graduated from Woodstock and taken a trip through Europe, arrived home on August 24 with thirteen cents in his pocket. His parents left a mission board meeting to greet him, and they all went out to find Joe and Judy.

A few days later Phil enrolled in Malone College, and the DeVols had many opportunities that fall and winter to be with him in Canton for soccer games and many long talks. They were shocked to realize that during their time-consuming battle to save Ezra's eyesight, they had somehow lost touch with their son.

"I want to live my own life, apart from God," Phil stated frankly.

Phil's father could not let him go. He could not bear for Philip to be less than all for Christ. He remembered the bows and arrows given him by the Superintendent of Police in Chhatarpur.

"These are used to kill deer and rabbits, but they are also used to kill big game, such as tigers," the superintendent of police had explained. "It's all in the way you use them. You don't have to subject the bow to great strain to kill a rabbit, but when you aim at a tiger, you must take a different position. You must sit on the ground, place both feet on the bow, take the string in both hands and pull to the farthest extent of the bow, and then let fly. The weapon is the same, but it takes a lot more 'man' to bring down a tiger."

Ezra could not bear for Phil to aim for less than the highest or to give less than his best. He pled with Philip to consider the dangers in rejecting Christ and playing into the hands of Satan, but though Philip went away sorrowful, he did go away.

The parents were shattered. *Where have we failed so miserably in bringing him up?* Disappointment was so deep that Ezra sank into a time of darkness. Then the stark reality of his inability to love folk—even a son or a daughter—who disappointed him brought him under deep conviction. He prayed that day to be filled with God's love, to be made perfect in love.

"Rid me from all un-love," he cried out, "and fill me with Thy love!"

Frances was also struggling.

"O God, create in me a deeper love for Thee," she prayed. *Love does work in everyday life*, she affirmed in meditation. *Christ's love in our hearts enables us to rise above all personal grievances and petty things. It enlarges the heart. It is a fountain of courtesy.*

Frances called Ezra's attention to Isaiah 54:13: " 'All your sons will be taught by the LORD, and great will be your children's peace.' " She added verse 17 as a promise for their future work: " 'No weapon forged against you will prevail, and you will refute every tongue that accuses you. This is the heritage of the servants of the LORD, and this is their vindication from me,' declares the LORD."

Phil went to California to spend Christmas with Joe. The DeVols called him and Joe on Christmas Day as they celebrated in Ohio with the twins and their families and held the new granddaughter, Cynthia Marie Haynes, born December 19, 1966.

The Return to India

In 1967 events leading toward the DeVols' return to India developed rapidly. In New York, the Woman's Union Missionary Society was planning a merger of their nurses' training program with Friends in India. The DeVols met with the WUMS president and worked out financial details for building a training center near the Christian Hospital in Chhatarpur.

To raise money for this new development, the mission board scheduled the DeVols in such heavy deputation that Dr. DeVol had to fight for time to organize his notes of new developments in medicine that he had taken while attending the American College of Surgeons' Convention in San Francisco with Dr. C. Everett Koop as moderator. To keep up with the times, he ordered and packed the necessary medicines, supplies, and equipment secured at very reasonable prices from the Medical Assistance Program (MAP) in Chicago.

The DeVols were not able to receive in person the honor Marion College bestowed on them as Distinguished Alumni of the Year of 1967. Daughter Priscilla agreed to be present to receive the plaques on their behalf.

One cold, rainy night just a week before their flight to India, the DeVols, on their way to Westgate Monthly Meeting in Columbus, skidded into a multiple-car accident due to the icy road. As the lady in the car they hit jumped out to notify the police, Dr. DeVol slid in beside the man at the steering wheel and checked him over to see if he had been injured. Finding nothing wrong, he handed the man his card and advised him to get a more thorough checkup. The policeman, harried by the many accidents that had occurred at that same slick spot of the downhill road, called out, "Keep moving!" Since neither car had been damaged and there was no evidence of injury, the DeVols heard no more of this before leaving for India.

Flying off via California to see Joe and Judy, the DeVols made stops in Honolulu and then in Taiwan for a visit with Charles and Leora DeVol. They were inspired by the zeal and enthusiasm of the Christians in Taiwan as they heard their testimonies. Ezra also shared experiences of India and Nepal. They were given two superb Chinese feasts and went to hear Charles preach in Generalissimo Chiang Kai-shek's church before proceeding to Hong Kong.

Of special delight in Hong Kong was meeting Dr. A. R. Hodgson of the University of Hong Kong's Department of Orthopaedic Surgery. Dr. Hodgson invited the DeVols to scrub and join him in the operating room. He specialized in operating from the anterior approach on the spine for tuberculosis, and the DeVols spent the day observing his techniques and assisting in an operation.

At Home in Chhatarpur

A year after leaving Nepal and India with bandaged eyes, Dr. Ezra and Frances returned to the early morning warmth of Delhi and Bob Hess's welcome. Bob was in the city to meet with the Board of Managers of the United Mission to Nepal, and the DeVols also joined them. Later, on board the train for Central India, they were flooded with familiar sights and sounds and overwhelmed by the sense of being home again. In Chhatarpur the people welcomed them graciously, and as they stepped into their house with everything in order and lunch on the table, they knew this was where they belonged.

No one was happier to see the DeVols return than Dr. Mategaonker, who had been accepted in Ludhiana Christian Medical College for the study for the Masters in Surgery course. The next day Dr. DeVol went with him into the operating room and assisted him in the first operation. The second operation that day was done by Dr. DeVol with Dr. Mategaonker assisting. Dr. Mategaonker congratulated him on his performance.

"I had no trouble with my eyes!" Dr. DeVol exclaimed. "It is as though I have never been away!"

Applying lessons learned from Dr. Hodgson in Hong Kong in treating a paraplegic patient, Dr. DeVol had remarkable success. Prof. A. R. Hodgson, F.R.C.S., F.A.C.S, on hearing of it, wrote on May 19, 1967: "I am delighted to hear that you have been able to go ahead with the radical procedure for Pott's Disease, and I am sure the young lady who has recovered from her paraplegia is indeed very happy with her treatment."

Dr. Mategaonker left for his training in Ludhiana in July. Famine in Bihar took the Colemans and the mission jeep away to save some millions of lives. The only other doctor in the Christian Hospital left for the army. Though Norma Freer and a loyal staff stood by, India's heat and the pressure of work quickly took a toll as the DeVols stepped into their roles of very heavy responsibility. Both lost weight rapidly.

"We don't have the old stamina we used to have," Frances observed.

When three staff members became ill, the daily care of nearly a hundred outpatients and fifty-seven inpatients exceeded their strength. Dr. Grace Jones Singh came to the rescue, taking calls on Thursday afternoons in order to give the DeVols half a day off.

Bilateral Detachments

The pressure in the Christian Hospital with no other doctor proved to be too much, and in late August Dr. DeVol experienced one of the worst calamities possible to a surgeon. He developed detached retina in both eyes. Having witnessed divine healing in others, he and his staff now prayed for restored eyesight. It soon became evident that this was not the way the Lord was leading, and in order to keep the Chhatarpur hospital open, Dr. Mategaonker returned immediately, forfeiting his opportunity for study that year. Norma Freer accompanied the DeVols to Delhi and telephoned St. Lukes Hospital in Cleveland to arrange for early admittance.

Catherine Cattell met the plane as it arrived in Cleveland, and friends from medical college days, Marie and Alice Hines, sped back from their vacation to be on hand to help.

Dr. Daniel T. Weidenthal, who had warned Dr. DeVol of just such a possibility, was on hand to operate. On September 1, he performed Cyro-Surgery on the left eye with 40 percent detachment, and ten days later he repaired the right eye with 50 percent detachment. Cardiac arrest gave the doctor and his team a terrible fright, but prayer was answered and Dr. DeVol's life was spared.

The Hines sisters opened their home to the DeVols for a period of recuperation, but Ezra continued having trouble with the right eye. He had to reenter the hospital for another operation in October. Again in January 1968, he went back for still another. Dr. Weidenthal used mercury vapor and photo coagulation to seal the retina in at least twelve places.

When this fourth operation in four months did not bring the desired results, discouragement mounted, and Ezra and Frances began to wonder if they would ever again be able to work as a surgical team. There was so much yet to be done.

In his regular devotional reading, Matthew 6:22 spoke to Ezra: "If your eye is pure there will be sunshine in your soul."

He shared this with Frances, and they thought about what it meant as they fought the darkness that seemed to be crowding in on them. In faith, Ezra accepted God's Word to him through this verse and said, "Whatever my optical vision may be, I want above all else to have this sunshine in my soul. After all, the all-wise and all-loving Potter has the right and power to make His vessel into just the kind that would serve His purpose best."

This lift in their inner spirits was quickly followed by improvement in the right eye, and by April the DeVols were cleared medically to return to India. Before leaving, they had the joy of flying to California to hold their new granddaughter, Nancy Tara, born to Joe and Judy DeVol February 3, 1968.

Mission and Hospital Staff Changes

During the time the DeVols had been away from Chhatarpur, two other doctors had joined the staff and one of them, Dr. Mathew, stayed. The Colemans had left India, and the Hesses left a month later. Kathryn Thompson, a new missionary nurse, had completed her language and was on hand to help. She was living in Chhatarpur with Norma Freer, and Anna Nixon was still in Jhansi eighty miles away. Soon after the DeVols arrived, Dr. Mategaonker left again for Christian Medical College to pursue his medical studies.

"Ezra feels bereft, especially being the only man now on the missionary staff," Frances wrote.

Another woman, Dr. Elizabeth Pothan, replaced Dr. Mathew who left at the end of that year. Dr. Pothan was trained in Ludhiana and had special degrees in pediatrics and obstetrics. Though not a surgeon, she proved to have unusual ability and courage, and when Dr. DeVol was absent at the time a patient needed a cesarean section, Frances advised, encouraged, and assisted her in the operation. Dr. DeVol returned to find both mother and baby doing well.

The Accident

Shortly after the new year, 1969, Ezra received a letter from the Franklin County sheriff alerting him to the fact that he was being sued for $175,000. Sixteen months after the accident occurring on that icy highway January 27, 1967, the man in the car had died of a heart attack, and just a few days before such a suit would have been invalid, his wife had been persuaded to blame his death on the accident and sue the doctor. This came as a shock because Ezra had reported the accident to his insurance company at the time of the accident and had taken for granted that the case had been settled. Letters went back and forth to no avail until finally on April 23, 1971, Nationwide Insurance Company's lawyer Wilbur Jones requested Ezra to return to the U.S.A. for the court hearing. The mission board paid Frances' way home.

On reaching Sunnyslope, Ezra rummaged through the attic to find his diary. As soon as the opposition lawyer heard about the diary, he came down from $175,000 to $8,500, and Wilbur Jones recommended that they settle out of court. Ezra readily agreed, realizing that though his salary was about a thousand dollars a year, no jury would believe it, and the sympathy would be with the "poor" widow rather than with the surgeon.

The DeVols thanked God that summer for the most restful, luxurious, beautiful vacation they had ever had, and Romans 8:28, "All things work together for good to them that love the Lord," proved true once again. While at home, they were able to see Sarah Anita Haynes, their new granddaughter, born July 28, 1968, and their new grandson, Philip Robert Cox, born June 29, 1969. They met Phil's wife, Peg, and had reunions with all their children in Ohio. Frances was present to comfort her sister Elsie at the time of her husband's last illness.

The grandchildren became close to them. "My grandpa is a doctor," was Mike's first sentence. The DeVols delighted in being grandparents.

The summer trip home was beneficial also in allowing Ezra to have another very crucial eye examination. The previous year a bump on the head had sent him sprawling. His eyes, of course, were the main concern. Two years later Dr. Weidenthal would again use argon laser to seal the retina in about twenty-five places. Though the right eye still showed some impairment and limitation of peripheral vision, the battle for sight had been won, and the surgeon continued his work, full of gratitude for each day of seeing.

Through the years of this fight, the DeVols were also engaged in other struggles, as they determined, in the short time they had left, to build a solid structure for the future of the church in India.

Phil loved everything living—especially horses. Woodstock High School graduate, 1966.

W. Robert Hess, superintendent, United Mission to Nepal Representative for American Friends Mission

A detached retina took the DeVols out of Nepal and India to the U.S.A. three months before Phil graduated from Woodstock High School.

The DeVols and the Mategaonkers (children—Dinesh, Mala, Shoba). The DeVols returned to Chhatarpur so that the Mategaonkers could go for further training.

The hospital in Chhatarpur to which the DeVols returned in 1967

Norma Freer, hospital business manager, with Frances

13 The Finishing Touch

Upon this rock I will build my church; and the gates of hell shall not prevail against it.　　　*Matthew 16:18*

The Unfinished Task

Thousands of times Dr. Ezra and Frances DeVol had lived through the dramatic hopes and tragedies of the Christian Hospital's operating theater. Both the agonies and the ecstasies were intensified by the awareness of the eternal significance of the roles they played in the lives of people around them. Cutting away the rottenness of human flesh to save the patient's life while keeping in focus the needs of his whole person, restoring health and the joy of living, reaching his heart with the love and forgiveness of Christ, helping others to accept him as a new creature in Christ Jesus, establishing him in the eternal kingdom of God—all of these aspects were a part of their vision.

"She's gone! It's all over!"

Oh, no! Teenage Elishba Silas Masih, just entering nurses' training, lay dead in the hospital. Her family were new Christians from the distant village of Ghuara where the church had been born out of fierce persecution. Elishba, arriving in Chhatarpur only that week to register her name for training, had been alive and well. Suddenly she developed severe abdominal pain. Emergency surgery followed, revealing the cause— volvulus. Cardiac arrest brought the whole staff to her bedside and sent the members of the church to their knees as Dr. DeVol battled to save her life. Fifty miles away in her village, Elishba's illiterate mother in a dream heard her daughter say, "I'm all right, Mother, but I'm going away."

The mother awakened with a heavy sense of foreboding, called her husband, and together they rushed to Chhatarpur. Elishba's brother and mother readily gave blood for transfusion, but the next day high fever swept in, and as they looked on, it took her away in spite of all they could do.

Dr. Ezra, Frances, and the staff, standing with the family around Elishba's bed, were stunned with grief. *Faith is so new to this little family. How can they stand up under such tragedy?* Such were their thoughts. As they softly wept and prayed, a holy hush settled upon the little group who became suddenly aware of the awesome, mysterious, but very real presence of the Living God lifting their spirits and filling them with peace. No, life was not all over for Elishba and her family; it had only just begun. The DeVols marveled at the evident grace of God at work in the hearts of Elishba's brothers, sister, and parents, so recently converted.

The newly converted did not always reveal such steady faith in the face of death. One such couple, Nathu and Rajabai, brought their sister to the hospital for her delivery. They were sure of their favor with God and the mission, for they had taken a public stand for Christ, braving strong anti-Christian legislation and questionings by authorities. Far removed from their minds was a consideration of any possibility that their sister could die in the Christian Hospital surrounded by love, prayer, and faith.

When she did die, Rajabai, overcome with grief and a sense of betrayal, hysterically shouted at the Indian doctor, "You have murdered my sister!"

Other members of Rajabai's family, newly converted, took up her chant, and their loud wails and accusations reached the ears of all the patients in the hospital. Bitterness went so deep that they did not even return to claim the newborn baby. The father, a Hindu, signed papers to have the baby given to Kulpahar orphanage.

In spite of this distressing display, life was not over for Nathu and Rajabai either. Neither the DeVols nor other members of the church gave up on that newly converted and troubled couple. The DeVols found time to go out to their village, sit by their well, and listen, encourage, and share. They guided and advised Nathu and Rajabai concerning the future education of their children. Gradually the faith of this family took deep root, producing a consistent walk with the Lord and resulting in other relatives of theirs becoming Christians. Nathu and Rajabai eventually became pillars of faith in the church.

The positive impact of the hospital in Bundelkhand left no doubt that keeping it open was a part of God's plan in the building of His Church, and the DeVols, in the short time left, longed to leave the finishing touches of their love upon it. Bringing genuine caring to birth in the life of a person was a long process. In the hospital the DeVols thanked God when people started caring enough to help save lives by giving blood. When Jagannath was so deathly ill everyone thought he would surely die, Pyare Lal Brown heard of it and, remembering Jagannath as a friend of his father's in the orphanage, he came to the hospital and offered to give blood. Despite all he had done to harass Dr. DeVol and the missionaries, he suddenly became an example of caring, and his act was soon the talk of the whole community.

Planning for the Future

"I hope we can settle down for a long, steady, profitable stretch of service," said Dr. DeVol as he searched for ways to stabilize the hospital. He longed to build and hold a highly professional and dedicated staff. But well-trained doctors, nurses, and pharmacists came and left again, often for higher salaries in the cities in spite of all efforts to hold them through scholarship grants, training programs, and good housing. After three years, family concerns pulled even Dr. Pothan away.

The brightest star in hospital development was, of course, the real hope of Dr. Mategaonker's return to Chhatarpur after completing his studies. Men with his determination and dedication were a rare find. Skilled leader that he was, his influence reached through the hospital to the church where he was a tower of strength and wisdom. He would take over as medical superintendent when he returned to the hospital, and the DeVols determined to build up the plant to facilitate his effectiveness. With the help of the Oxford Committee for Famine Relief (OXFAM), the DeVols enlarged the hospital, providing two operating rooms, a larger central supply and sterilization area, more rooms for nursing service, and offices for the nursing superintendent, for the hospital superintendent, and for each of the doctors. They added wards and improved the nurses' home and the outpatient department (OPD). They replaced army cots with hospital beds, bought a new autoclave, and improved the laboratory.

Through the Medical Assistance Program (MAP) they secured a new colorimeter, an incubator, analytic scales, a jeep station wagon, an air conditioner, an emergency operating room light, an operating table, and more oxygen equipment.

The hospital had come a long way from those days when Frances used to pump the kerosene Primus to pressure-cook the syringes and Joe used to hold the flashlight while his father operated.

Joe DeVol returned to India in October 1970 to teach science courses in Woodstock School. With his rich background in the flora and fauna of the Himalayas and having earned his masters' degree in entomology, he came well-qualified for this task. His wife, Judy, and daughter, Nancy Tara, came with him. They all came to Chhatarpur for winter vacation, and Joe had a great time recalling the old days and introducing Judy to his Indian friends. He loved the drive with his father out beyond Ghuara through the jungles and then out to all the old picnic places and hunting grounds. Judy, a nurse, enjoyed helping her father-in-law in the dispensary. Nancy Tara loved her Indian friends and her grandparents. A visit that year from Everett and Catherine Cattell and their daughter, Barbara Brantingham from Taiwan, made the 1970 Christmas a very happy time.

During the second Christmas holiday season from Woodstock, the DeVols entertained two grandchildren: Deborah Audrey, born in Landour, June 4, 1971, and her older sister Nancy. Joe and his father, with a group of students from Woodstock School, took a trip to Khana Reserve Forest in Central India to observe and take pictures of India's fantastic wild animals. It was their last such trip in the exotic jungles, and they would never forget it. Joe and Judy returned to the U.S.A. the following spring.

Cooperative Consolidation through EHA and ETANI

Training administrators, nursing superintendents, and doctors was a task far too enormous for the small Friends Mission, but they were in the forefront of cooperative efforts to do just that under the Evangelical Fellowship of India. Dr. DeVol and Dr. Mategaonker were both active in the movement to consolidate the management of small Christian hospitals throughout North and Central India. The Emmanuel Hospital Association (EHA), though not registered with the government until 1976, began long before that to locate and train medical workers for small Christian hospitals. Dr. DeVol served as vice-chairman and as a member of the EHA Executive Committee. The Christian Hospital in Chhatarpur became one of the sixteen charter members of EHA. Mission hospitals, they learned, supplied one in four hospital beds in India, and the smaller mission hospitals like Chhatarpur were serving the poor and socially underprivileged and were the type EHA sought to encourage.

A sister organization under the EFI was the Evangelical Trust Association of North India (ETANI) formed to hold properties on behalf of foreign missions, which were being slowly but surely squeezed out of India. Dr. DeVol found it necessary to take a full morning off each week for transferring hospital and education properties into ETANI and for registering all churches and parsonages under the BMMS (Bundelkhand Friends Church).

Advantages of being a part of EHA and ETANI became visible almost immediately through shared training programs, public health and family planning information, the establishment of a uniform salary scale, and an additional supply of doctors. From that time there were often two to four doctors serving in the Christian Hospital in Chhatarpur.

Dr. DeVol valued EHA, but he was not enamored by it merely as a large organization. "The important thing," he stated, "is to have men of integrity with real spiritual life in these key positions. If that fails, no amount of rule-making is going to bolster up an organization regardless of how well conceived."

Trouble and Triumph

Another source of help in the realm of staff came through the cooperation of the Woman's Union Missionary Society in Jhansi with the Christian Hospital in Chhatarpur in establishing a joint nurses' training school in Chhatarpur.

The building was in the hands of the general superintendent of the Bundelkhand Friends Church, K. D. Lall, whose work load was already unbelievable. The church and the mission depended on him for keeping accounts, maintaining motors, and supervising workers. He had grown up with the mission and had given years of efficient and faithful service. Planning the new building, securing supplies, and overseeing the project fell on his shoulders more or less by default since no one else could be found to do the job. Under the pressure, this most trusted leader in the church succumbed to temptation. When the first monsoons caused the roofs to leak like so much muslin, the inferior quality of materials he had purchased became evident. The auditor discovered the discrepancies, and the heartbreak of the situation robbed the health and broke the hearts of the DeVols and Norma Freer. A few years later K. D. Lall repented and was restored, but at this time the Christian community went through the fire.

This problem of integrity had been exposed just before Christmas, and no one had the heart to celebrate even though 1971 marked the 41st year of the opening of the Christian Hospital and the 75th year of the mission.

"No matter how we feel, we are going to celebrate Christmas in keeping with the faithfulness of God," Dr. DeVol announced as he rallied the entire staff to practice their parts for the drama and sent invitations throughout the city.

The hospital quadrangle became the setting for scenes at Nazareth, King Herod's Court, Bethlehem, the shepherds' field, and the dedication in the Temple. Joseph and Mary brought the child to the Temple and gave a pair of live pigeons to the high priest. Simeon and Hannah appeared as the prophecies were read by Chaplain Gabriel Massey, spotlighted on the roof of the hospital. The shepherds warmed themselves around the fire while tending their live sheep, and the Roman soldier rode in on a prancing horse. Through the front gate, the kings came majestically riding on camels. At the close, the whole cast gathered around the Bethlehem manger and sang, 'O Come, All Ye Faithful.' Then the spotlight again focused on the hospital rooftop as Chaplain Massey recounted briefly the reason Jesus came. When he mentioned the cross, the spotlight picked up a large, rough cross, suspended against the sky as the angel choir sang, "There Is One Who Was Willing to Die in My Stead." The audience of some nine hundred people sat spellbound.

Three days later, the weather was magnificent as in the same location and under a shamiyana dignitaries of the city of Chhatarpur again were seated to see the pictures and hear the story of the opening of the mission and the establishment of the hospital.

"What hath God wrought!" were the words of Moti Lal, when the hospital was built. The Civil Surgeon, Dr. G. S. Saxena, officially opened the new OPD. The guest of honor was His Highness Bhumani Singh, Maharaja of Chhatarpur, whose father had given the land for the hospital. The plan to have a tea after the celebration was canceled, and the money and offerings were sent to help the 10,000,000 Bangladesh refugees crowding into India in 1971 and 1972 to escape the atrocities of the Pakistan/India war. The new BMMS superintendent, George Masih, emptied his pockets, and Dr. DeVol emptied his rupee bank account. As the celebrations ended, the disappointment and failure were temporarily buried in a flood of thanksgiving and caring for others.

Illness

"We're busier than we've ever been and older than we've ever been," Frances remarked in a letter to Catherine. "Ezra is back to his old skinny self. He has had some dizziness ever since his last eye operation and is now and then unsteady, but we support each other walking! The arthritis in his neck is painful. I'm hoping it will clear up. The aspirin he takes for arthritis causes hemorrhage in his eyes."

Following a vacation in Pinepoint, Frances wrote, "I don't know what happened in the hills, but apparently the altitude doesn't suit me. It may never happen again. I have cut out tea and coffee except for the early morning cup, and the high blood pressure has come down to what is pretty normal for me. It was just a quick reaction to too much coffee, I guess. We naturally get tired."

Ezra wrote Sherman Brantingham that fall of 1971, "Frances has not been well lately. She tires easily, has had the flu, and is stiff with arthritis."

At the same time, Frances wrote, "Ezra has developed a very bad cough, and it is hanging on. He has been in bed with it. We may have to take a trip either to Ludhiana or Vellore to get to the bottom of it. Many are praying as I know you are."

The culture showed the problem causing the cough to be *moniliasis* caused by a fungus, Monilia, an infection almost impossible to treat.

There is still so much to be done in building the church, in strengthening EHA, in finishing the hospital plant, and in developing staff! These were the thoughts underlying the prayers of Ezra and Frances as they overcame obstacle after obstacle during these final years in India. *We must hold out at least until Dr. Mategaonker gets back!*

Dr. Mategaonker, however, was having his own struggles. In spite of his best efforts, he could not complete the work in the time allotted. At the time of the second examination, the officials previously decided they would pass only one-third of the students. Dr. Mategaonker came just a few points below the top third. His disappointment was keener than if he had missed it by a wide margin. He returned to Chhatarpur immediately, however, because another emergency made it imperative.

The emergency began January 17, 1972, as the DeVols faced another life-changing crisis. The EHA auditor demanded not only a balanced account of the hospital money, but an exact count of such things as syringes, medicine bottles, and catheters. In the midst of the counting, Norma noticed Frances.

"Frances!" she called, reaching out to her.

"Oh, I can't take any more!" Frances moaned, grabbing her chest.

Norma called for the doctor, and Dr. DeVol came running. He called the doctors of the Civil Hospital and together they did an X-ray and an EKG. The tests revealed an enlarged heart and many extra systoles. Frances had severe chest pain and palpitations and had to be put to bed. Ezra could hardly pull himself away from her bedside. In the hospital he felt he had almost lost his right hand. There was no one in sight to take her place. Where could a superintendent of nurses be found? Emmanuel

Hospital Association was searching, but now the need was imperative.

A second EKG of Frances' heart was sent to Ludhiana for evaluation, and Ezra's worst fears were confirmed. The diagnosis was myocardial infarction. The doctor in Ludhiana recommended that she see Dr. Roy in Delhi at the All-India Institute of Medical Science. As soon as Frances had gained enough strength to travel, Ezra had another EKG taken. Just as they were leaving for Delhi, Pastor Stuti Prakash came to say goodbye and to pray with Frances. His prayer was so filled with power that Frances was lifted by an unusual sense of the presence of God.

The pastor then turned to her and said: "Mrs. DeVol, you are healed. Now you just have to gain your strength."

Frances stood the trip to Delhi very well and was given a thorough examination by Dr. Roy, the cardiologist. Another EKG was taken.

As Dr. Roy compared his EKG tracing with the one taken the day before and the three previous tracings, he said, "I cannot believe it! I cannot believe it! There is nothing wrong with this tracing!"

Back home again, Frances tried very hard to be completely well, and though she was definitely making progress, she was not able to rise to her expectations. According to the doctors' orders, she sought to engage in progressive exercise. She often pushed this to the point where cardiac irregularity again put her in bed. The awful sense of failure depressed her. Her husband began walking with her in the early mornings and late evenings to help regulate the pace and to encourage her.

"Ezra," she confessed, "sometimes I feel such heavy burden for the unsaved in my family, and I am concerned about my brother Jonathan."

"But Frances, before he died, you prayed so much for him."

"I know. When I heard how ill he was, I wrote him, 'Johnny, keep saying over and over, *The Lord is my Shepherd!*' "

"And I remember the letter his wife wrote back to you, telling you they had read your letter to him, and how your brother-in-law went in and had prayer with him before he died."

"But I don't have any assurance that Johnny made his peace with God, and tonight I feel so anxious about it. Can you pray with me that I will find peace about this?"

Shortly after this conversation and prayer, Frances woke up her husband. "Ezra! I've had a vision—or maybe it was a dream. I saw myself walking at night up toward a river, and across the way was a large group of people. All of them looked happy! Two of them walked toward the water. One of them looked like Mendel, and I was puzzled until I realized it was Mendel's twin, Melvin! With him was Jonathan!"

Ezra thanked God for this assurance that had come to Frances and urged her to share it with her family in Michigan. As soon as letters could go and come, Frances received a letter from her brother.

"In your dream, or vision, Frances, when you saw Johnny, did he have his glasses on?"

Frances remembered the vision. No, Johnny didn't have glasses on!

The joy of the assurance that came to her through this experience filled her with happiness that lasted a long time.

Dr. Mategaonker, hearing of the situation in Chhatarpur and of Frances' illness, swallowed his disappointment at not passing his examinations and entered into the struggle with the DeVols. He urged the DeVols to move to the bungalow formerly occupied by the Cattells, about half a mile away from the hospital. Dr. Mategaonker's house was near, and he would thus be on call to bear the brunt of emergencies.

The move to the quiet "old bungalow" with its cooler atmosphere and peaceful garden in front, instead of the noisy bus stand, contributed much to healing. The hot season, however, was rapidly approaching, and Ezra knew Frances would not be able to stand India's summer heat, nor could she go to the high altitude of Landour and take refuge in Pinepoint.

"India seems almost too much for us," Ezra had to admit, "but our work is not yet finished."

Reporting to the mission board, he wrote: "I feel I need to be here until after more of the building is completed. Also, K. D. Lall is still under discipline. Dr. Mategaonker must be given another chance to pass his examinations, and Dr. Pothan has gone."

They truly did not know what to do to escape the heat. Providentially an answer to the dilemma came through their finding a place in Switzerland's Grundelwall Valley at an altitude some three thousand feet lower than Landour. Nearby were the David MacKee family, whom they had known in India. Planning to be away part of the summer, the MacKees offered the DeVols their home. So they found themselves going from 112°F. weather in Delhi to 76°F. overnight to Zurich to begin one of the most refreshing, beautiful vacations of their lives. Both gained ground physically, and the doctor was pleased with the progress Frances was making until just a few days before they were to leave for India again.

"Hmmm. Not so good. You should stay a month longer," Dr. Roth, the Swiss cardiologist, advised.

Frances was disappointed. She went back to the house and wrote down her prayer:

> Lord Jesus, you know these symptoms and why we can't return on Saturday to India. We have felt we have been following your leading, so we do not question. I believe you began the work of healing on March 5th . . . . How to regulate life—so that I push as much as I should and still not too much is the problem . . . . Make me fit for whatever lies ahead. I trust you right now to perfect that which concerns me.

As the days went by, the expected improvement did not occur. The DeVols tried to hear what the Lord was saying through this. Should they cancel their flight at the end of the month and stay on in Switzerland, hoping Frances' health would improve? This would cost quite a sum in cancellation fees. Should they accept this as indicating they should leave mission work and return to the U.S.A. to retire now? Or should they hold to their present plans?

By the middle of the month, Ezra felt that he had the answer: "I believe the Lord expects us to take the initiative. We're going to have to put our feet in the water."

Even though Frances was not free of symptoms, she and Ezra accepted the challenge of Joshua 3:13:

> And as soon as the priests who carry the ark of the LORD—the LORD of all the earth—set foot in the Jordan,

the water flowing downstream will be cut off and stand up in a heap.

This trip was really to be a test of faith. In the first place, as they reached Basel to board the train, they were directed to the wrong end of the track. Seat reservations were in a coach with a certain number, and no such number appeared on any of the coaches of that train.

Looking for someone who might understand English, Ezra saw a conductor.

"Where can we find this coach number?" he asked. The conductor, however, was in no condition to answer. He was dead drunk.

Lord, what shall I do? Send someone who understands English to help us! Ezra silently prayed.

A man suddenly appeared by his side and asked, "Can I help you?"

Ezra showed the man his ticket.

"Oh, you're at the wrong end of the station!" the man exclaimed. "You'll have to hurry, for it's a long way back, and the train is about to leave!"

Knowing full well that this rush and excitement was exactly what Frances did *not* need, Ezra, loaded with luggage, proceeded as fast as possible to the other end of the station.

The train was shaking and the whistle blowing, but they finally spotted their number on one of the coaches and jumped on. The luggage was thrown on as the train moved out.

Reaching Amsterdam to board the plane, they found a state of confusion. The authorities delayed the plane as they used all their persuasive powers to dislodge unauthorized passengers so that those with tickets and reservations could board.

By the time the DeVols got into the air, Frances was exhausted. Between Teheran and New Delhi she felt absolutely wretched. Her feet were swollen and she could not rest.

Ezra had some very dark moments. His thoughts turned to God, and he began to pray: "O God, now it is Your move! We have put our feet in the water!"

Leafing through his Bible, he found and read to Frances what he believed was God's answer:

God is not a man, that He should lie,
Nor the son of man, that He should change His mind.

Does He speak and then not act?
Does He promise and not fulfill?
(Numbers 23:19)

"Yes!" Frances responded, squeezing her husband's hand. "We must not doubt Him now!"

Ezra noticed that Frances seemed more relaxed and was soon asleep. They reached Chhatarpur without any further difficulty.

Finding Dr. Mategaonker alone, the pump not working, no water in the hospital, the autoclave broken, and India caught in a terrible drought, Dr. DeVol was thankful they had returned to help lift the load. Frances was able to take up light duty occasionally. They urged Dr. Mategaonker to resume his study, but he would not consider leaving Dr. DeVol alone. Providentially, Dr. Pothan wrote that she would return in August to allow Dr. Mategaonker time off to return to Ludhiana.

In a far different mood from previously, the Mategaonkers returned from Ludhiana by mid-November 1972—he with his master's degree in surgery, and she with a postgraduate nursing administration degree. What thanksgiving rang throughout the hospital!

While the Mategaonkers had been away, EHA had located two more doctors and a business manager. Had it not been for the need of her parents, Dr. Pothan would also have stayed, as the hospital setup was better than it had ever been. Dr. Mategaonker took over immediately as medical superintendent, and the EHA salary scale put his income considerably higher than that of Dr. DeVol, on a missionary allowance. Sosan Mategaonker took over the responsibilities of the drug room.

One key post still had to be filled—that of nursing superintendent. Early in 1973 the EHA sent Imelda Shaw, a highly qualified and experienced Anglo-Indian nurse. As she took charge with courage and efficiency, the DeVols felt the finishing touches were almost complete.

A missionary, seeing the hospital work first hand after being away for some time, said: "God surely loves the people of Bundelkhand to have given them the DeVols and this medical team. I have witnessed their patience and compassion in reaching out to human need with God's full answers. The work has grown beyond measure in the past fifteen years. The church is more mature. The hospital has been central in making Christ known throughout the many villages of Bundelkhand."

The Income Tax Trial

All the battles, however, were not over. Pockets of opposition to the fee system were still active, and a complaint went to government that Dr. DeVol could not possibly have reported all the fees he was collecting in the hospital. They charged him with embezzlement and called him into court.

"Can you give an account of the fees you have collected from this man?" the magistrate questioned.

"Yes, I can give an account of all the fees I have collected," Dr. DeVol answered. "I have a copy of his receipt."

"Then go home and get it."

Dr. DeVol returned to the mission office and with Norma Freer's help found the records and the receipt, and presented them in court.

"But there was another payment of Rs. 500 from Philane," challenged the officer.

Carefully examining the account and receipt book, Dr. DeVol discovered the entry. "Here it is," he said, pointing it out.

The case ended, and his accusers had succeeded in nothing except making themselves look ridiculous.

The income tax problems, however, did not end there. At this time the government gave an order to all mission organizations to register for income tax purposes by June 30, 1973. The mission was already registered and the hospital had always functioned as a part of it. But now complaints were going in that the Christian Hospital was no longer a charitable institution and should pay income tax, retroactively.

Dr. DeVol presented thirteen years of accounts, and the matter was dropped. Nevertheless, this alerted him to the need of a separate hospital organization. He wrote to the board:

> We are registering the hospital as Bethesda Hospital Society (for income tax purposes it is essential). This society will manage the operation of the Christian Hospital. In the constitution there is a provision whereby it can be taken over by EHA when that time is appropriate. Meanwhile it remains incorporated in EHA.

Caring for One Another

Heart and eye trouble took the DeVols to Cleveland for the summer of 1973 where they stayed with the Hines sisters. Their plan to return in August was frustrated when Frances fell and fractured her right wrist and Ezra had to go to bed because of a hemorrhage in his left eye.

"We're a couple of cripples," Frances wrote. "When too many people come, I shut the door on Ezra to keep him quiet. He tells me when to rest."

"She can never go back to the hospital to work," the doctor informed Ezra after Frances' final checkup. "But if you both must return to India for a few months, take good care of her."

Strength and Opportunity for Completing the Call

Returning to Chhatarpur in November, the DeVols cherished the cool, sunny days in the quietness of the "old bungalow" with its neat and colorful garden of roses and many other varieties of flowers cared for by Lalla Mali, the gardener. It seemed the orioles, the tree-pies, and the bulbuls in the trees had never sung so sweetly. The squeak of the garden gate let them know someone was coming for a visit, and the sound was almost constant during those last months, for the word spread rapidly that the DeVol Sahib and Memsahib were back again, this time to pack up for their final departure.

The rich and poor, the Hindus, Sikhs, Jains, and Moslems—as well as the Christians—came for visits, especially during the Christmas season when the bungalow was outlined in lights, the fireplace crackling, and Dharm Das was kept busy baking and replenishing the plates with cookies, the bowls with fresh fruit, and the teapot with hot, steaming tea. No one left the DeVols' hospitable home without having an introduction to the real meaning of Christmas through background music, stories, testimonies, and prayer. During these few months left, the hostility and opposition felt in the past seemed to have entirely disappeared. The DeVols were warmed in spirit by the friendliness, good will, and deepening interest in Christianity.

Time after time, the desire to stay on longer swept over the DeVols, and only the periodic flare-ups of heart palpitations, coughing, or some other health problem reminded them that their time was finished in India. Then they would be reminded of God's gracious provision for carrying on the work through the excellent staff God had provided. Two missionaries, Norma Freer and Anna Nixon, would be remaining to continue the channeling of mission help and to sell off or put into a trust the remaining properties not deeded to the church.

Dr. DeVol missed Frances by his side in the operating room, especially when Dr. Mategaonker had to be away, but he relished every day of being back on the team. On just one day—and there were others like it—he performed a hysterectomy, an appendectomy, a skin graft, a volvulus operation, the removal of a cast, and cared for Sheila, a woman with a severe case of tetanus, praying for her healing. She did get well.

Building still needed attention. Money came through to dig a deep well to meet the need for a more adequate water supply in the hospital. Getting permission and seeing the job completed taxed the patience and took many hours of the precious time Dr. DeVol had left, but his staff was grateful for the water.

"Dr. DeVol, we know we are now responsible, but do you have time to sit with us on the trustees' committee?" requested the chairman of the church property board.

Ezra was more than happy to sit at the back and give moral support to the Indian leaders now taking charge in every department. One of the great thrills of these last few months was to see the hospital staff participating in the selling of Christian literature in the villages. Such a hunger he had never seen before in all of Bundelkhand. It was not uncommon for the team to report at the end of a day in a mela that they had sold more than a thousand gospels that day.

If the DeVols were disappointed in not seeing many profess to believe in the Lord Jesus Christ and come into the church, they were, nevertheless, encouraged by the promises of God for a harvest in the future. "You did not choose me, but I chose you to go and bear fruit—fruit that will last." (John 15:16)

The DeVol Fellowship Hall

Because of their faith in a harvest in Bundelkhand, the DeVols continued to invest their lives and their money in plans for the future. They contributed from their own resources toward the building of a fellowship hall on the hospital compound. For years Ezra had dreamed of just such a building, large enough to house a library and reading room, serve as a center of worship, a hospital committee room, and a social fellowship center. The Christian Medical Society and the regional board of the EHA could hold medical conferences in it. Public health demonstrations and instructions could be promoted in it, and spiritual life conferences could be held for the staff.

At last the dream became a reality as on February 12, 1974, Dr. Mategaonker and Dr. DeVol together broke the ground. The building went up very fast. Even the bricklayers seemed to sense the urgency of getting it up and ready for use while the DeVols were still in India. The day before their departure, they were called from their packing to participate in the dedication. After an appropriate service, the climax came when the DeVols were called to stand outside the building for one last photograph. Just before the photographer clicked his camera, a bronze plaque on the side of the building was unveiled, revealing its name: *DeVol Fellowship Hall.*

Everyone cheered. Dr. Mategaonker, who first suggested the name, beamed. Ezra and Frances, totally surprised and overcome, wiped away their tears of love and gratitude for such thoughtfulness and honor of which they did not feel worthy.

Goodbye, India!

Farewells began a month early. The hospital staff, the schools, each of the churches, the women's fellowships, the youth groups, the missionaries in the area, and the servants all had to celebrate with formal farewells. The most significant farewell, however, seemed to be the one held on March 20 by the municipal board in Chhatarpur. Over three hundred dignitaries of the city and the hospital staff were invited for this high tea in honor of the DeVols. Held in the town hall, and chaired by Lawyer S. N. Khare and the chief municipal officer, Shri J. S. S. Chauhan, the function demonstrated that the barriers of hostility and opposition were at least temporarily down. Dr. Ezra and Frances DeVol were seated on the platform, loaded with garlands, given plaques both in Hindi and in English, and heard such speeches in their honor they dared not believe.

When asked to respond, Dr. DeVol grasped the opportunity to honor God through presenting a message that had burned in his heart for many months. With thanksgiving for such an opportunity and a prayer that his thoughts would be clearly expressed, he spoke to the leaders of Bundelkhand, caught in the battle of ridding themselves of the evils of a caste system that had bound them for centuries. His message concerned the dignity of man. In summary, this is what he said:

> We are overwhelmed with your love and kindness. We shall leave Chhatarpur with many happy memories of association with the Government Civil Hospital, the business people, the college, and a host of friends over these twenty-five years. I have learned much from many of you. In particular, I want to mention Dr. Grace Jones Singh who taught me much of what I have learned about oriental medicine.
>
> There are two reasons for our coming to India. First, God called us. Second, we realized the tremendous worth of every individual. I have noticed even in India that you have a color bar. I learned this from a Chinese gentleman about color: Very few people are actually black. Most are brown, wheat-colored, or tan. No one is actually yellow unless he has jaundice. It would be horrible if white folk were really white. White men are really pink! Every individual under his skin is of tremendous worth and of equal worth.
>
> The constitution of my own country declares that man is endowed by his Creator with certain unalienable rights. Among these are life, liberty, and the pursuit of happiness. The French National Assembly in their *Rights of Man* declaration on August 27, 1789, stated, "Men are born and remain free in their rights." Franklin D. Roosevelt during World War II talked about "Four Freedoms": Freedom from want, from fear, of religion, and of speech.
>
> In 1948 the United Nations in its *Universal Declaration of Human Rights* stated: "All human beings are born free and equal in dignity and rights." None of the rights and freedoms defined in the Declaration are to be denied a person because of race, color, sex, birth, or other status.
>
> These are recent declarations. Now let us look at history.
>
> Hammurabi, King of Babylon nearly 4,000 years ago, included the thought that the strong should not injure the weak. His code set up a social order based on the rights of the individual.

About 1500 B.C., the Ten Commandments gave instructions in human relationships and the protection of human rights. Leviticus 19:18 states: "You shall love your neighbor as yourself. I am the LORD."

Jesus the Christ (A.D. 28-33) gave us the Sermon on the Mount. (Matthew 5,6,7) He gave us the golden rule in Matthew 7:12: "So whatsoever you wish that men would do to you, do so to them, for this is the law and the prophets."

Jesus raised the standard of Old Testament times to a new level. Where the Old Testament said, "You shall not kill," Jesus said, "You must not insult." For "You must not commit adultery," Jesus said, "You must not lust." For "an eye for an eye and a tooth for a tooth," Jesus said, "Turn the other cheek," and "Love your enemies."

Jesus Christ was concerned about the *dignity of man*. Man is not to be insulted or falsely accused. He is to be loved and honored.

The most important commandment, Jesus said, was: "Hear O Israel, the Lord our God, the Lord is one. Love the Lord your God with all your heart and with all your soul and with all your mind and with all your strength.

"The second is this: Love your neighbor as yourself." (Mark 12:29) Not only did He set a much higher standard than had been previously set, but it is He who gives the power to live up to this standard as we live in Him and let His life flow through us.

The response to this message did not result in any open commitment to the Lord, and apart from one or two expressions of appreciation, Dr. DeVol had no indication of how much of it was heard. The truth of what he said, however, was underlined on his last day in Chhatarpur. To bid them farewell that morning, Lalla Mali, their gardener, who was a man from Hinduism's outcastes, brought his whole family—including a young son wearing heavy glasses fitted by the doctor—and loaded the DeVols with garlands.

Throwing off all his fears of persecution by his own outcaste friends and relatives, Lalla Mali said: "Dr. Sahib, you have shown us the way to the Lord. Now I want to pray in Jesus' name." He bowed his head, confessed the Lord Jesus Christ as his Savior, and committed his life and his family to God.

Ezra and Frances could not keep back the tears. Commenting on this final moment in Chhatarpur, Ezra spoke of it as "our most wonderful and unforgettable farewell. Hallelujah!"

That evening, April 14, 1972, as they flew out of Khajaraho on their way back to the United States, Ezra turned to Frances, took her hand, and said: "He doeth all things well. Praise His holy name!"

Frances smiled and confirmed his feelings, "Yes!" she replied. "With all the joys and sorrows, it has been a tremendous experience. I wish we were young again!"

Dr. DeVol with his son Joe and his
granddaughter Nancy in front of the
Christian Hospital, 1970. His
Highness the Maharaja of Chhatarpur
(above) in 1972 at the 41st
anniversary of the Christian Hospital,
built on land given by his father.

The day the Bundelkhand
Masihi Mitra Samaj
(Friends Church) registered
with the government as
independent of the
mission and received the
deed to all their churches
and parsonages. Front
row: K. D. Lall, Rev. Stuti
Prakash, (bystander),
Samson Huri Lal, and
Lawyer Shiv Narain Khare.

The Christian Hospital
staff, 1974

Chief Municipal Officer J. S. Chauhan (left) and Lawyer S. N. Khare honor Dr. Ezra and Frances DeVol in a farewell given them by the city of Chhatarpur as they retired from India, 1974

Imelda Shaw, nursing superintendent, to take the place of Frances on the staff, 1973

An honor and a surprise! 1974

14 Home in America

Trust in Jehovah and do what is good. Make your home in the land and live in peace; make Jehovah your only joy, and He will give you what your heart desires. Psalm 37:3, 4

Homecoming

The plane set down on the runway in Columbus on April 19, 1974, and Ezra and Frances were home to stay.

"This is the first day of the rest of your life," the radio blared.

As their children and grandchildren met them, how the memories flooded in, blurring vision and melting hearts! It was like coming-down day from Woodstock, in reverse! Were moments of excitement ever any higher than those days back in India when the bus rolled in with tin trunks, lunch baskets, bedding rolls, and the children—coming home from boarding— each two inches taller, and with their clothes in shreds? The cycle rides on Sundays, the picnics under the big mohwa tree and down by the lake, the hunting trips to Kishengarh and Bux-waha! Dharm Das cooking pies in the kitchen, and the rush to the pantry to find what was good to eat! The tinkle of the bell on the tongas! And now! Here the DeVols were looking at those same children, grown up, with their families about them! Grandpa and Grandma DeVol reached out their arms in antici-pation of all that was yet best to be in each of them.

Frequent letters back and forth through the years had helped "keep the banner high." If there were any regrets, any feelings of times when parents were too busy to listen, or chil-dren too taken up with their own interests to understand, they

271

were all washed down the drain at this high moment as the DeVols arrived home to stay.

"These are our own flesh and blood and the wonderful partners they have chosen!" Ezra exclaimed. "They will make a contribution to this next generation and to our grandchildren. I hope they will be able to do better than we did and that their children will be what God intends them to be. There is no future in growing old physically, but there is a real future in maturing in the things of the Spirit until we all are finally translated into the likeness of His dear Son."

Arriving at Sunnyslope, twenty-five miles from Columbus, the DeVols exulted in the crisp coolness and fresh beauty of spring. Their fantasies about home had never exceeded the experience of these early days of retirement as the excitement of change, love of family, and all that was best in America seemed to welcome them into their new way of life.

"Even the dandelions on the lawn have never looked so good!" Ezra exclaimed to Frances as they picked up hedge shears and rakes and went out to trim the bushes and tidy up the yard. Cardinals, bluebirds, and redwing blackbirds came out to greet them, and a family of rabbits played outside the kitchen window. Ezra built a wren house and put up a bird bath.

Early one morning the DeVols explored the place to decide where they could build a retirement home for themselves when Sunnyslope went into the hands of others. They chose a plot and began planning to build. God had other plans, however, which they would not know or understand until they met Him around another corner further on. Inflation and change had made their dream a financial impossibility. "Therefore will the LORD wait, that He may be gracious unto you." (Isaiah 30:18) This was the promise they claimed in their disappointment.

The children came often to Sunnyslope, first one family and then another, and the old farmhouse resounded with laughter, conversation, and the patter of feet. They would swing on the porch, run on the lawn, and go into the woods to hunt sweet william, trillium, yellow violets, and many other flowers. The pastor, Jim Brantingham, came over to lend a helping hand. He mowed the lawn and plowed the garden. They set out roses and gladioli. They planted melons, brussel sprouts, tomatoes, corn, lettuce, lima beans, and peas. Along with the chickens, cows, and steers, the family added a pony named Ginger and bought a cart—an addition that delighted the grandchildren.

In the summer Joe and Judy brought their children from California for a long visit. On the 37th birthday of Pat and Pris, all the DeVol sons and daughters, sons-in-law and daughters-in-law, and the nine grandchildren in the family up to that time were present. Never before had all nineteen of them been together.

The grandchildren entertained the grandparents with their accomplishments and unusual responses. The California cousins could not get enough of running through the open spaces. Cindy was particularly clever in school. Sarah tried hard to keep up with Cindy. Stephenie played beautifully on the piano.

Phil Bob begged to stay some extra days on the farm with his big brothers, Bill and Geoffrey, and with his cousin Mike. But when time came for family devotions, Phil Bob did not want to pray.

"Don't you pray at home?" his grandfather asked, kneeling beside him.

"If you spank me, I'll pray," Phil Bob said.

Grandpa complied with a gentle swat, and Phil Bob began to pray. He even included a prayer for Bill's puppy: "Keep Bucky out of trouble and out of the trash."

Joe and Phil spent as much time together that summer as possible, putting new siding on the barn and doing painting jobs with the same eagerness they had displayed in painting the X-ray room and dispensary in Nepal.

Ezra's brother Charles' children and their families, the Cattells and their daughter Mary and her husband Fred Boots often came to Sunnyslope for visits. So did Ezra's boyhood playmate in China, Dr. Walter Williams, Jr., and his wife Helen.

The first Christmas at home the DeVols celebrated twice. They went to California to be with Joe and Judy and watched the tournament of roses on TV. They took along their slides of Nepal and India and relived those days with their friends. Joe and his dad attended the Rose Bowl game.

Ohio Christmas was on January 11, 1975, as the three Ohio children and families came with food and prepared a fabulous Christmas dinner.

The DeVols were welcomed into the church and asked to share their experiences of the past twenty-five years. The Quarterly Meeting was richly blessed and many people lined the altar for prayer as Pastor Jim Brantingham anointed some with oil and called on various elders to pray for the sick and suffering. Just one thing clouded the weekend of Quarterly Meeting. Though Phil and Peg had been visiting them regularly, Phil did not attend the meetings. Later he telephoned and apologized for not going.

Renewing Ties with Phil

Phil and Peg lived nearer than any of the other families and were over to Sunnyslope frequently. Phil came nearly every day to help clean up the place, paint the barn, plant trees, or put in fence. He and his father worked together like brothers, enjoying each other's wit and the great out-of-doors. Only when the father spoke about the will of God did conversation trail off into silence. *It will take time, but he will come back*, the father assured himself as he assessed the qualities of his son and worked shoulder to shoulder listening to his stories.

In deep moments, Phil talked about the Viet Nam War. Earlier, against the advice of his parents, he had refused to sign up as a conscientious objector. Accepting the draft, he was soon slated to go to the front. He had no qualms about this until a soldier from Viet Nam, bragging about his exploits, showed Phil a picture of himself standing with his gun in one hand and his foot on the Viet Nam soldier he had just shot and killed.

Phil was horrified. "In India we wouldn't have put our foot on an animal we had killed, we esteemed it so highly! Why, even our dog wouldn't walk on the leopard skin on our living room floor in India! He walked around it, very respectfully!"

Phil suddenly felt quite ill. He could not keep his former Woodstock High School Chinese roommate, Larry Pao, out of his mind. He thought of his Indian friends. This flash of insight jarred him out of his attitude of noncommitment.

"Racism! This whole war is racist, and I'll have no more of it!" he declared. His anger burned even hotter when the church did not protest the bombing, not even the Christmas bombing of 1972. He lost his respect for people in the church who in the face of such injustice remained silent.

"They don't talk my language," he said.

Sometimes as father and son worked and talked, there was argument and confrontation. This point seemed to demand it, and Father spoke up: "A whole different philosophy seems to have taken over your class in Woodstock. I can't understand why you reject the whole Church of Jesus Christ because of your view on this one issue."

"Look, Dad, we live in different generations, and we have different points of view. Yours has been a powerful generation and still is. Mine is the anti-war, anti-establishment Viet Nam generation. We see the injustice, racism, and paternalism in the systems your generation has produced."

"There'll always be generations, at least I hope so," Ezra responded. "I'm glad I had a father and a mother. Early in World War I when I was five years old, we were traveling on an allied ship to China. We heard that the dreaded German cruiser, the *Emden*, was loose in the Pacific. It was comforting to know Father and Mother were not panicked. It was also nice to know the captain of the ship was *over five* years of age and that he knew what to do. Years of training make a difference that is understandable to all concerned."

Phil stopped his work and looked up at his father. "I feel that your generation generally takes a position that America is morally right. You want to transfer our ideas to others. That sometimes conflicts with the nationalistic spirit of others who don't buy democracy, capitalism, or our way of doing things."

Phil's father took a step nearer. "Look, Phil, being in one particular generation does not mean we can categorize all the others in that generation. Not every young person in the Viet Nam era was a flag-burning radical, nor were those sixty years and older all racists and warmongers. Yes, I would rather be a citizen of U.S.A. than any other country I know. But that doesn't mean I agree with everything we do. I haven't led any protest marches, but I have written to several of our presidents, senators, and governors and protested racism and unfair foreign policy. Copies of these letters and the replies are in my files if you care to read them."

"We're not talking apples and oranges, Dad," Phil argued. "I respect you, but I find no room in your churches structured and run by your generation."

"Look, Phil," Father said earnestly, "alienation occurs when there is a sharp difference in ideology that makes it difficult to carry on helpful dialogue. During our separation while you were in boarding, some alienation seems to have occurred. When it comes to the rejection of the faith of our fathers and the denial of the divinity of the Lord Jesus Christ, which leads to eternal separation, this becomes intolerable to me."

Father and son went back to work as silence fell. Phil was thinking of the two years it took for him to fight his way out of Viet Nam, out of the army, and back into civilian life. Finally he had won. He married Peg Mullett, and by the time the DeVols came home from India, he was living close to Sunnyslope, their home—so near, but in some ways so far!

As cool weather began to set in and the leaves turned color, making the woods a fairyland, Ezra found a lot of joy in sawing wood for the fireplace and putting up storm windows and gathering in the produce from the garden. By mid-November the first snow brought Phil and a friend Ed Patteson over to help him insulate the house. Frances cooked a marvelous dinner topped off with apple crisp.

In the spring Phil and his father set out ten spruce trees, after which they spent the evening viewing slides of India. Phil grilled steaks in the yard. That night Ezra dreamed he had returned to Chhatarpur. There he found trees growing everywhere out of rocky soil, replacing thorn trees. One tree, at least one foot high, was a spruce. Another was growing between two bricks in a wall, pushing them apart. When he awoke, he felt reassured that God meant to give fruit that would remain in India.

Life in Sunnyslope was nearly always a challenge, but there were times, like the fall the steers all got eye infections, that the work was very heavy. Phil helped put ointment in their eyes. When one broke loose, Phil helped his father hunt for it. After hours of searching, they returned almost too tired to put one foot in front of another only to find the lost steer in the barn.

Phil was always there to help, and at Christmas that year, he and Peg sent their parents a gift of food for Christmas dinner and attached this verse to it:

You've noticed that our gifts to you
Are things that we can share in, too.

Becoming friends after years apart
We want to share more than just our hearts.

So we're willing to share work, food, love
And all the squash you can spare!

Medical Practice

Before Dr. DeVol left India, Dr. Deffinger in Marengo invited him to return and share his medical practice. Dr. DeVol went back to work July 1, 1974. Though five times higher than his missionary salary, the amount he first received was hardly adequate for the American standard of living. Fortunately, increases were not long in coming, and thereafter they came regularly. An oil well on the farm also produced some income. The lesson learned in India, "Bow your neck and I will fight your battles," continued to prove true at Sunnyslope. Monthly earnings had never been central in the thinking of the DeVols, however, and the retirement years did not change that. Ezra went to work according to his usual pattern, accepting calls in the middle of the night, taking his turn on emergency, and driving his Dodge Dart twenty-four miles between Marengo and the Morrow County Hospital in Mt. Gilead. How he missed Frances as he got back into practice! Niece Esther Westbrook worked with him at Morrow County Hospital and met a real need. He found her to be an excellent nurse and one he could count on. She helped bring him up-to-date on procedures in the cardiac care unit.

Ezra immediately signed up for refresher courses in medicine. He enjoyed the privilege of learning new developments. These Ohio Medical Education Network (OMEN) courses included weekly instruction over the telephone supported with slides. In addition, he took Ohio State University seminars in Cleveland Clinic and in Columbus. When in Cleveland, the DeVols stayed with their friends, Marie and Alice Hines, and in Columbus, with Everett and Catherine Cattell. Once a month there was a CORE CONTENT examination. Through the purchase of books dealing with the latest developments, as well as the use of a tape deck in his car as he traveled back and forth, Ezra filled his mind with facts. On snowbound days he studied CORE CONTENT, interspersed with happy moments with Frances as they watched bluejays, cardinals, juncos, wood-peckers, nuthatches, and titmice at the bird feeder. Ezra always piled up more hours than were required because he enjoyed the study so much.

Dr. DeVol welcomed into his office patients he did not recognize but who knew him well.

"Doctor, do you remember when you drove out to my house in the dead of night to deliver my baby thirty-four years ago?"

"Well, I'd like to see that baby now!" exclaimed the doctor.

"You surely remember that automobile accident. I was nearly dead when they brought me in. You saved my life," said another.

"You may not remember me, but I'm sure you've never forgotten my brother."

"Who was your brother?"

"The one who bit your finger when you were trying to take out his tooth."

"So, he was your brother!" They both laughed heartily. "My guess is that he hasn't forgotten me either!"

Patients came crowding into the office as word spread that Dr. DeVol was back. On one day he saw 101 patients. Some of them were in deep trouble, like the former Marengo classmate's daughter who was not only ill but had lost all she owned when her house burned down. Dr. DeVol gave her treatment and money.

A man came in with arthritis, but questioning revealed that his deeper problem was that he was an alcoholic. Dr. DeVol did not hesitate to pray with him. He followed him, encouraging him to look to God for strength and healing until he was completely delivered.

The rising threat of the drug traffic struck home the day Dr. Deffinger's office was robbed. Fortunately, the stolen drugs were recovered. The same threat struck home again the day a young man came in for treatment and Dr. DeVol discovered he was taking cocaine. Dr. DeVol stood by him, praying for him and treating him. He required a lot of time, but eventually he became established as a Christian free from drugs.

Certain depressed patients improved with prayer and through reading books such as *From Prison to Praise* and *Power in Praise*. Dr. DeVol gave out books frequently when he felt the need of the patient was matched by the message of the book.

For a man dying of lung and brain cancer, without any inner assurance or joy, Dr. DeVol gave him treatment to ease his pain, but he also prayed with him and read to him from the Bible of the future hope in heaven. Dr. DeVol believed in treating the whole man.

Concern for the Church

As the medical practice grew and responsibilities became heavier, so did the concern for the church. Ezra was soon appointed as an elder and as clerk of the monthly meeting. In August they enjoyed Yearly Meeting and were presented a plaque for service in China, Nepal, and India. They were also presented a pewter teapot and tray, and a quilt.

The early thrills of meeting old friends, feeling their gratitude, and witnessing spiritual response faded as time went on and they began to compare what used to happen with present practices. Why was prayer meeting no longer a time for prayer? Why were the Sunday evening services sparsely attended? Where was the quarterly meeting preaching that convicted people and led them to repentance?

On the one hand they found lethargy, and on the other a tendency to throw off discipline and plunge headlong into the charismatic movement. Divorced people were being married in the church. The old ethical standards were slipping. Even God's people seemed to have soaked up the philosophy of situational ethics. Though saying they did not believe the theory, they tended to put it into practice. Where were the men when business meetings were held? These things were not only expressed as concerns but became burdens for prayer in family devotions.

The DeVols opened their home for Sunday school class and ladies' missionary fellowship gatherings. They spearheaded neighborhood prayer groups through the church and held one regularly in their own home. They encouraged the "tent-making" ministry and gave special attention to the young people willing to pull up stakes, locate in new areas, get a job, and establish churches. They threw themselves into missionary promotion and encouraged Faith Promise giving, which more than tripled in their church the next year, from $2,000 to $6,009.

Pastor James Brantingham felt the strong impact of Dr. DeVol's convictions, but he also felt the weight of cultural change that had drastically affected the lives of Christians in America.

"I've yet to find a guilty party in divorce," he said. "How can I make judgment on these issues which are cutting deep into our society? Dr. DeVol, I believe we're on the same train! We're going in the same direction! But I feel the train has moved on while you've been overseas, and we have to take it now from where it is. Some of us are in cars that are further down the track from where you are getting on."

These were issues not to be settled even in the next decade. Dr. DeVol encouraged the younger pastor in preaching the Word, and James Brantingham appreciated the forthright and earnest efforts of Dr. DeVol to strengthen his ministry.

"Faithful are the wounds of a friend," Jim Brantingham said in retrospect. "Your best friends are those who will be true to you even though the truth is painful. Dr. DeVol supported me and he supported the ministry. He was indeed a real friend."

Heartache in the Family

Tragedies in the DeVol family piled up in the next two years. In April Frances had an angina attack. It was her second of the year. In July she had a third, and the doctor felt her symptoms were due to coronary insufficiency.

Four days later on July 18 in a Sears department store, Frances had another attack.

"Oh, Frances, don't leave me!" groaned Ezra.

Nitroglycerine brought relief, but the next day she was worse and was rushed to the hospital in the squad car with Ezra and Pris following.

By the beginning of August, Frances was back home and able to enter into the activities of the family, all of whom came to Sunnyslope to enjoy the wholesome fun of husking and freezing corn. Headache and vertigo continued to plague her, and she prayed for relief. By her sixty-sixth birthday, she felt better.

Just before Christmas a tank blew up in Russell Haynes's face, fracturing his nose, critically injuring him, and causing him to lose a pint of blood.

Everett Cattell began experiencing serious illness with a shower of emboli in his lungs and a need of surgery. The DeVols felt great concern for his deteriorating health. He fought a courageous battle until he died in 1981. They felt concern, too, for Frances' brother Mendel, who with his wife, Kathryn, came for a visit. He was not at all well, and as Ezra tried to relieve him physically, Frances talked to him about his relationship with God. Mendel died in 1982.

On February 10, 1976, Frances had such a severe heart attack that Ezra called all the children. He remained by his wife's bed until three days later, on the anniversary of the first time he ever told Frances he loved her, he went out and bought her forty-five red and yellow roses.

"Do you remember forty-five years ago tonight?" Ezra asked as he placed the roses on a stand by her bed. "I told you then, and I tell you again, every rose means I love you! I mean that forty-five times as much today!"

Vascular change in Frances' eyes made it necessary for her to get greater power in her bifocal lens, and for her birthday that fall, her husband bought her a giant print Bible.

Ezra himself became very ill with an ulcer and had to be hospitalized for six days. By January 20, 1976, he was much worse, but a week later the report came back that there was no sign of cancer. But he had other battles to fight as his cough returned, caused by Monilla Fungus. A few months later he was troubled with high blood pressure.

At the same time Frances developed severe pain going through to the back. She had a duodenal ulcer.

As they wrestled with these illnesses, they ran across a statement by Robert Collyer that helped them: "The days in which Job wrestled with his dark maladies are the only days that make him worth remembering."

Most tragic of all at the end of 1975, the DeVols discovered that Phil and Peg were living separately. Their reasons were deep and heart-breaking, and in spite of talks with parents on both sides and efforts of the parents together, the end to their marriage had come right in the heart of Sunnyslope community. Deep convictions do not shake with the storms, but people who love each other suffer.

One night Ezra dreamed of heaven. It was a beautiful place, filled with beautiful, happy people, richly dressed in shining, colorful clothes. He saw the whole panorama of Christ working out His design of salvation. There was the small beginning with a few despised followers, followed by the ignoble death on a Roman cross, and down through the centuries of struggle and persecution to the culmination in glorious triumph. There was a manifest conquering of every opposing force, and the Lord Jesus Christ reigned without challenge as King of kings and Lord of lords.

"In this dream," Ezra explained, "the last thing I saw was the Lord stamping this with His approval: 'WROUGHT!'—meaning established, accomplished, finished. Finally, it seemed we were at the gates of heaven, a terminal where people, young and old, were coming through to greet relatives. As I was there, families were being united. I kept wondering, Will Phil be coming? When will he come? I felt myself glued to the spot with no desire to go in but a determination to wait at the gates of that glorious land until Phil arrived."

The day came when the father knew he had to confront the son.

"I don't see it your way," Phil replied. "I have no desire to carry on the DeVol tradition. I have no sense of need except for more money to live on, and maybe more education. As to my marriage, I plan to have it dissolved. Please don't worry about me. I still love you."

"What can we do to help you see the wrong course you are taking?" Phil's father pled. "Are you asking us to turn you over to Satan?"

"Oh no, not that!" was Phil's quick reply.

After this encounter, Phil's parents were completely drained. They could hardly discuss it. They silently prayed. The next morning Frances awoke early.

"Ezra, dear, wake up. I have a word to share with you about Phil. It is a word I received for him in 1967—Isaiah

59:21. Listen to what it says about those who repent of their sins:

> My Spirit, who is on you, and my words that I have put in your mouth, will not depart from your mouth, or from the mouths of your children, or from the mouths of their descendants from this time on and forever, says the LORD.

Phil did not always avoid his father after this strong encounter, but when the two of them met, it was difficult for either to find anything to say. Nevertheless, Phil could not bear to stay away from Sunnyslope. He would find his way over to the house while his father was at work. Frances would give him tea, and as they shared the events of the day, she would find a point at which to confront him with the wrong direction he was taking and talk with him about God.

"I could not stay away, I loved her so much," Phil said. "I appreciated her strength and her willingness to never let go. Dad is real dominant, but that doesn't mean that if Dad is a tree, Mom would be a vine. Not at all. Dad is a big, strong tree, and I think Mom is standing beside him, and maybe she's a more willowy, beautiful sort of a tree, but she's a tree in her own right. It's just that when it came to dealing with Mom and Dad, we dealt with a united front."

Even so, Phil did not change immediately, and the concern for him took a toll of the energies of his caring parents. Ulcers, coughs, and heart attacks, to say nothing of the ache of hearts and valleys of tears, added up to a lot of pain. As for Phil, he confessed to his sister that he had never felt lonelier in his life.

Significant Events

Some highlights pinpointed the dark sky of 1976. Always proud of his country, Ezra had ached with the downward trends he observed on his return from India.

"Last night on TV I heard abortion defended," he noted. "I turned on another channel and heard the conservationists expressing their abhorrence of killing coyotes endangering sheep. How far astray we go: wrong to kill coyotes but legitimate to kill the human fetus!"

Again he noted: "Last night on one channel I saw excessive gluttony and luxury. On another channel World Vision was trying desperately to raise funds to feed famine victims. By

11:00 p.m. they had raised $17,500. Frances and I pledged $250."

Faith in the U.S.A. was restored as he watched the bicentennial celebration with Walter Cronkite of CBS as the articulate commentator. The flag waved proudly over tall ships sailing up the Hudson, in San Franscisco Bay, and over Independence Hall. The camera focused on the wide sweep of "spacious skies and amber waves of grain." President Ford spoke of the concern since Gettysburg to correct wrongs and expand rights in national life.

Afterward, Ezra pursued this patriotic theme in a united Thanksgiving service at which funds were raised for famine relief.

On their fortieth anniversary, the DeVols drove their 1976 Dodge Aspen to Mohican Forest Lodge. All their children and grandchildren joined them except for Pat, Judy, and Peg. All the grandchildren went to Pat's house afterwards to see the new baby, Pat's fourth child, Julia Kay Haynes, born April 26, 1975.

The DeVols took time for Bible study. Through their lives together the Bible had become far more than a code of ethics or a book of laws. As a record of experiences of men and women who had dealings with the invisible God, they read it and claimed its promises concerning their family:

> Genesis 18:19: For I have chosen him [Abraham] so that he will direct his children and his household after him to keep the way of the LORD by doing what is right and just, so that the LORD will bring about for Abraham what He has promised him.
>
> Deuteronomy 4:9: . . . Teach . . . your children and to their children after them.
>
> Joshua 24:15: As for me and my house, we will serve the LORD.
>
> Colossians 2:2: This is what I have asked God for you, that you will be encouraged by and knit together by strong ties of love, that you will have the rich experience of knowing Christ with real certainty and clear understanding.

Later in August, the Friends Church held its Yearly Meeting. Because of Frances' heart attack, they had not planned to go until Frances herself expressed her feeling that this was something they dare not miss. They went for the weekend and got a new vision of their Quaker heritage.

This Quaker heritage did go far back in both of their families, and especially the DeVols and the Frenches who, the DeVols discovered, qualified to become members of the Mayflower Descendants Society on their father's side. They could trace their mother's line back to the Frenchman who, with William Penn, established a settlement at Burlington, New Jersey, on July 23, 1680. This, plus contact with a cousin, Tom DeVol, encouraged Dr. DeVol to arrange for a DeVol reunion which drew the family together.

Some Tests in Faith and Obedience

Philip Edmund DeVol and Donna Marie Suclescy Gerling were married in Mt. Gilead on February 19, 1977. The two of them and Christopher Aaron, Donna's six-year-old son, came to call on the DeVols, who welcomed them and planned for a celebration of their marriage on the DeVols' engagement day, February 27. Pat's and Pris's families came, too. They telephoned Joe and his family to include the complete family circle. Prayer and a reading of 1 Corinthians 13 set the tone for the reception. There was healing in the air, and Donna, warmhearted and receptive, felt the love of her new family.

About six months later, Phil told his parents of his intention of adopting Christopher. The adoption was complete on April 21, 1978, just a day before the birth of their daughter, Sarah Christine, the DeVols' twelfth and last grandchild. The first one of this new family circle to bow at the feet of Jesus was Christopher, who during the next summer Daily Vacation Bible School reached out to become a child of God. His grandparents gave him a Bible with his name engraved on it. Phil said nothing but he could not keep back his tears.

"There's something so splendid about each of them," Ezra commented to Frances as they left.

Out in California all was not well. Joe discovered a black spot on the back of his neck, and the diagnosis was melanoma. This called for a wide excision. Judy, a nurse, and the DeVols, along with the medical team who operated on Joe, pooled their knowledge, gave him the very best treatment possible, and bathed the situation in prayer. Joe was completely healed.

The greatest test of faith of the year came with a telephone call from Anne Lipes, a dear friend in Cleveland. Anne and her husband, Milton, had been employed in NASA for many years and had loyally supported missions, visited India, and prayed for the DeVols.

"Milton is deteriorating rapidly," Anne told Dr. DeVol. "It seems the doctors here have done all they can do. He is losing weight every day, and I would like to bring him to you."

Dr. DeVol gave her some suggestions of what to talk over with her doctors. Meanwhile he discussed the matter with his own hospital staff. On May 29, Anne called again.

The DeVols had been praying for guidance, and Dr. DeVol confessed, "Lord, unless You give healing, what can I do that others have not already done? Guide us in the treatment! If this is the course we should follow, we pray that You may give quick response!"

Believing as he did that healing comes from God and that in giving prescriptions he was only walking in obedience to the God who made us all, he agreed to take the case.

Milton Lipes had cancer of the colon, which had spread to the liver and perineum. Physically speaking, there was no hope, but as Dr. DeVol undertook the treatment, he lay hold of Isaiah 50:7 as his promise: "For the LORD God will help me. Therefore shall I not be confounded. Therefore I have set my face like a flint and I know that I shall not be ashamed."

That night he prayed for a verse for Milton. Lamentations 3:57, 58 came to his mind so clearly that he wrote it down: "You came near when I called you, and you said, 'Do not fear.' O LORD, you took up my case; you redeemed my life."

Following this, the positive promises poured in. Faith was greatly strengthened. Milton improved. In a short time he was up walking around with the help of a nurse. Within two weeks he had gained four pounds.

The healing did not last. By the middle of June, Dr. DeVol noticed a definite downward trend.

"Summon your power, O God; show us your strength, O God, as you have done before!" (Psalm 68:28) This became his prayer.

On June 18, the doctor faced a crisis. It was evident that a partial obstruction was hindering Milton's progress. If he was to live, the obstruction had to be dealt with by very difficult and dangerous surgery or by the miraculous intervention of the almighty LORD. Dr. DeVol called the Mt. Gilead pastor, Charles Robinson, who anointed Milton with oil and prayed. Anne Lipes and Elizabeth Hart were also present along with the doctor, and the whole group felt God's presence in their midst.

The next day Milton's fever had subsided for the first time in two weeks. He felt better and ate more. His pain was relieved. More positive verses than before came to Milton, Anne, and the doctor, who turned to Anne and read Luke 1:45:

"And blessed is she who has believed that what the LORD has said to her will be accomplished!"

Oh, how she believed! Anne's footsteps were light throughout the next week as she walked along the corridors of the hospital ministering to her husband and praising the Lord for His goodness!

June 27, however, proved to be another dark day. The metastasis growth in the perineal region, which had seemed to be getting smaller in size, had suddenly become much larger.

This is not healing; this is dying! the doctor realized. *What am I doing wrong? How shall I face this development? Whom shall I consult? What do all our verses of Scripture mean? Have we been deluding ourselves with cheerful Bible verses we just happened to find, or has God really spoken to us through these verses as He has so many times in the past? Is God trying to teach us something new?*

The darkness reigned for a month as Milton Lipes continued to grow worse. During those days Dr. DeVol looked back over his life and remembered other disappointing times and recalled how God had dealt with each of those circumstances in just the right way. There was the time he missed the ship and was delayed in China. It proved to be a vital turn of events to help the church in China at that time. He recalled the trip from Switzerland to India in 1972 when with Frances ill he had "put his feet in the water" and taken her back to India, trusting the Lord to heal her, and He did.

We have put our feet in the water, and now, God, it is your turn! That was what he had said to the Lord then, and now he prayed again, "It is time for You to act, LORD. I expect to see a miracle in the morning!"

The next morning the doctor found Milton worse. As he stood by his bed, he recalled other times in India when he had faced similar situations with death, not life, taking a patient away after he had done everything he could do. He remembered Kasturi Bai, a prostitute, injured in a fight with a man who had pushed her off the top of a building and broken her back. In the hospital, she heard of Christ for the first time.

"Last night Jesus came to me and revealed Himself. He told me I did not need to be afraid. He told me He had forgiven my sins."

"How did you know it was Jesus who came to you?" the doctor asked.

"Oh, I knew Him by the print of the nails in His hands!"

Kasturi Bai died in spite of all they could do for her, but she died in peace with inner healing that no one who was near could ever doubt.

All are not healed, but there is no reason why all cannot have inner healing, Dr. DeVol remembered this dark day. He continued to recall many situations in which he had turned corners in desperate circumstances and met God, and by Milton Lipes's bed that day, he reached a new level of faith:

> In none of these situations did God really leave me, but He veiled Himself that I might really seek HIM, not just seek relief from the immediate problem. He manifested Himself at the right moment and dealt with the problem in just the right way.

This was the time to exercise a tough faith. Right in the midst of these profound struggles, other tests also came. Word reached him of the death of a young mother in the community, Viola Mosher Rawson, killed in an automobile accident. Frances had another severe heart attack and was taken to the hospital. Two days later Milton slipped away peacefully in his sleep, and the Lord gave peace and comfort to Anne. Five days later Frances was able to go home again. For all of them through the crucible of the fire of suffering, Habakkuk 3:17-19 gave them comfort: "Yet I will rejoice in the LORD."

Retirement

By early January 1977 the DeVols began serious planning for retirement. Plans to build on a plot near Sunnyslope were financially not feasible. They had no real desire to live anywhere else, but through Everett and Catherine Cattell they had heard of Friendsview Manor in Newberg, Oregon, and they opened their hearts and minds to consideration and prayer about this. Oregon seemed very far away and remote from their three Ohio families. It was also quite far from their California family. Telephones and modern transportation, of course, helped to overcome these distances, and they realized, too, that each family had to work through its own dreams and problems without too much parental interference. Distance would not need to stop the caring and the praying. In the spring, however, as they took a drive through the Ohio hills and valleys and went for a brief retreat to Mohican Forest Lodge, they were filled with a great longing just to stay on forever in the Sunnyslope locality.

During a seminar in Cleveland while staying with Marie and Alice Hines, they talked about all these possibilities and difficulties of retirement and shared the news of what they had heard about developments in Newberg, Oregon, under Milo Ross and the George Fox College Foundation. Marie and Alice listened intently, for they also were considering a move, and this was a brand-new idea. By the end of the year they were at home in Oregon and were so thrilled with what they had found that they urged the DeVols to pursue the matter.

Such a major change required much thought. In their regular prayer times they sought for guidance from the Bible.

"Whither it seemeth good and convenient for thee to go, thither go." (Jeremiah 40:4)

"If this is God's will," Ezra suggested to Frances, "let us ask Him to provide the $5,000 for the down payment by helping us sell that stock willed to us by your mother, which is at present bringing in very low dividends."

That same week, Paul Langdon, who helped them with financial matters, called and said he had sold that stock for $5,300.

"Now let us take the next step," Ezra proposed. "If the Lord wants us to buy a condominium in Spaulding Oaks, let's pray He will give us a clear indication by June 9 that the Michigan property is being sold. Gideon put out more than one fleece, and I feel just as timid, I am sure, as Gideon did."

There were many other steps along the way, each one covered with prayer, and each one led them in the direction of Newberg, Oregon. The last giant step was the sale of their part of Sunnyslope property. When Charles DeVol's son-in-law,

Edwin Westbrook, agreed to buy it and began making payments, the DeVols were able to make payments on Apartment Number 6 in Spaulding Oaks in Newberg.

"To practice or not to practice," was the next question to be dealt with. To get an Oregon license to practice medicine required another examination by their state authorities. Ezra decided at least to try, and an appointment was made for Friday, January 13, 1978, at 2:00 p.m. at the Loyalty Building in Portland. The DeVols prepared to go, but on January 9 a snowstorm hit Ohio such as they had not seen. It left them snowbound. The weather cleared enough by afternoon of the 12th to allow them to reach Columbus, where they stayed in a motel near the airport for the night. Finally in the air over O'Hare Airport the next day, they began to circle around because O'Hare was also covered with snow. *Lord, if you want me to get this license, you will help me get there in time for the examination*, Ezra began to pray silently.

In almost no time the pilot found a hole in the clouds, and they landed at O'Hare. The next plane, however, was late in leaving Chicago, and it seemed unlikely that they would reach Portland on time. Ezra quit looking at his watch. Friends met them at the airport. The Rectors took Frances directly to Newberg. George Moore took Ezra and sped down Portland's series of one-way streets, getting lost on the way, but finally reaching the Loyalty Building. Parking was the next frustration, but at last they found themselves in the building and on the elevator up ten flights. As they stepped into the office where the examinations were to be held, Ezra looked at the clock. It was exactly 2:00 p.m., and within thirty seconds he heard his name called.

The examination covered the use of digitalis, the treatment for urinary infections, the use of chloromycitin, and the treatment for tuberculosis. It was so easy Dr. DeVol was amazed. The doctors then began asking him about his medical experiences in India and Nepal and the examination turned quickly into a friendly visit.

"Do you have any questions you want to ask us?" they asked in conclusion.

"Yes. Do you need doctors out here?" Dr. DeVol responded.

"Pick up your license on your way out!"

In Newberg the DeVols stayed two days with Marie and Alice Hines and looked over the muddy bog that was the site for their new home. They rode around the city and discovered— just three miles from where they would live—the wide, flowing Willamette River, providing boating and supplying water to the paper mill, one of the few industries in the town. They learned that industries dealing with fruits, berries, and nuts, the A-dec dental equipment factory, and a few shopping centers provided most of the other employment opportunities to the town of less than 12,000 people. Portland airport was only fifty minutes away, and the Pacific coast could be reached in an hour-and-a-half.

Dr. DeVol met Dr. Stanley D. Kern and visited the hospital. Smaller than Morrow County Hospital, the Newberg Community Hospital boasted only fifty beds, but they had a plan to remodel at a cost of about $2,500,000. There seemed to be no shortage of doctors.

On Sunday, the DeVols attended the Newberg Friends Church, heard Ron Woodward preach, met the parents of Jamie Sandoz, who had served in Nepal with them, and recognized other friends they had known down through the years. They already began to feel at home in Newberg. They appreciated the mild winter climate and the beauty of the hills. On the day they left, heavy rain left no doubt about how the lush richness of western Oregon was nourished. The point of no return had been reached in plans to move to Oregon, but two questions yet to be answered were: *When should we go to Oregon?* and *Should I practice medicine again or leave it altogether?* The answer to the first question was determined through the financial arrangement of getting a renter for property in Oregon while waiting for final payment on the Sunnyslope property. This led to the termination of Ohio medical practice at the end of September 1979.

A unique set of circumstances brought the answer to the other question. On receiving his official license from the Oregon Medical Board of Examiners in March, Dr. DeVol had turned it over to his secretary to frame. She had evidently forgotten all about this. More than a month went by. As Dr. DeVol continued to pray about his future practice, he felt he should put out another "fleece."

"Lord," he prayed, "if you want me to use my license to practice medicine in Oregon, then cause Lois to bring it framed into my office today."

When Dr. DeVol arrived at his office, he realized that it was Lois's day off. He felt a bit foolish and frustrated. What did his prayer mean now? In a few minutes, here came Lois bringing the license neatly framed. She had made a special trip to the office to give it to him. He called Frances to tell her. The whole experience turned into a positive affirmation of God's guidance. They laughed and cried together.

"I marvel at the way God has been making His way known to us!" Frances replied. "Even the way His controlling hand helped you get to Oregon on time to get the license—and now this! It all seems like another miracle!"

"Frances, I have discovered over and over again that a few moments on my knees with the door shut and my heart open to my heavenly Father above produces more peace, more courage, and more decisiveness in action than hours of sitting around in an armchair trying to think out all the pros and cons of a complicated issue."

Frances laughed. "Would you call this a complicated issue? Anyway, dear, I haven't seen you spending much of your time in an armchair! Maybe in retirement!"

Final Months in Marengo

In October Joe had to come to Chicago in connection with his new appointment with World Books, Inc. He made a quick trip to Sunnyslope, and all the brothers and sisters came over to see him. The whole family, including Phil, went to church that Sunday. What a special time it was! Nothing much was said, but all realized changes were in process that would put distances between them. Nothing would ever be quite the same again. Sunnyslope would never again be "home base" for the extended family.

Joe seemed to feel the finality of it and expressed all their feelings as he said, "Our growing up under your care has left each of us children with wonderful, warm memories to last us a lifetime. I have always been so proud of you. You make the perfect couple!"

Pat could hardly bear to see her parents move away. Pris shared some of her heartaches as the responsibilities of parenting teenagers weighed heavily on her. Stephenie, her oldest daughter, had emptied all her savings for college at a Faith Promise appeal. It amounted to $300. She had given her all and had nothing left. Stephenie felt she had obeyed God, but she could not see the next step ahead. Then Grandpa suddenly got a light in his eye.

"Stephenie, would you like to go to George Fox College in Newberg? It would be good to have you near us."

Stephenie and her parents agreed, for what had appeared to be an impossible problem had suddenly been solved. Stephenie preceded her grandparents to Oregon to enter George Fox College and graduated from there in 1983.

Dr. Deffinger was reluctant to let Dr. DeVol go. The staff had a farewell party and gave Dr. DeVol a set of binoculars. Dr. Deffinger gave him a gift of a thousand dollars, and one of the staff wrote a poem and read it at his farewell:

Our Dear Souls

"Good morning, Governor—How's your Royal
    Highness?"
(A greeting often heard without a hint of shyness.)
"Come on, Sister Sue—Let's go make rounds—
This patient needs a Philbrook diet to gain a few more
    pounds."
"We'll check and see with this one how his night has
    passed.
Where's my stethoscope?—J. P. Young, must you always
    walk so fast?
"O Stars! I'd like some coffee (check my pressure if
    you've time)
Just a little milk and sweetener, My—this sure tastes
    fine!"
"Are you giving green stamps in ER?" and "Good night
    Nurse!"
"Let's walk upon the water." "Can you show me the
    chapter and verse?"
Do any of these phrases sound familiar, Dr. DeVol?
They really should, you know, as you have said them all.
As you leave us for retirement, for a well-deserved rest,
We send with you our love and wishes for life's best.

We'll miss your wit and humor, we'll miss your words of
cheer,
We'll miss your Christian witness, prayer at bedside, easing
fear.

In Philippians we read, "I thank God for each remem-
brance of you."
We hope each time you think of us you'll feel the same
way, too.

—*Nancy Reid, R. N.*
September 28, 1979

Farewells were many. Colleen Copp, an eight-year-old girl
who attended the neighborhood Bible studies every Friday
night in the DeVol home, expressed the feelings for the group in
their farewell: "I like going to your Bible study. You make hard
things easy to understand."

Between sales, packing, and farewell dinners, three weeks of
October slipped by rapidly. The church presented the DeVols
with a silver coffee set. Farewell times with the Hayneses, the
Coxes, and the Philip DeVol family were all deep and meaningful. Russell and Pat were in their new home in Painesville; Tom
and Pris had bought a home in Columbus; Phil and Donna
were buying a home near Cardington.

"Keep the Banner High!" each one called out at the time of
parting.

The movers backed in to Sunnyslope on October 22, 1979,
and loaded up ninety-eight items to take across the country to
Oregon. The DeVols left soon after and spent that night with
the Cattells in Columbus. The next day they said goodbye to
Ohio and drove to California for a visit with Joe and Judy and
family.

"Keep the banner high!" they also shouted when the goodbye time came.

Between the time the DeVols left Joe and Judy at Riverside
and their arrival in Newberg, waves of nostalgia washed over
them as the reality of the growing distance from their children
became increasingly real. There were agonizing moments as
they longed to turn the car around and go back. They knew
what to do at such times, and as they rolled their burdens on the
Lord and recounted the steps through which He had led them

this direction, peace and assurance returned though the loneliness remained.

"My God in His love will meet me at every corner" (Psalm 59:10) came afresh to their minds. They arrived at Number 6 Spaulding Oaks, Newberg, Oregon, on November 8, 1979.

Family gathering on Pris and Pat's 37th birthday, 1974. Left to right, back: Tom, Pris Cox; Grandma, Grandpa; Pat, Russell Haynes; Phil, Joe DeVol; middle: Stephenie, Geoffrey Cox; Michael Haynes; Judy DeVol (wife of Joe); Bill Cox; Peg DeVol (wife of Phil); front: Sarah, Cindy Haynes; Debbie DeVol; Phil Bob Cox; Nancy DeVol

Joe, Debbie, and Nancy in the cart pulled by Ginger

Granddaughter Julia Kay Haynes, born April 26, 1975

Alum Creek Friends Church—Merrill Cowgill, Cecil Wiley, Mary Staley, Lawrence Westbrook, and Mr. Jeffrey. Lawrence Westbrook ran the farm while the DeVols were overseas. Dr. and Mrs. William S. Deffinger (below right). In 1974 he asked Dr. DeVol to share in the medical practice that Dr. DeVol had turned over to him in 1949.

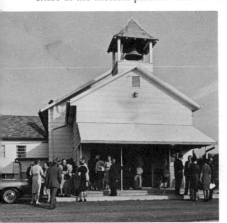

Cindy, Sarah Haynes, Phil Bob, Nancy, and Debbie. Christopher Aaron (Gerling) DeVol, born November 3, 1970, and adopted April 21, 1978; Sarah Christine DeVol, born April 22, 1978, with Phil and Donna Gerling DeVol

A DeVol family reunion, including cousins, nephews, nieces. The DeVol side of the family (below)—Everett and Catherine Cattell, Ezra and Frances, Leora and Charles.

The Hodgin side of the family (below)—Frances, Mendel, Kathryn, Daniel, Elsie (Eyler)

15 The Golden Years

As for me and my house, we will serve the LORD.
Joshua 24:15

Discovering Oregon

The papers reported snow in Ohio. Newberg was still green and gold with the invigorating climate and scents of fall as the DeVols settled into their new apartment, exchanging visits with Marie and Alice Hines, who lived near and who undergirded their moving-in days.

As soon as the house was ready, their granddaughter Stephenie Cox came over from George Fox as the DeVols' first guest. They spent weekends and holidays together as the kitchen became an outlet for Stephenie, who baked dozens of cookies for Christmas. Together they went for rides out over the beautiful hillsides, past huge fallow fields and filbert, pear, and cherry orchards. They became acquainted with the birds, were thrilled to see western bluebirds, and even caught sight of deer.

The DeVols soon transferred their membership to Newberg Friends Church, one of the two larger churches in the town known to have more evangelical churches per capita than any other town in the U.S.A.

Just a month after the DeVols got settled in their new home, Carl and Winifred Sandoz moved in beside them. Ezra helped them move in the heavy furniture and was glad to find out that Carl was an uncle to Jamie, who had worked with him and Frances in Nepal.

"As they say in India, *Duniya gol hai!* The world is round!" Ezra responded. "It means that you are always running into people who know people you have met before!"

As the DeVols and the Sandozes became better acquainted, they learned of even earlier connections. During World War II, Carl Sandoz had worked in a Japanese camp in Idaho. When the U.S.A. and Japan agreed to exchange nationals in 1942, Carl arranged passage for the Japanese in the camp who wished to be repatriated. They sailed on the *Gripsholm*. When the ship returned in 1942, Ezra was on board.

The Sandozes were true "web-footers," having been born in Oregon. They had both graduated from the college now called George Fox, and were thirty years in Portland before moving back to Newberg. Therefore, they knew many people in the area and introduced the DeVols to them. Both Carl and Ezra were elected as two of the five members of the Spaulding Oaks Board, and they enjoyed working together in the care and maintenance of the fifty-six units there. Carl also knew about Oregon's wildlife, trees, flowers, mountains, parks, game reserves, and birds. He discovered Ezra was a true lover of nature, too. Both families had bird feeders in front of their houses. House finches, junkos, chickadees, scrub jays, nuthatches, and humming birds frequented them. So did sparrows and starlings, though they were not so much appreciated. Both families planted varieties of roses and reveled in the flora and how quickly and beautifully flowers and trees grew in Oregon.

Without the Sandozes, the first five months in Oregon would have been rough. It rained most of the time, and the constant cloudiness was depressing. The DeVols were not yet established in the medical community, had not begun to practice, and had no roots as yet in the church.

The Sandozes and the DeVols began taking trips together. They went to Malheur National Wildlife Refuge, a large freshwater marsh in Southeast Oregon. While Dr. Charles DeVol, the botanist, was visiting his brother, they went to Sauvie Island, a bird refuge on the Columbia River.

At Klamath Falls, where Ezra and Carl saw and photographed about a hundred bald eagles, Ezra suddenly discovered the film in his camera had not moved forward! They walked over a very rough trail to see a national monument where the lava had made natural trenches. This was where Captain Jack and his band of Indians had defended themselves in the 1880s. In the winter the Sandozes and DeVols took a trip up along the Columbia River where they saw trumpeter and whistling swans. In the spring they went up Hood River to see the country in pear and apple blossom time. The azaleas and rhododendrons vied for brightness of color.

The trip to Mt. Rainier National Park was unforgettable. There the DeVols and the Sandoz saw a special species of bird that thrives at high elevation called the Clark's Nutcracker. These birds came quite close, and Carl and Ezra fed them popcorn. After every four or five pieces of salty popcorn, they would fly to a nearby puddle for a drink and then come back for more popcorn. Towering snowcapped peaks walled the trails through meadows filled with alpine flowers.

By the time Carl took off for a three-week canoe trip, Ezra had opened an office in his house and started treating patients who came to him. He fixed Carl up with a first-aid kit for his trip. Later the Sandozes took a trip to Europe, and Winifred came down with gout. The medicine prescribed helped, though it had some side effects. Back home and still having trouble, she went next door to ask Ezra to write a new prescription for more of the same medicine. He first examined her and also the medicine.

"Now this is okay," he said, "but there's a newer medicine that's better and that doesn't have side effects."

Winifred later visited a doctor in Portland who confirmed that the medicine prescribed was the latest thing and the exact one for her. She was interested to know that Ezra, a retired missionary doctor, was up on the latest medicines. The doctor in Portland was also surprised. As Winifred got to know Ezra better, she said, "I found this was typical of him."

Getting into Medicine

Newberg Community Hospital did not seem to have any shortage of doctors at this time, and Dr. DeVol—this older man coming in from who knew where and who knew how far out-of-date—was not immediately welcomed. Also his papers had been lost in the hospital, and he may never have been

recognized had it not been for three providential developments: First, Dean Campbell, the Friendsview Manor director, offered him an office where he could see patients, particularly those from the Manor. The second was that the lost papers were found, and he became linked to Newberg Community Hospital. The first patient he admitted was his good friend Marie Hines. The third development came through a new relationship with Dr. Greg Skipper, who had arrived in Newberg just a month after the DeVols.

Dr. DeVol had met Dr. Skipper in the hospital in 1981. He had been helpful in assisting Dr. DeVol get his first patient admitted and helped him find the equipment he needed.

"My first impression of Dr. DeVol was as an old, dour, probably out-of-date, and perhaps even a bit senile person from a different generation," Dr. Skipper said.

Even Dr. DeVol's dress put him in another generation. He always wore a starched shirt, usually white, with a tie and sweater or sport coat, or he wore a three-piece suit. He never looked really casual as Dr. Greg Skipper usually did.

It was not until Dr. DeVol met Dr. Greg and Dr. Anne Skipper in the foyer of the church that the relationship changed. The Skippers had become interested in protesting nuclear arms buildup, and in their effort to get a platform, they had appealed to the Newberg Ministerial Association, even though they were not known in the community as Christians. Dr. Greg Skipper was president of the medical staff of Newberg Community Hospital, and his wife, Dr. Anne Skipper, had been practicing psychiatry in Portland. The only response they received from the churches came from a Sunday school class in Newberg Friends. They accepted the invitation and went to present their cause and show their slides.

The Skippers were on their way through the foyer to pick up their children when they met the DeVols. They responded immediately to the DeVols' warmth and friendliness.

"Oh, you just must stay and hear Ron Woodward's sermon today," insisted Ezra, having attended the first service. "I know you'll appreciate it. There's children's church for the little ones."

The Skippers were amazed at Ezra's vitality and the warmth of Frances' support. They stayed. Dr. Greg had, in his heart, been following Christ for about a year, but his wife was a professed agnostic. That day, however, Pastor Ron Woodward gave a message on the prodigal son and forgiveness, using illustrations and comparisons from Dostoyevsky's *Crime and Punishment*, a novel that has long intrigued psychiatrists. Dr. Anne Skipper was amazed.

"We must come back!" she said.

The Skippers did come back and kept on coming. Both not only became keen Christians, but in spite of the generation gap, they developed a close friendship with the DeVols. Other young couples joined them for evenings at the DeVol home. Among them were Hank and Jo Helsabeck, who were teaching and on the staff at George Fox College. When all the chairs were taken at one of these occasions, Jo was amazed to see Ezra fold up his legs and sit on the floor like a teenager.

"Ezra doesn't seem to worry about protecting his image as a dignified surgeon," Jo commented to Hank afterwards, calling attention to his display of youthful glee, his humor, and the way he put others at ease.

"Ezra and Frances always show such care for one another," Jo commented to a friend. "He treats her as his bride and often refers to her that way. Have you noticed how he extends courtesies to her, and how she honors him in accepting them? Their example of married life centered in Christ and now spanning fifty years challenges Hank and me in our marriage."

As the DeVols became better acquainted with these young people, they offered to show slides of India and Nepal.

"Now don't let us bore you to death!" Ezra said after showing two or three carousels full of pictures.

The guests were not bored. They were fascinated.

Dr. Skipper said, "I'm astonished to see the wide range of cases you have recorded with these photographs. Fantastic! You must show them to our staff at the hospital."

Dr. DeVol was pleased with the opportunity.

"Another thing. We need your help on the hospital credentials committee. You have background that we are lacking. Will you serve there?"

The people in the hospital who opposed Dr. DeVol's appointment to the credentials committee soon revised their opinions when they discovered his fair and conscientious way of dealing with problems and his fearless willingness to make hard decisions. When they saw his pictures and heard his testimony, they began to understand who he was. An orthopedic surgeon invited him to assist in an operation. Many asked questions, and Dr. DeVol answered forthrightly, giving credit to the Word of God and to how the Lord had provided.

"The other staff members were really moved by his courage and commitment, and they could see his faith," Dr. Skipper said. "I had tears in my eyes, watching him work."

The relationship between these two doctors became close enough that even though Dr. DeVol did not wear a beeper, Dr. Skipper would look in on his hospital patients in an emergency.

"The DeVols are our dear friends," Dr. Skipper said. "My wife and I go to see them, and even though we're in our mid-thirties and they're in their late seventies, they are totally our peers."

One night, from Friendsview Manor, Dr. DeVol admitted to the hospital a very sick patient with meningitis. He called Dr. Skipper.

"Can you please come help me out?"

Dr. Skipper went right over, and after consultation, the two doctors decided the patient needed a lumbar puncture, but because of the calcifications in her spine, it was very difficult to find a spot for the needle.

The doctors turned the patient on her side, and Dr. DeVol said, "Dr. Skipper, why don't you do it?"

"Okay," Dr. Skipper replied confidently, because he had a reputation of being pretty good at this sort of thing. He tried, and tried again numerous times, but he could not get into the spinal column.

Frustrated, he gave up and handed the needle to Dr. DeVol. "Why don't you try?"

Dr. DeVol took the needle and tried about fifteen times with no results. Both doctors felt they just had to conquer this, and the nurse with them was also aware of the seriousness of the situation.

"I'll go out and find someone else to try. The orthopedic surgeon ought to be in by now," said Dr. Skipper.

Dr. DeVol took up the needle once again, and as Dr. Skipper went out the door, he heard Dr. DeVol praying: "Help me get in here, Lord! We're just trying to help this lady!"

By the time Dr. Skipper returned with the orthopedic surgeon in tow, he found a smiling Dr. DeVol who had already collected the spinal fluid and was coming out of the room.

"Oh, you got in!" Dr. Skipper exclaimed.

"It's a miracle!" answered Dr. DeVol. "You know I prayed, and it just went right in, and we'll just have to thank the Lord for this."

Three doctors and a nurse knew that thanking the Lord was the right thing to do as they reached to shake Dr. DeVol's hand. Dr. Skipper, turning to go, blinked back the tears and said, "Ezra, keep the banner high!"

After becoming linked to the Newberg Community Hospital, Dr. DeVol faithfully attended the staff meetings. After Dr.

Greg and Dr. Anne Skipper became linked with the Newberg Friends Church, he as president of the medical staff, wanted to begin staff meetings with an invocation. He felt prayer would help them in staff relationships. He knew of a precedent for this in St. Vincent's Hospital in Portland. When the chaplain took up the matter, the debate over the issue became somewhat heated and went on for a period of months.

"It is the Great Physician who does the healing," Dr. DeVol said. "We are just His instruments. It seems appropriate to honor Him by having a prayer before our meetings."

The vote was finally taken with an even number of *yes* and *no* votes.

"Well, the president should vote," a staff member said, "to break the tie."

"I am the president," answered Dr. Skipper, "but I have already voted!"

"You shouldn't have done it. We must vote again."

That meant the cause was lost, and Dr. Skipper's heart sank.

"Don't worry, it will come out right!" Dr. DeVol said softly, encouraging him.

After the second round of votes were in, the count showed two extra votes for *yes*. Two of the staff had changed their votes, and this seemed like another miracle to Dr. Skipper.

Following this, the Christian doctors organized prayer meetings under the chaplain. Dr. DeVol was nearly always one of the six or eight who attended. Each took turns at a short devotional, and then they prayed for patients, problems, concerns, and for people going through difficult times.

Another concern of Dr. Skipper's in which Dr. DeVol and two other Christian doctors became involved was to provide a free medical clinic to the indigent population of Newberg. The clinic was operated under the auspices of "Give Us This Day," and the four doctors took turns giving a day of their services freely every two weeks.

Friendsview Manor found that a doctor so easily accessible often saved them medical bills and hours of pain. Such was the case when Elsie Campbell, a resident, sprained her ankle. Dr. DeVol came at once, took her to the hospital, x-rayed the ankle, and bandaged it.

"Now leave it on," he instructed.

But the next day Elsie wanted a shower and took the bandage off. The bandage was not back on yet when she heard a knock at the door.

"Just dropped in to see how the ankle—What? You've taken the bandage off?" Dr. DeVol exclaimed in disbelief.

Elsie was embarrassed. She was not used to having a doctor come right into her room to check up on her. Dr. DeVol went to work this time and put on a plaster cast.

"Now leave that on. If you ever want to 'dance' again, leave it," he advised.

Interaction

Dr. DeVol's reputation of being one who really cared began to grow. Few people realized, however, that the caring led him to continue medical studies far beyond the call of duty, to keep up-to-date. Because of his relationship to older people in Friendsview Manor, he enrolled in and completed a course in Advanced Cardiac Life Support under the American Heart Association.

The DeVols lived five years in Spaulding Oaks, but as previous health problems persisted, they moved to a single-level apartment in Friendsview Village nearer the Manor with life-care privileges.

Friendsview Manor women soon found Frances DeVol had those qualities of empathy and understanding that lifted. Elsie Campbell, with her ankle healed, was one of those.

"Frances is sensitive to my problems," she confided to a friend. "I've just had a long walk with her and I felt she heard even what I didn't say. We stopped once right on the sidewalk to pray. When we got home, she had this book she thought would throw light on my problem."

"When I talked to Frances on the phone about a problem I had," Jo Helsabeck said, "she prayed for me right then and there! Hank and I were literally agnostics even though we had been faithful churchgoers in our earlier years. It was only in adult life that we learned we could have a personal relationship with Christ. In the DeVols we recognize people with a deep hunger for the Lord, and they have helped us get to know the Lord better. Their faith has been kept fresh. It's never old hat. We forget the age difference, for they make us feel they are learning right along with us. When we're in our seventies, Hank and I want to be like that, too—*on the cutting edge*."

Frances was by Ezra's side at every service and prayer meeting. Some of the younger people noticed she often waited patiently in the back as Ezra interacted with others. They also noticed there were times he whisked her off quickly because he knew for her health's sake she should not continue to stand and talk.

The Sandozes, their neighbors, observed Ezra's care of Frances' health and their devotion to one another. Ezra often borrowed books from them, like *The Life of Emmett Gulley*, a ponderous volume, or books about nature. He would read them to Frances since her eyesight prevented her from reading, sharing with her as she did with him when he was going through the eight operations on his eyes.

After a week in the hospital, when Frances was brought home, Ezra went out and put up the flag. It was not the Fourth of July or Flag Day.

"Why is your flag up today?" a neighbor asked curiously.

"That means the queen is in residence," Ezra explained.

Service in the Church

Ezra was soon at work in the church, and his strong convictions immediately exposed the "laid-back" attitude of many. He was appointed as an elder, a member of the local church missions committee, and a member of the missionary board and their administrative committee.

"I appreciate Ezra's boldness and the prophetic quality about him," remarked Pastor Ron Woodward, even though later, when Hank Helsabeck and Ezra DeVol locked horns to polarity on the purpose of Sunday night services, Ron agreed with Hank.

The issue was whether Sunday night services should be directed toward helping Christians obey the Lord and practice what they had already heard, or whether they should be devoted to preaching strong, evangelistic gospel messages to lead people to repentance and renewed commitment. Ezra strongly supported the latter. This was neither the first nor the last time such convictions would be expressed, for Dr. DeVol remembered well how much he owed to just such meetings in the early days of his spiritual life. He sorely missed these opportunities in the church in the 1970s and 1980s.

Ezra did not feel very happy with the pastor or the outcome of the meeting. He returned home defeated, having lost not only his cause, but also his peace. He had long since learned what to do in such circumstances, and when the opportunity came in open worship in the manner of Friends on a Sunday morning, he rose from his seat, went up to the pulpit, put his arm around Pastor Ron, and said:

"I am convicted for my uncharitable thoughts of you because you opposed me in the last elders' meeting. Forgive me."

Pastor Ron was choked with emotion and overcome with deep feelings of respect for the godly qualities he recognized in a man of deep conviction willing to be vulnerable.

At special sessions of prayer called by the church, the DeVols were always present. When Ezra's sister Catherine Cattell came to Friendsview Manor to live in 1981, after the death of her husband, she also joined in this ministry of prayer and counseling and felt strengthened and comforted by their nearness and support. They formed a small weekly group meeting of those particularly interested in praying for India.

Others might serve better as chairmen of committees, but none excelled Ezra as a leader in prayer. That is why Ron Woodward requested him to lead the Wednesday night prayer meetings in the church. He found Ezra always willing to serve without protest or reluctance. He valued the quality of the prayer meeting devotionals, which showed Ezra had prayed over his messages and dug deep. People left with something really edifying and helpful. The attendance doubled.

People who came to Wednesday night prayer meeting began to pray specifically and look for answers. A woman was saved just one day before she died. A man, crushed and hopeless, who had lost a job he had held for a long time, was restored to Christ and got a job as a cherry sorter. They prayed about the abortion issue and the right way to handle it. They saw a doctor turn away from it. There were many such answers, and people began to believe more and more in the effectiveness of prayer and to practice it.

The DeVols were both growing in their spiritual lives even as others looked on them as models—even models of the process of growing.

"Ezra is publicly vulnerable, but Frances is privately vulnerable," a young friend remarked. "She is also a seeker."

"Brother," Ezra said to Hank after another stormy elders' session, "I came on too strong. I hope you'll forgive me. With my children I was too black and white. I realized that last Christmas Eve while I was visiting my son Joe in California. At Rose Drive Friends Church I heard Charles Mylander preach a sermon on the prodigal son, and it opened my eyes."

The Prodigal's Return

That 1982 Christmas Eve sermon Ezra heard in California had come as a surprise. He remembered how just such a message had blessed his soul the day he invited Drs. Greg and Anne Skipper to church. He had not expected to hear another message on the subject, particularly on Christmas Eve, but there it was. As he listened, he began to think about his own son Phil. His other children had all accepted the Lord, and though none were preachers, missionaries, or Christian workers, they were all in the church and knew how to pray. Relationship with Phil, though surfacely cordial, had been strained ever since the strong confrontation at the time of the divorce.

Phil definitely had started "home" but there was not yet an indication that he had fully arrived, and the father was still waiting to hear the words, "I have sinned against heaven and in thy sight."

Phil had been working with alcoholics in Morrow County, and when a young woman seriously threatened suicide, Phil began to realize how powerless he was. *Only God can help her*, he thought. *How I wish I could pray for her, but how can I when I am not right with Him myself?* He began to pray for himself and also for the alcoholic woman, asking for God's help. He acknowledged God's hand in the woman's recovery. He did not, however, return to his father's house, and the father was still waiting and watching.

Charles Mylander's voice was penetrating as he read, "And the father ran out to meet him!"

Ezra heard no more. Sudden conviction blinded him as he realized with fresh insight that his attitude of inner demand for apology had kept him from running out to meet his son. He could hardly wait for the service to end.

As soon as the DeVols reached home, Ezra immediately picked up the telephone. It was already past midnight in Ohio when he heard the click of the receiver and the familiar voice.

"Hello?"

It was Phil. Everyone else was in bed.

As Ezra cleared his voice, that one sentence kept ringing through his mind: *The father ran out to meet the son.*

"Son, I'm calling to tell you that I know I have been too hard on you. Back there in 1978, I said things in anger to you that I should never have said. I am sorry! I ask your forgiveness."

Before anything else could be said, both father and son were in tears, and both were talking at the same time, asking forgiveness and expressing love. Fear and bitterness disappeared, and no one thought of the time as father and son talked and talked. The prodigal was home again.

Soon after that a letter came from Phil:

> Dear Mom and Dad,
> Christmas was very nice at our house. Opening gifts in the morning in the traditional way. Santa drank all the milk and polished off the cookies, he stuffed the stockings, too. Sarah is still dreaming about it.
>   All of that was wonderful, but the best thing of all was your phone call. I have wanted to deal with those issues for a long time. Your forgiveness is something I have needed. I'm afraid that I have disappointed you many times and given you many reasons to be angry. Thank you for calling....
>   KEEP THE BANNER HIGH!
> Your son,
> Phil

A few months later Phil had a real homecoming as he flew to Portland and came down to Newberg for the personal touch and embrace, which confirmed complete reconciliation as the DeVols and their son loved, talked, and prayed as peers. Though they did not as yet see eye to eye, they could discuss differences in an atmosphere of trust.

"I still can't find people in your church who understand where I'm coming from," Phil commented wistfully. "I've come to the same spiritual life and beliefs. I know how powerless I am and how much I need the Savior. I came to this understanding while working with alcoholics, and I found myself just as powerless as they are. Their answer is spiritual, too. It is among them that I find the people who seem to understand the nature of my spiritual life."

"Look, Phil, neither my generation nor yours formed the Church. Jesus said, 'On this rock I will build my church and the gates of hell will not prevail against it.' You need the Church and the Church needs you."

"But I can't forget what I've learned, and they don't seem to want to hear it. But I'm still open. I'm searching."

The son and his parents sat silently for awhile, and as they did so, Phil thought deeply about his parents' happy marriage. *It has worked*, he realized, *because of their Christian faith. Because there's something larger than each of them that they've given their lives to. How thankful I am that they pointed the way for me!*

Pat visited her parents in Oregon in 1980. Pris came in 1986. Joe, from California, has come for several visits. The DeVols have averaged a visit a year to California and Ohio. Thus the family continues to keep close.

These Fifty Years

Not many people have the privilege of celebrating a fiftieth anniversary with all their children and grandchildren, not because people do not live that long, but often because families become separated.

The DeVols' Golden Wedding Anniversary furnished an occasion for reunion, and a year before it took place, the telephone lines were kept busy. Even granddaughter Stephenie Cox, now married to Mark Thomas and living in California, offered to help in the planning.

The place chosen for the celebration was Mohican Forest Lodge in Ohio, and the date was August 15, 1986. This immediately followed the Yearly Meeting in Canton, where many of their former friends would be gathered for the annual banquets, business meetings, and spiritual life convention. Plans were carefully made to include all who could come. Joe and

Judy, with daughter Debbie's help, made a "This Is Your Life" set of slides to present at the student center at Malone College on the afternoon of the 14th when relatives and friends could be present. Pris and Pat made the plans for the 15th at Mohican Forest Lodge where the DeVols and their children and families would have the full day together.

As the time of the celebration drew near, a number of events tested the faith and perseverence of those making the plans. Ezra's sister, Catherine Cattell, died in Friendsview Manor on July 3. Two weeks later, Frances had such a severe heart attack that she had to be hospitalized for nearly a week. It seemed unlikely that she could make the trip, but at the last moment her doctor gave his consent.

"Under your care, Ezra, I believe she can go," Dr. Skipper agreed. From that moment on Frances began to improve.

Their flight to Canton had been booked at night, and it left Portland over two hours late; therefore, they missed their connection in Chicago. They had to take a flight via Detroit, changing planes there for Canton. The luggage was missing in Detroit, and as Ezra tried to find it, the dark feelings he had to fight were reminiscent of the flight they took from Switzerland to India in 1972. He prayed again in the same way, feeling as he did then, that they had "put their feet in the water." They arrived in Canton late, but friends and relatives were still waiting to greet them. Three days later the luggage followed.

The celebrations exceeded their expectations. Frances' sister Elsie Eyler and sister-in-law Kathryn Hodgin came from Michigan. Charles and Leora DeVol came from Marengo. Walter Williams, Jr., and his wife, Helen, came from Florida. Cousin Ethel, daughter of Uncle Charles DeVol, flew in from California. Many nieces and nephews were present, as well as a host of friends who remembered times of fellowship and blessing with the DeVols down through the years.

At Malone College there was thanksgiving that Drs. George and Isabella DeVol's three children all had celebrated fiftieth wedding anniversaries, and that two and a half weeks earlier, Charles and Leora had celebrated their sixtieth.

The next day at Mohican Lake Lodge after a sumptuous meal, Joe gave opportunity to the children and grandchildren to express their love. What they said was not necessarily new. They had often in letters or on other occasions expressed such thoughts:

PAT: We've had super visits over the phone. You really listen even with your mind. People can be together for great periods of time and not communicate that well. But it is wonderful to be together. Dad has been strong. Mother has been a gentle, loving mother. You are both tremendously precious.

PRIS: Few can give their children such roots or example of oneness and trust in marriage. We should make banners, "Givers of Security." People don't believe me when I tell them I have never heard my parents argue. Your communication and understanding of one another is amazing!

JOE: I have always been proud of my parents. I have never been embarrassed by anything about you. We love visiting you in Oregon and sharing in your positive trust in the Lord. It is a comfort to know you are praying daily for us. You've been a really happy married couple. I want my marriage to be the same way. A happy one, a trusting one!

PHIL: Keep the banner high!

By the time the sons-in-law and daughters-in-law and grandchildren got through expressing themselves, everyone was in tears and the love flowed. Julia and Sarah, the two youngest, expressed themselves in body language, a hug for Grandma and Grandpa. It was a tender time, a golden moment, never to be forgotten.

The time then came for Ezra and Frances to express their love to their children and grandchildren. They had given long and prayerful consideration about how to do this in order to say all they wanted to say in a way it would be remembered. They finally decided to give each son, son-in-law, daughter, and daughter-in-law a gold Krugerrand along with a golden verse from the Bible.

"You are my parents!" Russell said.

"You've given me the best verse of all," said Tom who had gotten up from a hospital bed to come.

"You've always treated me like your own daughter," Judy commented.

"I love you!" said Donna.

"I am the only son of my generation in this family who bears the name of DeVol, and I promise to carry forward the DeVol tradition," said grandson Christopher.

To each grandchild the DeVols gave E. E. bonds and a message. They felt the wonder of God's grace in giving them such a rare opportunity to share their deepest feelings with those they loved most and for whom they felt most responsible. They had saturated their thoughts with prayer and prepared with the greatest care.

Ezra, as father and grandfather, in the dignity of a true prophet of God, stood to address his children and grandchildren:

> The gold that we have given your parents will fluctuate in value with the stock market. But these bonds that Grandma and I are about to give you will increase in value until they reach maturity. So KEEP them until they reach their full value. In this "throw-away" society, there are some things that it PAYS TO KEEP.

As he proceeded with his message, he felt the power of the Holy Spirit. He knew he was speaking to a responsive audience, but he was not prepared for what happened as he was emphasizing the point, KEEP YOUR COVENANT TO GOD!

As he explained this point he said, "Our family has a covenant with the Lord. It is: "As for me and my house . . . ""

With a jubilant shout, every member of the family present that day stopped him midverse with a fervent unison affirmation:

"WE WILL SERVE THE LORD!"

Both Ezra and Frances were so overcome by this solid proclamation of faith, the answer to their deepest prayers, that it took awhile to gain composure. They looked at each other, laughing and weeping at the same time. It was hard to pick up the threads of the message and carry on. Their hopes were already fulfilled. But finish they did before saying goodnight, leaving the younger generations to stay on enjoying each other's fellowship far into the night.

Mary Green and Frances DeVol,
sailing off the Pacific Coast

Stephenie Cox Thomas stayed
with her grandparents in
Oregon and graduated from
George Fox College in 1983

The DeVols,
roughing it
(It is not a
"Senior Log")

Mission Board President Ron Woodward (left), pastor of Newberg Friends Church, appreciated Ezra's involvement in the missionary board and the prayer meetings. "None excelled Ezra as a leader in prayer," said the pastor.

A weekly prayer group for India (left to right) included Marie Hines, Anna Nixon, Frances DeVol, Alice Hines, Catherine Cattell, (below) Edna Deuell Springer, Louis and Betty Coffin, and Ezra DeVol.

The doctors' prayer breakfast includes, left to right: Dr. DeVol, Chaplain Manley, Dr. Rosenau, Dr. Skipper and son Shannon.

Dr. Walter R. Williams, Jr., and his wife, Helen. He has been a life-long friend.

Paul Langdon and his wife Marjorie, friends for nearly half a century. He has been the DeVols' financial adviser. Dr. DeVol delivered and named their son Larry.

George Fox College President Ed Stevens, recognizing Ezra and Frances as members of the Leadership Circle of the President's Council

The DeVol parents, Newberg, Oregon

Pris Cox (above left), homemaker, nurse at Mercy Hospital, Columbus, Ohio. Pat Haynes, homemaker, teacher, Stow, Ohio. Joe DeVol (lower left), Branch Manager of Northern California World Books, Inc., El Dorado Hills, California. Phil DeVol, Director of the Morrow County Council on Alcohol & Drugs, Inc., Cardington, Ohio.

Russell and Pat; Michael, Sarah (left), Julia (front), and Cynthia

THE FAMILY OF
RUSSELL AND
PATRICIA DeVOL HAYNES

Cynthia Haynes spent
the summer of 1986
with her grandparents
in Oregon.

THE FAMILY OF
TOM AND
PRISCILLA DeVOL COX

Tom and Pris

Mark and Stephenie Cox
Thomas, Geoffery (above),
Philip Robert (left),
and Bill

Joe and Debbie; Judy and Nancy

THE FAMILY OF JOSEPH AND JUDY DeVOL

Phil and Donna

THE FAMILY OF PHILIP AND DONNA DeVOL

"I bear the name DeVol, and I promise to carry forward the DeVol tradition."
—Christopher DeVol

Christopher   Sarah

Postscript

August 15, 1986

*The golden verses—a message to the children
from Ezra and Frances DeVol*

Patricia: "A word fitly spoken and in due season is like apples of gold in a setting of silver." *Proverbs 25:11, Amplified*

Russell: "Happy . . . is the man who finds skillful and godly Wisdom, and the man who gets understanding—drawing it forth [from God's Word and life's experiences]. For the gaining of it is better than the gaining of silver, and the profit of it than fine gold." *Proverbs 3:13, 14, Amplified*

Tom: "Wherein ye greatly rejoice, though now for a season, if need be, ye are in heaviness through manifold temptations: that the trial of your faith, being much more precious than of gold that perisheth, though it be tried with fire, might be found unto praise and honour and glory at the appearing of Jesus Christ." *1 Peter 1:6, 7*

Priscilla: "He knows the way that I take—He has concern for it, appreciates and pays attention to it. When He has tried me, I shall come forth as refined gold [pure and luminous]." *Job 23:10, Amplified*

Joseph: "The (reverent) fear of the Lord is clean, enduring for ever; the ordinances of the Lord are true, and righteous altogether. More to be desired are . . . they than gold, even than much fine gold; sweeter also than honey and . . . the honeycomb." *Psalm 19:9, 10, Amplified*

Judy: "I love your commandments more than (resplendent) gold; yes, more than [perfectly] refined gold. Therefore I esteem as right all, yes,

325

all your precepts; I hate every false way." *Psalm 119:127, 128, Amplified*

Philip: "A good name is rather to be chosen than great riches, and loving favor rather than silver and gold." *Proverbs 22:1*

Donna: "And the twelve gates [of heaven] were twelve pearls, each separate gate built of one solid pearl. And the main street of the city... was of gold as pure and translucent as glass." *Revelation 21:21, Amplified*

There are some things it pays to keep— a message to the grandchildren

"**Keep thy heart with all diligence;** for out of it are the issues [the springs] of life." *Proverbs 4:23*

"But you, **keep your head in all situations,** endure hardship, do the work of an evangelist, discharge all the duties of your ministry." *2 Timothy 4:5, NIV* "He that is soon angry dealeth foolishly." *Proverbs 14:17* If you are always "blowing your top"—maybe it is because you have more "blow" than "top." So be calm, cool, and steady.

"**If you really keep the royal law** found in the Scripture, '**Love your neighbor as yourself,**' you are doing right." *James 2:8, paraphrase*

"Do not... share... in another man's sins—**keep yourself pure.**" *1 Timothy 5:22b, Amplified*

"My son, **keep your... [God-given] commandments** and forsake not the law of [God] your mother [taught you]." *Proverbs 6:20, Amplified* There is a stability found in these principles not duplicated anywhere else.

"**Keep His covenant.**" *Psalm 25:10* All society is based on covenants of one sort or another. There **must be some sort of fabric**—some type of definable relationships to prevent utter chaos.

If car drivers did not covenant to drive on the right side of the road and stop for red lights, there would be terrible slaughter on all our highways—even if we drove only at 10 miles per hour. What if every football player was his own quarterback? There could be no hope of a winning team. What if there were no umpires and every tennis player was a MacEnroe? When treaties between nations are broken, this leads to *war.*

Keep your covenant with your marriage partner—to one another at all costs. We must be able to count on each other!

Keep your covenant to God! "The fear of the Lord is clean, enduring forever; the judgments of the Lord are true and righteous altogether. More to be desired are they than gold, yea, than much fine gold: sweeter also than honey and the honeycomb. Moreover by them is thy servant warned: and in **keeping of them there is great reward.**" *Psalm 19:9-11*

Our family has a covenant with the Lord. It is: "As for me and my house—**we will serve the Lord!**" *Joshua 24:15*

"Keep yourselves in the love of God." *Jude 21*

"Dear children, **keep yourselves from idols** (from substitutes for God). *1 John 5:21* Do not let anything take God's supreme place in your life.

* * * * *

These admonitions may seem like a lot of impossible demands—but see Jude 24. "To him who is able to **keep you from falling and to present you before his glorious presence without fault** and with **great joy**—to the only **God our Savior** be glory, majesty, power and authority, through Jesus Christ our Lord, before all ages, now and forevermore! Amen." *(NIV)*

When you and I come down to the end of life, it will be worth all that it costs to be able to say honestly and confidently, **"I have kept the faith!"**

All of the above is included when we challenge one another with

"KEEP THE BANNER HIGH!"